I0332439

Translated Texts for Historians

300–800 AD is the time of late antiquity and the early middle ages: the transformation of the classical world, the beginnings of Europe and of Islam, and the evolution of Byzantium. TTH makes available sources translated from Greek, Latin, Syriac, Coptic, Arabic, Georgian, Gothic and Armenian. Each volume provides an expert scholarly translation, with an introduction setting texts and authors in context, and with notes on content, interpretation and debates.

Editorial Committee
Sebastian Brock, Oriental Institute, University of Oxford
Averil Cameron, Keble College, Oxford
Marios Costambeys, University of Liverpool
Mary Cunningham, University of Nottingham
Carlotta Dionisotti, King's College, London
Peter Heather, King's College, London
Robert Hoyland, University of St Andrews
William E. Klingshirn, The Catholic University of America
Michael Lapidge, Clare College, Cambridge
John Matthews, Yale University
Neil McLynn, Corpus Christi College, Oxford
Richard Price, Heythrop College, University of London
Claudia Rapp, University of California, Los Angeles
Raymond Van Dam, University of Michigan
Michael Whitby, University of Warwick
Ian Wood, University of Leeds

General Editors
Gillian Clark, University of Bristol
Mark Humphries, Swansea University
Mary Whitby, University of Oxford

A full list of published titles in the Translated Texts for Historians series is available on request. The most recently published are shown below.

Lactantius: Divine Institutes
Translated with introduction and notes by ANTHONY BOWEN and PETER GARNSEY
Volume 40: 488pp., 2003, ISBN 0-85323-988-6

Selected Letters of Libanius from the Age of Constantius and Julian
Translated with introduction and notes by SCOT BRADBURY
Volume 41: 308pp., 2004, ISBN 0-85323-509-0

Cassiodorus: Institutions of Divine and Secular Learning and On the Soul
Translated and notes by JAMES W. HALPORN; Introduction by MARK VESSEY
Volume 42: 316 pp., 2004, ISBN 0-85323-998-3

Ambrose of Milan: Political Letters and Speeches
Translated with an introduction and notes by J. H. W. G. LIEBESCHUETZ and CAROLE HILL
Volume 43: 432pp., 2005, ISBN 0-85323-829-4

The Chronicle of Ireland
Translated with an introduction and notes by T. M. CHARLES-EDWARDS
Volume 44: 2 vols., 349pp. + 186pp., 2006, ISBN 0-85323-959-2

The Acts of the Council of Chalcedon
Translated with an introduction and notes by RICHARD PRICE and MICHAEL GADDIS
Volume 45: 3 vols., 365pp. + 312pp. + 312pp., 2005, ISBN 0-85323-039-0

Bede: On Ezra and Nehemiah
Translated with an introduction and notes by SCOTT DEGREGORIO
Volume 47: 304pp, 2006, ISBN 978-1-84631-001-0

Bede: On Genesis
Translated with introduction and notes by CALVIN B. KENDALL
Volume 48: 371pp., 2008, ISBN 978-1-84631-088-1

Nemesius: On the Nature of Man
Translated with introduction and notes by R. W. SHARPLES and P. J. VAN DER EIJK
Volume 49: 283pp., 2008, ISBN 978-1-84631-132-1

For full details of Translated Texts for Historians, including prices and ordering information, please write to the following:
All countries, except the USA and Canada: Liverpool University Press, 4 Cambridge Street, Liverpool, L69 7ZU, UK (*Tel* +44-[0]151-794 2233, *Fax* +44-[0]151-794 2235, Email J.M. Smith@liv.ac.uk, http://www.liverpool-unipress.co.uk). **USA and Canada:** University of Chicago Press, 1427 E. 60th Street, Chicago, IL, 60637, US (*Tel* 773-702-7700, *Fax* 773-702-9756, www.press.uchicago.edu)

Translated Texts for Historians
Volume 50

Sources for the History of the School of Nisibis

Translated with an introduction and notes by
ADAM H. BECKER

Liverpool
University
Press

First published 2008
Liverpool University Press
4 Cambridge Street
Liverpool, L69 7ZU

British Library Cataloguing-in-Publication Data
A British Library CIP Record is available.

ISBN 978-1-84631-161-1 limp

Set in Times by
Koinonia, Manchester
Printed in the European Union by
Bell and Bain Ltd, Glasgow

CONTENTS

Acknowledgements	vii
Abbreviations	ix
Introduction	1
The School of Nisibis	1
Identifying Barḥadbeshabbā	11
On the Manuscripts, Translation, Notes and Terms	16
The Transliteration of the Syriac Alphabet in this Volume	18
Texts	
Simeon of Bēt Arsham, *'Letter' on the 'Nestorianization' of Persia*	21
Introduction	21
Translation and Notes	25
Barḥadbeshabbā, *Ecclesiastical History*	40
Introduction	40
Translation and Notes	47
Chapter Thirty One: 'The Life of Narsai'	47
Chapter Thirty Two: 'The Life of Abraham of Bēt Rabban'	73
Barḥadbeshabbā, *The Cause of the Foundation of the Schools*	86
Introduction	86
Translation and Notes	94
Mingana Fragment of the *Cause*	161
Translation and Notes	161
Portion of the *Mēmrā on the Holy Fathers* by Rabban Surin	163
Translation and Notes	163

Appendix I: On the Manuscript Tradition of the *Cause of the Foundation of the Schools* 165
Appendix II: The Tree of Porphyry in the *Cause of the Foundation of the Schools* 172
Appendix III: The Literary Dependence of the *Cause of the Foundation of the Schools* on the *Ecclesiastical History* 181

Brief Glossary of Selected Terms 192
Maps 194
Bibliography 196
Index of Biblical References 203
Index of Proper Names 206
Subject Index 211

ACKNOWLEDGEMENTS

This volume offers annotated translations of several of the most important sources for the study of the history of the School of Nisibis, the most prominent centre of learning in the Church of the East (the 'Nestorian' church of the Sasanian Empire) in the sixth century and an institution that played a key role in the creation of Christian intellectual culture in Mesopotamia in Late Antiquity and the early Islamic period. I hope that it will help to encourage other scholars to continue in the study of the School of Nisibis and East-Syrian intellectual culture in general (I use the term 'East-Syrian' throughout this volume for those Syriac-speaking Christians commonly known as 'Nestorians'). A number of works remain unexamined, such as several examples of the East-Syrian 'cause' genre, an aetiological genre typical of East-Syrian scholastic culture, while the role of Syriac Christians in the intellectual history of Mesopotamia, as well as the important comparative evidence Syriac Christianity offers for the study of the other contemporaneous religious communities, has still not been fully appreciated.

This project derives from translation work I began while writing my dissertation in the Religion Department of Princeton University and at the Oriental Institute, Oxford University. The dissertation, which was an intellectual and institutional history of the School of Nisibis and the broader East-Syrian scholastic culture, has since been heavily revised and published with University of Pennsylvania's *Divinations* series as *Fear of God and the Beginning of Wisdom: The School of Nisibis and the Development of Christian Scholastic Culture in Late Antique Mesopotamia* (2006). Because of the similar nature of the material it was inevitable that there would be a number of overlaps between the former volume and the present one. I hope these redundancies are not too tedious for those who notice them. Some material from chapter 7 of the *Fear of God* has been placed verbatim in the notes to the more philosophical portion of the *Cause of the Foundation of the Schools*. I would like to thank Sebastian P. Brock for, aside from encouraging my studies over the past several years, first suggesting that I submit these texts to be published in Translated Texts for Historians and for his numerous editorial comments and suggestions. Mary Whitby, as General Editor for the series, provided numerous useful suggestions and criticisms. I would like to thank Michael Peachin for several helpful references and Ilaria Ramelli for sharing with me her annotated Italian translation of the *Cause of the Foundation of the Schools* when it was still in manuscript form. A number of people have helped me with obscure references and bibliographical queries on the *Hugoye* Syriac Studies electronic list. I appreciate their help. I re-read a large chunk of the *Cause of the Foundation of the Schools* with my Syriac *ḥavruta* buddies, Jeffrey Rubenstein and P. V. 'Meylekh' Viswanath. I thank them for their feedback on this text as well as their companionship (along with Mike Pregill) in reading Syriac texts. I thank Leyla B. Aker for listening to me drone on about obscure things during much of the work on this volume. Special thanks to Bridget M. Purcell for her encouragement during its completion. The brevity of this work is inverse to the immensity of love I feel for my two sisters, Danielle Speckhart and Rachel Petev, to whom this small volume is dedicated.

ABBREVIATIONS

AB	Analecta Bollandiana
CAG	Commentaria in Aristotelem Graeca
CS	*Cause of the Foundation of the Schools*
CSCO	Corpus Scriptorum Christianorum Orientalium
JA	*Journal Asiatique*
JECS	*Journal of Early Christian Studies*
JTS	*Journal of Theological Studies*
LA	Life of Abraham of Bēt Rabban
LM	*Le Muséon*
LN	Life of Narsai
NPNF	Nicene and Post-Nicene Fathers (Peabody, MA: Hendrickson, 1994)
OC	*Oriens Christianus*
OCA	Orientalia Christiana Analecta
OCP	*Orientalia Christiana Periodica*
OLA	Orientalia Lovaniensia Analecta
OLP	*Orientalia Lovaniensia Periodica*
OS	*L'Orient Syrien*
PdO	*Parole de l'Orient*
PG	Patrologia Graeca
PO	Patrologia Orientalis
SC	Sources Chrétiennes
SL	Letter of Simeon of Bēt Arsham

INTRODUCTION

The Christianization of the ancient Mediterranean and Near Eastern world led to radical innovations both in the content and the locus of learning in Late Antiquity.[1] The Christian study circle and eventually the monastery created a new literary culture, which would be maintained and transmitted for centuries to come in both eastern and western monasteries. However, traditional Greco-Roman institutions of learning persisted deep into the Middle Ages and this new Christian culture of learning continued to be influenced by the ancient classroom until the end of antiquity. For example, Neoplatonism, the final floruit of ancient philosophical learning, especially in the later schools of Athens and Alexandria, left a deep imprint upon the Christian learning of the Middle Ages.[2] In varying degrees the diverse Christian cultures of Late Antiquity brought with them into the Middle Ages a combination of late antique monastic spirituality, patristic exegesis, and Greek philosophical and rhetorical learning.

THE SCHOOL OF NISIBIS

One such innovative combination of the late antique intellectual heritage is attested in the East-Syrian 'schools', a series of institutions which began to spread through much of Sasanian Mesopotamia in the sixth century. These institutions could range from gatherings in local churches for the elementary study of scripture to informal study circles which met in specific locations

1 A recent study of one example of this new kind of learning is Richard A. Layton's *Didymus the Blind and His Circle in Late-Antique Alexandria: Virtue and Narrative in Biblical Scholarship* (Urbana and Chicago: University of Illinois Press, 2004). For a general discussion of classical learning, late antique developments, and the Syriac context, see Becker, *Fear of God*, 6–12. For a more recent discussion, see Paolo Bettiolo, 'Scuole e ambienti intellettuali nelle chiese di Siria', in *Storia della filosofia nell'Islam medievale*, Vol. I, ed. Cristina D'Ancona (Torino: Giulio Einaudi, 2006), 48–100.

2 For the most recent cultural analysis of the later Neoplatonic schools, see Edward Watts, *City and School in Late Antique Athens and Alexandria* (Berkeley: University of California Press, 2006).

within monasteries to independent institutions with a multi-tiered hierarchy of offices, where students engaged in a detailed study of biblical exegesis and acquired an acquaintance with Aristotelian logic.[3] The foremost and most influential of the East-Syrian 'schools' was the School of Nisibis, which is also the most well-known.[4]

The School of Nisibis was founded after the so-called 'School of the Persians' in Edessa (Syr. Urhāy, or, [Şanlı]Urfa in modern Turkey) was closed in 489 by the bishop of the city, Cyrus, under orders from the Emperor Zeno.[5] At least part of the community from Edessa travelled approximately two hundred kilometres eastward to re-found this institution of learning in Nisibis, an important border city in the Sasanian Empire.[6] Evidence suggests that some form of collective gathering for the sake of learning may have existed in Nisibis prior to 489 and that some of the members of this group may have even joined ranks with the immigrants from Edessa. However, the events of 489 and afterward were a watershed in the history of the institutionalization of learning in upper Mesopotamia. In the late fifth century, under the leadership of Narsai, the last head of the School of the Persians before its closure, and with the aid of Barṣaumā, the controversial bishop of the city, the community in Nisibis created for itself formal rules, similar to those of a monastery, and began the process that within a few decades would lead to the School of Nisibis becoming the primary centre of learning within the Church of the East.[7] By the turn of the seventh century prospec-

3 For a typology and discussion of the different East-Syrian schools, see Becker, *Fear of God*, 155–68.

4 Nisibis is modern Nusaybin in south-eastern Turkey, across the border from al-Qamishli in Syria.

5 For a reassessment of the sources and an attempt to fit them into a new framework, see Becker, *Fear of God*, 41–76. The discussion of the School of the Persians below summarizes the arguments therein. In the following pages I will refer to the School of the Persians and the School of Nisibis as 'School' for short and not 'school'. Although the sources refer to them by the Greek *scholḗ* and especially the Syriac *eskolē*, which obviously comes from the Greek, I try to avoid referring to them, especially the former, as 'schools' since it can lead to an anachronistic understanding of them as institutions similar to our own. On Edessa in general, see J. B. Segal, *Edessa, 'The Blessed City'* (Oxford: Clarendon Press, 1970; repr. Piscataway, NJ: Gorgias, 2005). For an earlier period, see Steven K. Ross, *Roman Edessa: Politics and Culture on the Eastern Fringes of the Roman Empire, 114–242 CE* (New York: Routledge, 2001).

6 On the Christian history of Nisibis in general, see Fiey, *Nisibe*. The most important works for this period are Gero's *Barṣauma* and Vööbus's *History*. For geography, see Dillemann, *Haute Mésopotamie Orientale*.

7 There are numerous articles on and translations of Narsai's works, but a full synthetic study of his work and life is still lacking, despite his importance in the history of the Church

tive students flocked to Nisibis from across the Sasanian world and the reputation of the School would be an inspiration as far West as Italy where Cassiodorus imagined creating a similar centre of learning at Vivarium.[8] A disproportionate number of the significant figures in the Church of the East of the sixth and seventh centuries studied at the School.

The School of Nisibis served as a model for other East-Syrian schools as well, and the sources reveal a proliferation of this type of institution of Christian learning throughout Mesopotamia by the late sixth and early seventh century. Furthermore, the significance of the School of Nisibis and the scholastic movement in which it played a major role remains to be fully integrated into the historiography of the institutionalization of learning among Jews in late antique Mesopotamia and the rise of the Babylonian Jewish academies (*yeshivot*), as well as into the study of the reception of Greek philosophical and medical literature into Arabic in the early 'Abbasid period.[9] Although an awareness of the importance of the School of Nisibis for both of these respective fields has existed for some time, the sources have not been sufficiently examined and integrated into a concrete scholarly discussion of the relevance of East-Syrian scholastic culture for the history of learning in Sasanian and early Islamic Mesopotamia.

The sources for the School of Nisibis are diverse. The three that provide the majority of our chronological and narrative information are the

---

of the East. In general, see Baumstark, *Geschichte*, 109–13. On his importance to the School of Nisibis, see Vööbus, *History*, 57–121. On Barṣaumā of Nisibis, see Gero, *Barṣauma*, the primary study of this important ecclesiastical figure, and Peter Bruns, 'Barauma von Nisibis und die Aufhebung der Klerikerenthaltsamkeit im Gefolge der Synode von Beth-Lapat (484)', *Annuarium Historiae Conciliorum. Supplementum* 37 (2005): 1–42.

8 On one member of the school who travelled from Qatar to study there, see Becker, *Fear of God*, 1–4. A close connection is made between the School of Nisibis and Cassiodorus in Robert Macina, 'Cassiodore et l'école de Nisibe. Contribution à l'étude de la culture chrétienne orientale à l'aube du Moyen Âge', *LM* 95 (1982): 131–66; however, Macina's specific claims are refuted in Gianfranco Fiaccadori, 'Cassiodorus and the School of Nisibis', *Dumbarton Oaks Papers* 39 (1985): 135–37. On travel for the purposes of study, see Edward Watts, 'Student Travel to Intellectual Centers: What was the Attraction?', in *Travel, Communication and Geography in Late Antiquity*, ed. Linda Ellis and Frank L. Kidner (Aldershot: Ashgate, 2004), 13–23.

9 For example, see Richard Kalmin's *Jewish Babylonia between Persia and Roman Palestine: Decoding the Literary Record* (New York: Oxford University Press, 2006), 3–8; Rubenstein, *The Culture of the Babylonian Talmud*, 35–38; Adam H. Becker, 'The Comparative Study of "Scholasticism" in Late Antique Mesopotamia: Rabbis and East Syrians', *Association of Jewish Studies Review* 33 (2009); and Cristina D'Ancona, 'Greek into Arabic: Neoplatonism in Translation', in *The Cambridge Companion to Arabic Philosophy*, ed. Peter Adamson and Richard C. Taylor (Cambridge: Cambridge University Press, 2005), 18–20. On the utility of the term 'scholastic' for this material, see Becker, *Fear of God*, 12–17.

Ecclesiastical History of Barḥadbeshabbā of Bēt 'Arbāyē; the *Cause of the Foundation of the Schools*, often attributed to the same Barḥadbeshabbā; and the canons of the School. From these three texts we can establish the basic narrative, however schematic, of the School's foundation and history through the sixth century. The first two of these are translated in this volume, while the third, the canons, which provide an important perspective on the day-to-day life of the School, were translated into English by Arthur Vööbus.[10] A reprint of these canons is pending and thus I have decided not to retranslate them here.[11] There are other texts extant that were composed at the School. For example, Ḥenānā of Adiabene, the head of the School at the turn of the seventh century, has left us two examples of the aetiological 'cause' genre apparently typical of the more advanced East-Syrian 'schools'. However, his *On Golden Friday* (the first Friday after Pentecost) and *On the Rogations* (i.e. on the different types of prayer) tell us little about the School's history, despite the light they shed on its intellectual life.[12]

Mention should also be made of other sources which may eventually help to contribute to the history of the East-Syrian schools and to the history of the Church of the East in general. Although Arthur Vööbus occasionally used the later Arabic sources in his reconstruction of the history of the School, more work could be done, especially after source critical analysis, on a number of these texts. For example, there are parallels to the events in the 'Life of Narsai' (i.e. Chapter 31 of Barḥadbeshabba's *Ecclesiastical History*), translated in this volume, in Mārī ibn Sulaymān's late Arabic *Kitāb al-Mijdal* and Ṣalibā ibn Yuḥannā's borrowing of 'Amr ibn Mattā's use of the *Kitāb al-Mijdal*.[13] These two texts as well as Ibn aṭ-Ṭayyib's *Fiqh an-naṣrāniyya*

10 *Statutes of the School of Nisibis*. Becker, *Fear of God*, 81–87 offers a summary of the contents of the canons. See also I. Guidi, 'Gli statuti della scuola di Nisibi', *Giornale della Società Asiatica Italiana* (Rome) 4 (1890): 169–95; Chabot, 'L'école de Nisibe, son histoire, ses statuts'; E. Nestle, 'Die Statuten der Schule von Nisibis aus den Jahren 496–590', *Zeitschrift für Kirchengeschichte* 18 (1898): 221–29; N. V. Pigulevskaja, *Les villes de l'état iranien aux époques Parthe et Sassanide. Contribution à l'histoire sociale de la Basse Antiquité* (École Pratiques des Hautes Études, VIe section, 'Documents et Recherches' VI; Paris: Mouton, 1963), 244–51 (see note 24 above); Vööbus, *History*, 90–99, 147–48, and 269–75.

11 Gorgias Press has planned a reprint, but as of publication of this volume it was still unclear to whom the rights of the volume belong.

12 Ḥenānā, *On Golden Friday* and *On Rogations* in Scher, ed., *Traités*, 53–82.

13 E. Gismondi, ed., *Maris ibn Salmonis, De Patriarchis Ecclesiae Orientalis Commentaria* (2 volumes; Rome: C. de Luigi, 1899). On these texts, see G. Graf, *Geschichte der christlichen arabischen Literatur* (Studi e Testi 133; Vatican: Biblioteca Apostolica Vaticana, 1947), II: 200–02 and 216–18 respectively.

and especially the *Chronicle of Siirt*, which is employed occasionally in this volume, may offer information not found in the earlier Syriac sources.[14]

Furthermore, numerous other texts mention the School of Nisibis in passing. However, these sources often offer only further references to the School and no detailed evidence. For example, references from the late sixth and seventh centuries to saints and church leaders spending their formative years there are commonplace and point to the School's prominence within the Church of the East. Unfortunately the sources take for granted what their audiences know about the School and therefore do not provide information useful for the reconstruction, for example, of the School's curriculum or its leadership.

The main question regarding the origin of the School of Nisibis is its historical relation to the School of Edessa, or the School of the Persians in Edessa, as it is more commonly referred to by the earlier sources. As stated above, the School of the Persians was closed in 489 CE under the auspices of Cyrus, Bishop of Edessa (471–98), by order of the emperor Zeno, at which point its members migrated into the Persian Empire, some of them, most notably Narsai, going on to found the School of Nisibis.[15]

The School of the Persians seems to have been one of several intellectual circles in fifth-century Edessa.[16] Although many of the details are open to dispute, it is clear that it played a significant role as the predecessor to the School of Nisibis.[17] For example, it is possible that a number of the school offices later institutionalized in Nisibis developed first in Edessa and that the core of the exegetical tradition as well as some of the curriculum from the latter institution originated in the former.

The standard view of the School of the Persians in modern scholarship

14 W. Hoenerbach and O. Spies, eds., Ibn aṭ-Ṭaiyib, *Fiqh an-naṣrānīya*, 'Das Recht der Christenheit' (CSCO 167–68; Louvain: Secrétariat du CSCO, 1957), II:168.12–169.4. For a discussion of the sources of the *Chronicle of Siirt*, see L. Sako, 'Les sources de la Chronique de Séert', *PdO* 14 (1987): 155–66.

15 This date has been disputed in the secondary literature. Vööbus takes Narsai's exodus from Edessa for Nisibis to be in 471 (Vööbus, *History*, 33–47). I have argued against this elsewhere, Becker, *Fear of God*, 74–75.

16 The Acts of the so-called Robber Council of Ephesus of 449 briefly and tantalizingly mention schools of Armenians, Syrians, and Persians in Edessa; *Akten der Ephesinischen Synode vom Jahre 449*, ed. J. Flemming. Abhandlungen der Akademie der Wissenschaften zu Göttingen, Philologisch-historische Klasse, New Series 15.1 (Berlin: Weidmannsche Buchhandlung, 1917), 24:22–24. In English, see Doran, *Stewards of the Poor*, 148, despite the idiosyncratic translation.

17 Drijvers, 'The School of Edessa'.

has suffered from an uncritical reading of the sources and an anachronistic understanding of what type of institution the term 'school' may have referred to in antiquity.[18] Modern scholarship has attributed greater significance to the School than it perhaps deserves, arguing, for example, that commentaries on Aristotle's logical works were composed and studied there[19] and misleadingly extending its history back to the time of Bardaiṣan of Edessa (d. 222) by using the title 'School of Edessa' more broadly to refer to the intellectual culture that existed in the city of Edessa.[20] The origins of the School of the Persians are unclear, lying somewhere in the late fourth century and perhaps related to the immigration of Christians from the East after Jovian's concession of several provinces to the Sasanians in 363, following the debacle of the emperor Julian's invasion of Sasanian Mesopotamia. Furthermore, a tradition developed from early on that Ephrem the Syrian, the master of Syriac poetry (d. 373), taught in and even founded the School, but this is a later retrojection.[21]

Its appellation ('of the Persians') and the background of those persons immediately associated with it in the sources suggest an originally ethnically-based intellectual circle, which in time, perhaps due to the influx of Christians from the East and the changing theological standards in the West, became the centre of a more conservative Antiochene theology. Christianity originally spread to Mesopotamia in part from Antioch and therefore the Antiochene theological emphasis on the humanity of Christ as well as a hesitant stance towards allegorical exegesis – a practice commonly associated with Alexandria – were shared by the Church of the East. This shared theological heritage between the Church of Antioch and the Church of the East would explain the popularity at the School of the works of the so-called Nestorian fathers, such as Diodore of Tarsus and Theodore of Mopsuestia, which were translated in part by those associated with the School.[22] Moreover, it seems that the School only became controversial within Edessa as it developed a pedagogical hierarchy and began to resemble a more formally organized institution of learning.

18 The standard volume on the School commits this same error (Vööbus, *History*). See comments at Becker, *Fear of God*, 41–42.

19 E.g., on Probus, see Vööbus, *History*, 104–05.

20 E.g., E. R. Hayes, *L'école d'Édesse* (1930); more recently, Drijvers, 'The School of Edessa'.

21 *Cause* 381.8.

22 The West-Syrian Jacob of Sarug describes the study of such texts occurring at the School in the mid to later fifth century, *Letter* 14, 58.21–59.8.

As I have discussed in detail elsewhere, all but one of the sources for the School derive from after its closure and thus reflect the ongoing controversy between the West Syrians, for whom the School was a source of heresy, and the East Syrians, who understood it as the intellectual predecessor of the School of Nisibis. The question remains unresolved as to how much continuity there was between the School of the Persians in Edessa and that of Nisibis. The two richest sources for the former, *The Cause of the Foundation of the Schools* and the *Ecclesiastical History*, both of which are translated in this volume, were composed at the School of Nisibis and describe the School of the Persians in the fifth century. However, inconsistencies between these two texts suggest that their knowledge of this predecessor institution is hazy.

In any case, in the late fifth century the School of Nisibis was founded by Narsai, the prior head of the School of the Persians in Edessa and the first of the School of Nisibis, and Barṣaumā, the bishop of the city. The details on this and subsequent events in the early history of the School are not always clear, especially since the two main accounts, the *Ecclesiastical History* and the *Cause*, disagree on occasion. Apparently the first set of canons established for the School did not work, and a new set of canons, which are extant, were established in 496.[23] Further canons are extant from 590 from the time of the leadership of Ḥenānā of Adiabene. These were reconfirmed in 602, perhaps due to the crisis during Ḥenānā's tenure of office that contributed to the decline of the School. Between Narsai (d. c. 503) and Ḥenānā (d. c. 612) there were several heads, or 'exegetes' (Syr. *mphashshqānē*) as they were called, of the School, but none left his mark more deeply upon the institution than Abraham of Bēt Rabban, who may have led the School for up to sixty years. It is thus no wonder that the author of the *Ecclesiastical History* followed his chapter on the life of Narsai with a chapter on the life of Abraham, the final chapter in the work as a whole.

The basic chronology of the School's leadership can be reconstructed only for the sixth century, and even this has a number of uncertainties. Arthur Vööbus's *History of the School of Nisibis*, the standard study and reference tool for the School, offers the fullest attempt to develop an accurate chronology for the School's leadership:[24]

23 This is discussed at *Statutes of the School of Nisibis*, 31–32.

24 Vööbus's results are schematized in Tamcke, *Der Katholikos-Patriarch Sabrīšō I. (596-604) und das Mönchtum*, 68.

Narsai	until 503
Elisha bar Qozbāyē	503 to 510
Abraham of Bēt Rabban	510 to 569
John of Bēt Rabban	after 547 or 561/2 or 564
Isho'yahb	two years around 565/8
Abraham	?
Ḥenānā of Adiabene	571 to before 612

Much of this chronology derives from the *Ecclesiastical History* and the *Cause*, neither of which demonstrates a strong interest in accurate dating and chronology. Therefore, it seems that unless radically new information is uncovered Vööbus's dating provides the best overall chronology, although his reading of the sources is questionable at a number of points.[25]

It is difficult to determine the School's precise curriculum, if curriculum is even the appropriate term to use for pre-modern centers of learning such as this, where learning was more informal than in modern institutions in which a clearly delineated course of study is often, if not practised, the ideal.[26] The titles used in the sources for the different types of teacher may point to the varying levels of study: the elementary instructor (*mhaggyānā*), the reader (*maqryānā*), and finally the exegete (*mphashshqānā*),[27] who was the sole occupant of this office and the head of the School. It is likely that there was some fluidity between the pedagogical focus of one type of teacher and another. There were also other instructors, whose role in the hierarchy is less clear: the teacher (*mallphānā*) and the interpreter (*bādoqā*). The School had an administrator in charge of the daily routine, the steward (*rabbaytā*). The term 'schoolman' (*eskolāyā*) appears as well in the sources, not only for students, but also for more advanced persons associated with the School.

The level of learning at the School ran across a wide spectrum, from basic literacy to the study of Aristotelian logic. One unifying factor was the sociality of study. Unlike the East-Syrian monasteries, where monks were encouraged to study scripture on their own in the privacy of their own cells and collective gatherings were limited to weekly Eucharistic meetings, students at the School studied together and, as the canons attest,

25 For example, he uses the *Chronicle of Arbela*, a text of questionable, if not authenticity, then accuracy, to resolve problems in dating (Vööbus, *History*, 132–33).

26 For a more detailed discussion of the curriculum, the offices, and life at the School, see, e.g., Becker, *Fear of God*, 87–96.

27 The term *mphashshqānā* is often rendered 'interpreter' in translations and secondary literature.

lived together. This common life of study began with acquiring basic literacy for those who arrived without the ability to read. Literacy was based on the Psalter and probably also entailed the study of the liturgy. Some documents point to a thorough study of much of the New Testament and the Christian Old Testament.[28] Reading eventually led to interpretation, but it is not clear where one level of study ended and the next began. For example, we may assume that the 'reader' guided students in more than simply reading, since below him was the 'elementary instructor'. However, if the 'reader' also provided interpretation, it is not clear how this differed from the higher interpretation of the 'exegete', who, we are told, led the 'choir', a collective gathering the aim of which is uncertain.[29]

The exegesis of the School was heavily derived from the exegetical works of Theodore of Mopsuestia as they had been translated and subsequently received by the Church of the East. That Theodore was simply referred to as 'the exegete' by the East Syrians demonstrates both the authority his works held but also the easy correlation that could be drawn between him and the head of the School, who was also called 'the exegete'. Most of the exegetical tradition of the School itself is unfortunately lost with the exception of the works of Narsai, the first head of the School.[30] Of the numerous poetical works attributed to Narsai, at least some must have been composed at the School. Furthermore, even those composed at the School of the Persians in Edessa may shed some light on the School of Nisibis, inasmuch as the former was the predecessor of the latter. The sources mention works by a number of other figures associated with the School of Nisibis, especially its various head exegetes, but none of these are extant.[31] Traces of these works can be found in quotation in later exegetical collections, which are no doubt in part the reason for the disappearance of these earlier works. The numerous other works attributed to members of the School, for example, collections of letters, are also, alas, lost.

28 *Statutes of the School of Nisibis*, 107–09. See also *Syriac and Arabic Documents*, 185–88.

29 The Syriac term *si'tā* simply means 'troop' or 'group', but here seems to be some type of collective liturgically-based study.

30 Robert Macina, 'L'homme à l'école de Dieu. D'Antioche à Nisibe: Profil herméneutique, théologique et kérugmatique du mouvement scoliaste nestorien', *Proche-Orient Chretien* 32 (1982): 87–124, 263–301; 33 (1983): 39–103. Molenberg, 'The Silence of the Sources'. More recently on the East-Syrian exegetical tradition in general, see for example Clemens Leonhard, *Ishodad of Merw's Exegesis of the Psalms 119 and 139–147: A study of his interpretation in the light of the Syriac translation of Theodore of Mopsuestia's commentary* (CSCO 587; Louvain: Peeters, 2001), 50–61.

31 The majority of the references to this material are gathered in Vööbus, *History*, *passim*.

The learning that occurred at the School and the kind of intellectual interaction are possibly represented by the East-Syrian 'cause' (*'elltā*) literature, an aetiological genre focusing primarily on explaining the origins of certain holidays and ritual practices.[32] Several examples of this genre are extant. In fact, the *Cause of the Foundation of the Schools* seems to belong to a subset of this genre, one that provides an explanation for the origins of the 'school session (*mawtbā d-eskolē*)'. The aetiological interests, the structural division of information around a formalized list of questions, the emphasis on sacred days and theological questions, as well as other features of this genre may be representative of the intellectual interests and approach found at the School. Texts such as these are written in a rhetorical fashion and may have been addressed to large audiences.

The use of basic philosophical logic in a number of texts from the School points to the study of certain Greek philosophical texts, particularly Syriac translations of the Aristotelian *Organon* and parts of the Neoplatonic commentary tradition on it.[33] Philosophy itself was not studied at the School, but rather philosophical texts and ideas were incorporated into the curriculum where they were practically useful for exegetical and theological inquiry. The titles of other texts mentioned in the sources yet no longer extant suggest that students were also introduced to theological polemic and debate, thus preparing them for proselytising and disputing with Zoroastrians, Jews, and heterodox Christians.

The School of Nisibis seems to have gone into decline in the early to mid-seventh century.[34] After the death of Ḥenānā of Adiabene (c. 610), who was head of the School in the late sixth and early seventh centuries, the sources become thin, apart from a number of passing references to East Syrians studying there. It is possible that this decline was due to the controversy which developed around Ḥenānā, who was accused of introducing heterodox exegesis and theology into the curriculum and condemned at a council under the Catholicos Sabrisho' in 605. The *Chronicle of Siirt* describes a mass exodus during his tenure of office.[35] However, there were a number of events at this time, including the Arab defeat of the Sasanian Empire, which led to radical political, economic, and cultural changes in the region.

32 On this genre, see Becker, *Fear of God*, 98–112.

33 The *Organon* (lit. 'tool') is the common appellation for Aristotle's *Categories*, *De Interpretatione*, and *Prior Analytics* I.1–7.

34 For a more detailed discussion of the School's decline, see Becker, *Fear of God*, 197–203.

35 *Chronicle of Siirt* 2.2.511–12.

Furthermore, it is possible that the School's decline occurred due to its great success as a model institution of learning. Many of the leading figures of the Church of the East, especially in the sixth and seventh centuries, had studied at the School of Nisibis and no doubt introduced its learning and institutional structure as they ascended through the ecclesiastical hierarchy and spread throughout the Church to various positions of authority, becoming bishops and heads of monasteries. By the end of the sixth century East-Syrian schools could be found through much of Sasanian Mesopotamia and a new scholastic culture had been infused through much of the Church of the East. The School of Seleucia, which was farther south in the Sasanian capital, was also another important intellectual centre.[36] However, the sources refer to numerous schools throughout Mesopotamia, even some in towns of lesser importance. As mentioned above, these schools varied from complex, independent institutions, like the School of Nisibis, to small study circles attached to the local village church.[37] The School of Nisibis fades from our sources in the early seventh century, but its influence on the Church of the East is clearly discernible for long time after its apparent decline.

IDENTIFYING BARḤADBESHABBĀ

Two of the most important sources for both the history of the School of Nisibis and the intellectual life engaged in there are the *Cause* and the *Ecclesiastical History* – specifically the last two chapters of the latter, which treat respectively the life of Narsai (d. c. 503), the first head of the School, and that of Abraham of Bēt Rabban (d. c. 569), its director through much of the sixth century. These two texts have both been attributed to a Barhadbeshabbā, but some scholars have identified two distinct persons in the sources, Barhadbeshabbā 'Arbāyā and Barḥadbeshabbā of Ḥulwān. No one has formally examined the question of the authorship of the *Cause* and the *Ecclesiastical History*, though scholars have in passing expressed views on this problem. This question and the possibility of clearly differentiating between the two Barḥadbeshabbās needs to be addressed, especially since the *Cause* may rely on the *Ecclesiastical History*, or at least share a source with it, despite the discrepancies between the two.

Two contemporary figures named Barḥadbeshabbā are attested in the sources: Barḥadbeshabbā 'Arbāyā and Barḥadbeshabbā of Ḥulwān.[38]

36 Becker, *Fear of God*, 157–59. On its founding see the Mingana Fragment in this volume.

37 See note 3 above. For the School of Seleucia, see Becker, *Fear of God*, 157–59.

38 Barḥadbeshabbā is not an uncommon Syriac name. It is the equivalent of 'Kuriakos' or

'Arbāyā is a locative appellation used for someone from the region of Bēt 'Arbāyē, called 'Arabistān' in Middle Persian, named after the Arabs who settled there.[39] In antiquity it was the diocese of the city of Nisibis. Ḥulwān, or Ḥalwān, was in eastern Iran, near Hamadan, not far from the contemporary border with Iraq.[40] Aside from these two figures there are also several references to a Barḥadbeshabbā that may correspond to either or even neither of the two.

The early fourteenth-century catalogue of 'Abdisho' has the following entry for Barḥadbeshabbā 'Arbāyā:

> Barḥadbeshabbā 'Arbāyā wrote a book of treasures in three parts, and disputes (*drāshē*) with all religions (*deḥlān*) and their refutation, and an ecclesiastical (history), and a cause of the followers (Syr. *bēt*, or 'school') of Diodore, and a commentary (*mashlmānutā*) on Mark the evangelist and (the psalms of) David.[41]

Scholars have commonly understood the 'ecclesiastical history' mentioned here as referring to the text entitled in its manuscript 'The History of the Holy Fathers Who were Persecuted because of the Truth'.[42] A late manuscript attributes a hymn to the same person.[43] Perhaps the commentary on Psalms mentioned by 'Abdisho' is the source of the quotation attributed to a Barḥadbeshabbā in a later psalm commentary.[44] Similarly, the seventh-century monastic writer, Dadisho' of Bēt Qaṭrāyē, cites a 'Book of Treasures', which he attributes to Barḥadbeshabbā the Teacher (*mallphānā*), probably the same person.[45]

Barḥadbeshabbā of Ḥulwān is referred to by the *Khuzistan Chronicle*, an East-Syrian chronicle probably composed no later than the 660s CE (the last

'Dominicus', i.e. born on Sunday.

39 For a discussion of the place name, see D. L. Kennedy, 'The Place-Name "Arbeia"', *Britannia* 17 (1986): 332–33.

40 J.-M. Fiey, *Pour un Oriens Christianus Novus*, 92–93; idem, 'Médie chrétienne', 360–68.

41 *Bibliotheca Orientalis* III.1.1.169 (Chap. XCIII).

42 Barhadbeshabba, *La second partie de l'histoire ecclésiastique*, 495 and 631.10–11.

43 Cambridge manuscript of the 16th or 17th century, William Wright, *Catalogue of Syriac Manuscripts* (2 vols.; Cambridge, 1901), II: 1083 (Oo. 1. 22).

44 Ms Ming. Syr. 58. His name is in the list of those quoted on 17b of this manuscript, Alphonse Mingana, *Catalogue of the Mingana Collection of Manuscripts* (Cambridge, 1948–1963), col. 159.

45 Dadisho' Qatraya, *Commentaire du Livre d 'Abba Isaïe (logoi I-XV)*, ed. and trans. R. Draguet (CSCO 326–27; Louvain: Peeters, 1972), 263.22 (trans. 203); Discourse 15.12. This is cited by Vööbus as a reference to Barḥadbeshabbā 'Arbāyā (Vööbus, *History*, 281).

datable event is in 652 CE).[46] In a discussion of figures from the early seventh century the text states: 'Famous in composition was Barḥadbeshabbā of Hulwān'.[47] This same Barḥadbeshabbā is listed in the *Synodicon Orientale*, a collection of council acts of the Church of the East, as one of the signatories to the record for the Council of Mār Gregory I of 605 CE.[48] The strong reaffirmation of the orthodoxy of all the writings of Theodore of Mopsuestia at this council and the one before it in 596 can be read as a positioning against Ḥenānā of Adiabene, the director of the School of Nisibis praised in the *Cause*, who was accused of flouting Theodore's authority in his own exegesis.[49]

The *Chronicle of Siirt* suggests that these two figures referred to as Barhadbeshabbā are the same person.[50] The *Chronicle* contains a list of those who left the School of Nisibis due to the controversy caused by Ḥ enānā of Adiabene.

> Among those who left the School of Nisibis there were Isho'yahb of Gedālā, who later became Catholicos (i.e. Isho'yahb II), Ḥadbeshabbā 'Arbāyā who became metropolitan of Ḥulwān; Isho'yahb of Adiabene who became Catholicos (i.e. Isho'yahb III); Paul the exegete in the monastery of Abimelek, Michael the teacher, and many other wise men.[51]

This passage would seem to settle the question. However, there remains the possibility that its author is conflating two distinct figures. The *Chronicle* is rather late, composed in either the tenth or eleventh century CE. Ambiguities in the sources also seem to derive from the apparent fame of at least one Barḥadbeshabbā: for example, that sources such as the ninth-century biblical commentator Isho'dād of Merv and the later *Gannat bussāmē* (*Garden of Delights*, a commentary on the East-Syrian lectionary) merely

46 Also known as 'Guidi's Chronicle', after the editor of the *Chronica Minora*; 'Chronicum Anonymum', ed. and tr. I. Guidi (CSCO Scr. Syr. 1–2; Leipzig, 1903). Hoyland, *Seeing Islam As Others Saw It*, 185. Brock, 'Syriac Historical Writing', 25, gives the date of c. 670–80. For a recent English translation of the text from the beginning (15) up to 30.19 (the text ends at 39), see Geoffrey Greatrex and Samuel N. C. Lieu, eds., *The Roman Eastern Frontier and the Persian Wars: Part II AD 363–630, A narrative sourcebook* (London: Routledge, 2002), 229–37.

47 'Chronicum Anonymum', 22.25-26 (Latin 20.23–24).

48 *Synodicon Orientale*, 214 (491).

49 E.g., Brock, 'The Christology of the Church of the East', 127, 139. See also Becker, *Fear of God*, 197–203.

50 Hoyland, *Seeing Islam As Others Saw It*, 443–46.

51 *Chronicle of Siirt* 2.2.511–12. Note the minor corruption of the name 'Barḥadbeshabbā' in the Arabic.

refer to Barḥadbeshabbā without any appellation suggests that he was well known enough not to require explicit designation.[52]

The *Cause* was composed between 581 and c. 610 CE. The text's reference to Isho'yahb of Arzon, who became Isho'yahb I, the Catholicos of the East, provides the *terminus post quem* of 581 CE.[53] A definite *terminus ante quem* is more difficult to determine; we only know that the text was written within the lifetime of Ḥenānā of Adiabene, who lived until c. 610. The text would have been written perhaps before the mid-590s if the author is identical with the Barḥadbeshabbā who participated in opposing Ḥenānā at the Council of 605 CE and left the School some time after.

Unfortunately the manuscript tradition of the *Cause* does not help us in identifying the author. The older manuscripts upon which Addai Scher, the editor of the text, based his edition were either lost in 1915 when he was murdered or may have eventually been deposited in Baghdad, but at this point in time it is not possible to verify whether they are there and if they have survived to the present. The extant manuscripts are late copies made by scholars such as Scher and Alphonse Mingana and therefore attributions to Barḥadbeshabbā 'Arbāyā are of lesser value.[54]

If the same Barḥadbeshabbā who rejected Ḥenānā also composed the *Cause*, how are we to understand the significant praise the *Cause* gives Henānā? It could be the standard laudatory comments made about the head of the School, composed before he became a controversial figure, or an apology for a leader under attack – or even an attempt to prescribe to Ḥenānā how he *should* be.[55] This is a matter of interpretation. The *Cause*'s statements linking Ḥenānā to Theodore of Mopsuestia may be taken as a standard practice tying the head of the School to an authoritative figure of the past or as an intentionally defensive posture, since Ḥenānā had been accused of flouting Theodore's exegetical authority. If the author is defending Ḥenānā, this would suggest the text was written later in his career, after his views became subject to attack. This would then date the text to the early 590s,

52 Isho'dad of Merv, *Commentaire sur l'Ancient Testament*, ed. J.-M. Vosté et C. van den Eynde (CSCO 126–86 [*passim*]; Louvain: L. Durbecq, 1950–1981), Genèse I:81. *Gannat bussāmē*: Ms Manch. Ryl. Syr. 41. Baumstark, *Geschichte*, 136 n. 6 also refers to a citation of a Barḥadbeshabbā in an anonymous New Testament commentary.

53 *Cause* 397.11–398.2. cf. Ortiz de Urbina, *Patrologia Syriaca*, 133. See also Vööbus, *History*, 295.

54 On the manuscripts of the *Cause*, see Appendix I.

55 *Cause* 390.7–393.3; on the controversy surrounding Ḥenānā, see also the discussion in Becker, *Fear of God*, 197–203.

when Ḥenānā began to cause a controversy, but before this controversy had stirred up the Church at large.

The main problem in identifying the author of the *Cause* depends on whether he is the same Barḥadbeshabbā ‘Arbāyā who composed the *Ecclesiastical History*. This text, the *terminus post quem* for which derives from the death of Abraham of Bēt Rabban in 569 CE, is the other major narrative source for the history of the School of Nisibis.[56] As stated above, few scholars have treated in any detail the questions surrounding the identity of the author of the *Cause* and his relationship to the author of the *Ecclesiastical History* and whether Barḥadbeshabbā ‘Arbāyā and Barḥadbeshabbā of Ḥulwān were one and the same person.[57] More often the issue has been mentioned in passing.[58] The scholars who have addressed this issue in any way at all include: Mingana,[59] Scher,[60] Nau,[61] Baumstark,[62] Hermann,[63] Ortiz de Urbina,[64] Vööbus,[65] and Fiey.[66] Following Fiey, Stephen Gero ignores the ‘Arbāyā / Ḥulwān question and argues that the *Ecclesiastical History* belonged to Barḥadbeshabbā, but that the *Cause* could not be his because its adulatory tone towards Ḥenānā of Adiabene does not fit with Barhadbeshabbā’s later stance against him.[67] Gero suggests that ‘[s]ince orations of this sort were fairly common, one could argue that a medieval

56 For this date, see, e.g., Vööbus, *History*, 210.

57 Various authors have employed both of these sources and not taken a stand regarding their relationship or the identity of their authors (e.g. Martin Tamcke, *Der Katholikos-Patriarch Sabrīšō I. (596–604) und das Mönchtum*).

58 E. g., G. J. Reinink, ‘“Edessa Grew Dim and Nisibis Shone Forth”’, 81 and n. 15; *Synodicon Orientale*, 479 n. 3; Jérôme Labourt, *Le Christianisme dans l’Empire Perse, sous la Dynastie Sassanide (224–632)*, 223; Rubens Duval, *La littérature Syriaque* (Paris: V. Lecoffre, 1907), 204. Chabot seems to be ignorant of the issue: J.-B. Chabot, *Littérature Syriaque* (Paris: Bloud et Gay, 1934), 59.

59 Mingana, *Réponse à M. l’abbé J.-B. Chabot, à propos de la chronique de Barhadbšabba*, 4ff.

60 *Cause* 322; see also Scher, ‘Étude supplémentaire sur les écrivains syriens orientaux’, 15.

61 Barhadbeshabba, *La second partie de l’histoire ecclésiastique*, 494.

62 Baumstark, *Geschichte*, 136.

63 Hermann, ‘Die Schule von Nisibis vom 5. bis 7. Jahrhundert’, 94 implies that he sees the texts as by two different authors.

64 Ortiz de Urbina, *Patrologia Syriaca*, 132–33.

65 Vööbus, *History*, as he sees them as two persons, he treats them respectively, 280–82 and 294–96.

66 J.-M. Fiey, *Jalons pour une histoire de l’église en Iraq* (CSCO 310; Louvain: Secrétariat du CorpusSCO, 1970), 25–26.

67 Gero, *Barṣauma*, 5–6 and notes.

scribe who knew merely that Barḥadbeshabbā and Ḥenānā were contemporaries, but was not acquainted with the history of their relationship, attributed the (anonymous) oration to this 6th-century writer'.[68]

However, while it has been noted that the Council of 605, along with those of 585 and 596, seemed to be aimed at the theological aberrations of Ḥenānā of Adiabene and his followers, and while it is true that the *Cause* contains a veritable panegyric of the same Ḥenānā, this does not necessarily prove, as Gero would argue, that the author is not the same person who signed the acts of 605 and left the School. From a *terminus post quem* of 581 to the early 590s or even later Barḥadbeshabbā could have reevaluated his relationship with Ḥenānā and shifted his support to Ḥenānā's adversaries. In other words, he could have changed his mind.

The identity of the two authors of the *Cause* and the *Ecclesiastical History* could be maintained if we take 'Abdisho''s reference to the 'Cause of the Followers of Diodore' as a recherché reference to the *Cause*.[69] There certainly does not seem to have been an actual group of 'Diodorians' within the Church of the East. 'Abdisho''s odd appellation for the work could be explained as an attempt to fit the seven-syllable metrical line. However, this reading could in turn be countered by suggesting that even if 'Abdisho' is referring to the *Cause* he may be conflating the two Barḥadbeshabbās, as the *Chronicle of Siirt* may also be doing, or that he may simply be attributing a text of an unknown author to a known one, as Gero suggests. Further evidence may come to light in the future, but to a certain extent the question of whether the *Cause* and the *Ecclesiastical History* have the same author is insignificant. Individual personalities are of lesser relevance here, since both texts, whether by the same author or not, were written in the same institution within a few years of one another. Furthermore, as I argue in Appendix III, the *Cause* is dependent on the *Ecclesiastical History*, or at least shares a common source with it.

ON THE MANUSCRIPTS, TRANSLATION, NOTES AND TERMS

Manuscript variants, especially the numerous minor ones for the *Cause*, are not included in the translation and commentary, except when they are of particular interest. For the 'Letter' of Simeon of Bēt Arsham I relied on

68 Ibid. n. 26.

69 Scher himself mentions this connection but then rejects it because Diodore does not play a major role in the text (*Cause* 322).

Assemani's text, as well as the one manuscript, Ms Vatican Syriac 135, which has been reproduced on DVD by Brigham Young University.[70] Although I used the manuscript in preparing this translation, I do not provide a thorough commentary on it. I employed it specifically where it differed from or illuminated Assemani's text. I was able to glance at the one manuscript of the *Ecclesiatical History* several years ago, but I have not had the luxury of consulting it while producing this volume. I wanted this volume to serve as a handy introduction to these texts and the larger cultural world from which they derive. It seemed superfluous to do excessive manuscript work on them, especially since there are numerous other texts that have not been published at all. Apart from the extra material published by Mingana (i.e. the 'Fragment'), the translation of the *Cause* is based on Scher's text and notes (see the discussion of the manuscripts in Appendix I). My translation often agrees with Scher's French version, even when he at times translates T from the apparatus without mentioning that he is altering his base text. I comment in the notes on those few occasions where I resort to his critical apparatus in disagreement with him on the text. Furthermore, I usually note where my translation differs radically from his, and I am usually far more literal in my rendering.

In translating these texts I have tried to be as literal as possible without making the English too awkward for the reader. My only addition to the texts themselves are the italicized section headings included throughout. Occasionally I have taken some liberties to bring out the particular sense of a phrase, but in general I preferred to keep the English as close to the Syriac as possible. I have on occasion translated biblical quotations to fit the context of quotation, rather than employing the sense they would have in the original biblical context. For example, it would be misleading to translate *talmidā*, the standard word for a 'disciple' of Jesus (equivalent to Gr. *mathētḗs*) as simply 'disciple,' since this would lose the vividness of the pedagogical understanding of Christianity that we find in the *Cause*. Therefore I translate it as 'student' to better convey how the author would have probably understood this term.[71]

The notes have been written in order to clarify and highlight certain aspects of the texts. I have provided some parallels where pertinent, but did not do an extensive and systematic reading of the Syriac and Greek sources that might have been used to further illuminate these texts. The notes would

70 Kristian S. Heal and Carl W. Griffin, eds., *Syriac Manuscripts from the Vatican Library*, Volume 1. DVD-Rom (Bibliotheca Apostolica Vaticana; Brigham Young University, 2005).

71 E.g., *Cause* 373.2.

have become cumbersome, if I had noted every connection, for example, between the *Cause* and the works of Narsai and Theodore of Mopsuestia. Nor was I systematic in pointing out Greek loan words. I ignore those words that had already become standard in the Syriac language by the fifth century CE. I employed the following abbreviations for cross-references to notes in other works: SL = 'Letter' of Simeon of Bēt Arsham; LN = Life of Narsai; LA = Life of Abraham of Bēt Rabban; CS = *Cause of the Foundation of the Schools*.

Finally, there is a glossary of selected terms at the back of the book. I have used more accurate and less theologically offensive terms in this volume and they are explained there.

The bibliography only includes those volumes mentioned more than once in the notes.

THE TRANSLITERATION OF THE SYRIAC ALPHABET IN THIS VOLUME

I have transliterated Syriac words throughout the volume, instead of rendering them in a script legible only to those who know the Syriac language. In this way, readers can see, for example, the derivation of certain Syriac words from Greek, and those who know another Semitic language, such as Hebrew, can make further sense of the notes. In transliterating I have tried to use a system that would be both simple and accurate. Of the so-called *bgadkephat* letters, that is, consonants that have both aspirated and unaspirated forms, I have only distinguished between the unaspirated 'p' and the aspirated 'ph', since this distinction requires a major change in pronunciation for an English speaker. I have added 'e' to some names where a half vowel would technically appear (ĕ), like Ḥenānā and Barḥadbeshabbā, to make pronunciation easier. Since they are not marked in the Syriac script, I have not differentiated by means of a macron between historically long and short vowels (o/ō and u/ū). In the table of parallels below I provide the Syriac alphabet and the transliterated equivalents used in this volume, as well as some of the alternative transliterations readers may find in other volumes.

Syriac	**Transliteration**	**Other Volumes**
ܐ	’/unmarked when frontal/vowel letter	’
ܒ	b	b/bh
ܓ	g	g/gh
ܕ	d	d/dh
ܗ	h	
ܘ	w/vowel letter	
ܙ	z	
ܚ	ḥ	h
ܛ	ṭ	t
ܝ	y/vowel letter	
ܟ	k	k/kh
ܠ	l	
ܡ	m	
ܢ	n	
ܣ	s	
ܥ	‘	unmarked
ܦ	p/ph	p
ܨ	ṣ	s, ts
ܩ	q	
ܪ	r	
ܫ	sh	š
ܬ	t	t/th

SIMEON OF BĒT ARSHAM, *'LETTER' ON THE 'NESTORIANIZATION' OF PERSIA*

INTRODUCTION

All but one of the sources for the School of the Persians in Edessa derive from at least several years after its closure, and some of them are from decades after its heyday. Furthermore, the various passing references to the School and its closure have only recently been examined.[1] One of the most commonly cited sources for the reconstruction of the history of the School, the sequence of events surrounding its closure, and what was known by scholars in the past as the subsequent 'Nestorianization' of the Christian communities of the Sasanian Empire is a 'letter' by Simeon of Bēt Arsham, the contentious West-Syrian bishop of the early sixth century. Simeon's letter is extant in one manuscript, Ms Vatican Syriac 135. The text was first published with a Latin translation by Joseph Simeon Assemani (1687–1768 CE) in his *Bibliotheca Orientalis Clementino-Vaticana*, a collection which served as the main resource in Syriac Studies until the rapid growth of the field in the late nineteenth and early twentieth centuries.[2]

Simeon's life is described by his student, John of Ephesus, in his *Lives of the Eastern Saints*.[3] He played a role in the Church not unlike that of Philoxenus of Mabbug (d. 523), Severus of Antioch (d. 538), John of Tella (d. 538), and Jacob Burd'ānā (d. 578), after whom the West Syrians received the name 'Jacobites'. All these men struggled to promote the Miaphysite

1 Becker, *Fear of God*, 41–61.

2 *Biblioteca Orientalis* I.346–58. On the *Bibliotheca Orientalis* and its influence, see Sebastian Brock, 'The Development of Syriac Studies', in *The Edward Hincks Bicentenary Lectures*, ed. Kevin J. Cathcart (Dublin: Department of Near East Languages, University College Dublin, 1994), 98–99, 109. There is also a French translation in Garsoïan, *L'église Arménienne* at 450–56, but this is clearly based on Assemani's Latin text.

3 John of Ephesus, *Lives of the Eastern Saints*, 17: 137–58 (Chapter X). See Wright, *History*, 79–81; Barsoum, *History*, 97; Baumstark, *Geschichte*, 145–46. The one full study of this text is Harvey, *Asceticism and Society in Crisis: John of Ephesus and 'The Lives of the Eastern Saints'*. Later sources on Simeon seem to depend on John's account (e.g., Garsoïan, *L'église arménienne*, 186 n. 136).

cause and in doing so helped to develop a separate Miaphysite ecclesiastical hierarchy.[4] They are the true fathers of today's Syrian Orthodox Church. Simeon became bishop of Bēt Arsham, possibly near the Tigris, not far from Seleucia-Ctesiphon,[5] and seems to have spent his career canvassing for the Miaphysite position. He was known as 'The Disputer', because he engaged in public debate with East Syrians, most notably winning against the East-Syrian Catholicos Bābai, after which Simeon received his bishopric (between 497 and 502/3 CE).[6] The latest reference to Simeon places him in Constantinople some time before the death of the empress Theodora in 548 CE.

Simeon's works include an anaphora (the Eucharistic portion of the divine liturgy) attributed to him and, more importantly, a document on which much research has focused, his letter describing events in Arabia, including the persecution of Christians by Dhu Nuwas, the Jewish king of the Himyarites.[7] This text, which is an important attestation of Christianity in southern Arabia at the turn of the sixth century, comes down to us in more than one recension and has received far more scholarly interest than the so-called 'Letter on Barṣaumā, Bishop of Nisibis and the heresy of the Nestorians'. 'The Letter' has been studied closely only once and this is in a recent publication.[8] Elsewhere I have examined the structure and rhetoric of parts of this document.[9]

4 See Ernest Honigmann, *Évêques et Évêchés Monophysites d'Asie Antérieure au VIe Siècle* (CSCO Subsidia 2; Louvain, 1951) and more recently, Volker-Lorenz Menze, 'The Making of a Church: The Syrian Orthodox in the Shadow of Byzantium and the Papacy' (PhD thesis: Princeton University, 2004).

5 Barsoum, *History*, 211 n. 224, suggests an etymology for the place name and that it was most likely near Ctesiphon.

6 The Catholicos is the spiritual head of the Church of the East, equivalent to the Pope in Rome. His see was in Seleucia-Ctesphon.

7 Arthur Jeffrey, 'Three Documents on the History of Christianity in South Arabia', *Anglican Theological Review* 27 (1945): 195–205; Axel Moberg, *The Book of the Himyarites* (Lund: C. W. K. Gleerup, 1924); Irfan Shahid, *The Martyrs of Najran: New Documents* (Subsidia Hagiographica 49; Bruxelles: Société des Bollandistes, 1971), esp. Syriac text in Section III and translation in Section IV (43–64). More recently, see Christian J. Robin, Joëlle Beaucamp, and Françoise Briquel-Chatonnet, 'La persécution des chrétiens de Nagran et la chronologie himyarite', *Aram* 11–12 (1999–2000), 15–83. Aloys Grillmeier with Theresia Hainthaler, *Christ in Christian Tradition* 2/4 (Atlanta: John Knox Press, 1996), 309ff., with a general analysis on pp. 305–23.

8 Grillmeier and Hainthaler, *Jesus der Christus*, 262–78 ('Fünftes Kapitel: Der persische Disputator Simeon von Bet Aršam und seine antinestorianische Positionsbestimmung').

9 Becker, *Fear of God*, 47–51.

It is difficult to date this text precisely, although scholars have generally placed it in the very early sixth century.[10] It contains a reference to Anastasius (491–518 CE),[11] which may point to a date before 518, but this depends on how we interpret the relevant passage. Simeon's failure to refer to Justin and Justinian may be simply an attempt to avoid the uncomfortable fact of the new anti-Miaphysite regimes of these emperors, who would oversee the reassertion of Chalcedonian orthodoxy from 518 onward. References to the East-Syrian Catholicos, Bābai, and to Philoxenus of Mabbug, if they are taken to be deceased – again a matter of interpretation – suggest that it was composed after 502/3 and 523 respectively.[12] De Halleux and others have speculated that it could be from the time of the Armenian Council of Dvin (505/6), to which the document makes reference.[13]

Hainthaler divides the text into five parts: 1. The Genealogy of 'Nestorianism' (*Bibliotheca Orientalis* I.346–51); 2. The School of the Persians (351–354); 3. The Apostasy of the Khuzites and the Persians from the true faith of the fathers (354); 4. The Orthodox Faith (354–356); and 5. Anathemas against those with dissenting views (356–358).[14] It is in fact not even clear whether this text was originally a letter. The title itself is questionable.[15] It is labelled as a letter in its single attestation, Vatican Syriac 135, an undated manuscript probably from the seventh or eighth centuries.[16] The text itself seems to begin *in medias res* and lacks any references to an addressee nor does it have an epistolary closing.

However useful Simeon's letter is as a description of the larger historical context for the School of the Persians in Edessa and the origin of the School of Nisibis, we must remain aware of his own polemical goals and the position he held as one of the first West-Syrians to foray into the East-Syrian dominated realm of Persia. This document, composed by a West Syrian known for his polemical skills and fiery rhetoric, does not provide a clear and unbiased account of the events of the late fifth and early sixth centuries. In fact, it can be taken as a textbook example of the creative flair of heresio-

10 Garsoïan, *L'église arménienne*, 450 says the date is imprecise; Gero, *Barṣauma of Nisibis*, 9: 'an early 6th-century letter'; No date given: Wright, *Short History of Syriac Literature*, 81; Baumstark, *Geschichte*, 146.

11 Simeon of Bēt Arsham, *Epistola*, 356.

12 Ibid. 358 and 352–53.

13 Ibid. 356; De Halleux, *Philoxène de Mabbog*, 4 n. 9; Grillmeier and Hainthaler, *Jesus der Christus*, 265; Garsoïan, *L'église arménienne*, 161–66, 455 n. 63.

14 Grillmeier and Hainthaler, *Jesus der Christus*, 266.

15 Ibid. 265; Gero, *Barṣauma*, 9–10.

16 *Biblioteca Apostolica Vaticana* (Paris: Maisonneuve, 1926), III.213–15.

logical literature, with its harsh polemic and slippery argument by association. One noteworthy feature of Simeon's text is its use of a genealogical tree to demonstrate how contemporary 'heretics' are the ideological descendants of a long line of errant, evil thinkers extending back to Jesus' day.[17] This creation of a spurious chain of transmission running from 'heretic' to 'heretic' through the generations is in fact the inverse of the kind of scholastic chains of transmission one finds in East-Syrian texts, such as the *Cause of the Foundation of the Schools*. Such a usage of the same literary technique by both those endorsing an institution and those criticizing it derives from a common Christian practice going back to the second century CE, which in turn reflects a common Greco-Roman technique for detailing the lines of transmission in medical and philosophical schools and which also appears in Rabbinic sources.[18]

What Simeon describes as the spread of 'Nestorian' heretics into the Sasanian Empire does not reflect an innovation in the theology of the Church of the East.[19] In fact, it seems the Church of the East had long-standing ties to the theology wrongly characterized as 'Nestorian'. This is because the early spread of Christianity eastward into the Parthian and then Sasanian Empires was in part through Antioch. Antiochene theology lies behind what was labelled 'Nestorianism', and therefore the flight of Dyophysite Christians eastward only reinforced certain theologically conservative tendencies in the East. In other words, I do not think Simeon's letter is as important as it has been taken to be by historians. It does not demonstrate the 'Nestorianization' of the East, but rather the deep historical connections that created an affinity between 'Nestorians' and the Church of the East. Apart from serving as an example of a heresiological attempt to malign certain Christians in the East, Simeon's letter confirms a link connecting late fifth-century Edessene followers of a traditional Antiochene theology, the School of the Persians in Edessa, and the newly founded School of Nisibis.

17 For a similar chain by one of his contemporaries, see André de Halleux, 'La dixième lettre de Philoxène aux monastères du Beit Gaugal', 1–17 (pp. 28–40); see also idem, 'Die Genealogie des Nestorianismus nach der frühmonophysitischen Theologie', *OC* 66 (1982): 1–14, and Witold Witakowski, 'Syrian Monophysite Propaganda in the Fifth to Seventh Centuries', in *Aspects of Late Antiquity and Early Byzantium. Colloquium of the Swedish Research Institute in Istanbul 31 May–5 June, 1992*, ed. L. Rydén and J. O. Rosenqvist (Swedish Research Institute in Istanbul *Transactions* 4; Stockholm, 1993), 57–66.

18 See, for example, Elias Bi[c]kerman[n], 'La Chaîne de la Tradition Pharisienne', *Revue Biblique* 59 (1952): 44–54.

19 Becker, *Fear of God*, 73–74.

THE 'LETTER' OF SIMEON OF BEIT ARSHAM: TRANSLATION AND NOTES

[346] (24a1)[1] The Letter of the Blessed Mār Shem'on of Bēt Arsham,[2] which he wrote on account of Barṣaumā and the Heresy[3] of the Nestorians,[4] which demonstrates whence was its beginning and at what time it descended to the land of the Persians.

The Genealogy of 'Nestorianism'

For just as the true faith of us Christians took its beginning from Abraham, the first[5] of the fathers, by the promise, which was from God: *In your seed the nations will be blessed*,[6] that is, Christ,[7] as it is written, and because of the true faith of Abraham – he was called the father of all nations to which we ourselves belong[8] – in this way also the error of the Nestorians began from Hannan and Caiphas, the high priests, as well as from the rest of the Jews of that time.[9] For those Jews regarded Christ as a human being, as they were saying: *You are blaspheming and, although you are a human being, you make yourself God.*[10] This (opinion) was passed down (24a2) from the Jews of that time. Some were calling him a human being, others a righteous man, others a prophet, a good teacher, and the king [347] of Israel. But others were calling him Beelzebub, the head of the demons,[11] a blasphemer, and a transgressor of the law, and there was a division among the Jews on account of him, but both sides thought he was human. It is this same

1 I provide both the Assemani page numbers as well as the columns in Ms Vatican Syriac 135.

2 The Ms is corrupt here. It has *rshm* without the aleph and with a short *e* vowel marked between the letters *sh* and *m*. Such vowels are rare in the manuscript.

3 Syr. *heresis*, from Gr. *haíresis*.

4 Syr. *Nesṭuryānē*.

5 Syr. *rēsh*, lit. 'head'. The source of this expression is Rom 4:1 of the Peshitta version. For the same expression, see notes LA 77 and CS 518.

6 Gen 22:18.

7 The Syriac word 'Christ' (*mshiḥā*) may also be rendered 'Messiah' in English.

8 Cf. Gal 3:6–9.

9 Cf. Lk 3:2; Jn 18:13–14, 23–24; Acts 4:6.

10 Jn 10:33. Cf. 'Is there a greater insult than that which the new Jews of our day utter, blaspheming Christ face to face, subtracting from the honor (due to) Him, reviling His glory, and saying to Him, "Thou art a man, and Thou makest Thyself God?"', Philoxenus, *Three Letters*, 107 (text 148–49) ('First Letter to the Monks of Beth-Gaugal').

11 Cf. Mt 12:24; Mk 3:22; Lk 11:15.

opinion which has been passed down among the Nestorians until today.[12] Now Simon the Sorcerer,[13] whose Samaritan race was akin to the Jews in certain matters,[14] succeeded[15] the Jews, and he opposed the Apostles in the city of Rome, while extolling himself and saying, 'I myself am great!,' and he thought himself Christ,[16] just as he succeeded[17] Hannan and Caiphas, his companions and masters.

Ebion[18] succeeded Simon, and Artemon[19] Ebion, and he was succeeded

12 Those on the Miaphysite side of the Christological spectrum tended to equate Dyophysite positions with Judaism since both were thought to deny the divinity of Christ. Cf. Lucas Van Rompay, 'A Letter of the Jews to the Emperor Marcian Concerning the Council of Chalcedon', *OLP* 12 (1981): 215–24. Furthermore, the text reflects standard Christian anti-Jewish arguments. By placing the roots of heresy within Judaism the author shows implicitly how 'heretics' continue the persecution of Christ and his followers supposedly begun by the Jews.

13 Simon Magus. Following New Testament and later usage, the Syriac employs the Greek form of his name, Simōn, although it may originally derive from the Semitic Shem'on. The Syriac translates the pejorative epithet 'Magus' with *ḥarrāshā*, a standard word for 'magician' or 'enchanter'. It was common to attribute the origins of heresy to Simon Magus. This point as well as much of the following early Christian history probably derive here from Eusebius's *Ecclesiastical History*, which was in circulation in a Syriac version at least by the early fifth century, perhaps earlier. See the edition of W. Wright and N. McLean, *The Ecclesiastical History of Eusebius in Syriac*.

14 It is possible that Simeon composed this text later in his career, in which case this connection between the Jews and the Samaritans would also call to mind for his audience the failed Samaritan Revolt of 529 CE. A Christian audience would certainly be aware of the 'rebelliousness' of the Jews and their subsequent 'punishment' after the revolts of the first and second centuries.

15 The idiom here and in the following is Syr. *qabbel min*, lit. 'he received from'. I translate it as 'succeed' because *qabbel* does not have an explicit object as it is used here and also by analogy with the use of the same idiom to translate the Greek *diadéchetai* in the Syriac version of Eusebius's *Ecclesiastical History*, e.g. 1.7.12.

16 Acts 8:9ff.

17 Assemani's vocalized text has the passive form *mqabbal (h)wā*, though his Latin translation renders it as the active. The Syr. *lēh* is either the object of the active *mqabbel*, or an ethical dative with it, or it expresses agency with the passive *mqabbal*. The Ms does not help to resolve this ambiguity.

18 Already by the second century heresiologists were referring to the founder of the eponymous Ebionites, a commonly condemned group of 'Jewish-Christians' whose name actually reflects what is apparently their own self-allocation, 'the poor' (Hebr. *ebyōn*) (cf. Gal 2:10). E.g. Hippolytus, *Refutatio Omnium Haeresium*, ed. M. Marcovich (Berlin: de Gruyter, 1986), 7.22.

19 This figure about whom little is known lived until the late third century, since he seems to have been alive at the time that Paul of Samosata was accused of following his teaching (Eusebius, *Ecclesiastical History* 5.28; 7.30).

by Paul of Samosata,[20] who was for some time bishop of the city of Antioch in Syria in the days of the pagan kings of the Romans, when Constantine,[21] (24b1) the faithful (and) true[22] king of the Romans, had not yet begun to rule, because there was no fear (of God) among[23] the kings of the Romans. This Paul of Samosata was bold and he blasphemed more than Simon the Sorcerer, Ebion, and Artemon, his masters, and he said about the blessed Mary, 'Mary gave birth to a mere human being[24] and she did not remain in her virginity after she gave birth'.[25] He called Christ created, made, mortal, and a son by grace.[26] He spoke about himself, 'I too, if I wanted, would be Christ because I and Christ are one nature'. By Paul of Samosata the heresy of the two natures, their individual properties and operations,[27] was demonstrated.

[348] Paul was succeeded by Diodore of Tarsus[28] – the city of Cilicia – who from his youth was on the side of the Macedonian heresy, which blasphemes against the Holy Spirit.[29] When Diodore became a student of

20 Paul of Samosata, the third-century bishop of Antioch (c. 260–68), was deposed for his controversial Christological views (Eusebius, *Ecclesiastical History* 7.28–30). See U. M. Lang, 'The Christological Controversy at the Synod of Antioch in 268/9', *JTS* 51 (2000): 54–80.

21 Constantine the Great (306–37).

22 Assemani perhaps correctly translates this asyndeton as 'orthodox' (*orthodoxus*). See note 103 below.

23 Syr. *men*, lit. 'from'.

24 East-Syrian texts regularly refute this Christological title (cf. Gr. *psilós ánthrōpos*) (*Nestorian Christological Texts*, 61.22–23 [38.27f.]).

25 For the source and authenticity of this attribution, see Grillmeier and Hainthaler, *Jesus der Christus*, 268–69.

26 Syr. *brā d-ṭaybutā*, lit. 'son of grace'. 'Hence since what is by grace is not by nature and what is by nature is not by grace, there are not two sons, according to thy mode of reasoning. He indeed who is son by grace and not by nature is not truly son, it remains that the glory of true Sonship exist in Him Who is so by Nature not by grace, that is, in God the Word Who is forth of God the Father.' P. E. Pusey, 'Cyril of Alexandria, Against Diodore of Tarsus and Theodore of Mopsuestia (fragments of book 2)', *Library of the Fathers of the Church* 47 (1881): 347.

27 Syr. *iḥidāyāthon* and *ma'bdānwāthon* (each has the plural masculine possessive suffix) are equivalent to the Greek Christological technical terms, *idiótētes* and *enérgeiai*.

28 Diodore of Tarsus, d. c. 390, is the third of the 'Nestorian' triumvirate of authoritative Greek fathers, along with Nestorius and Theodore of Mopsuestia. His extant works, often only in fragments due to his post-mortem condemnation, demonstrate his Antiochene theological and exegetical leanings. Diodore's influence also derives from his institutional work: he was a major player at the Council of Constantinople in 381 and founded a monastery outside Antioch known for its scriptural study. Theodore of Mopsuestia and John Chrysostom were among his pupils. Most recently, see Robert C. Hill, trans., *Diodore of Tarsus: commentary on Psalms 1–51* (Boston: Brill; Atlanta: Society of Biblical Literature, 2005).

29 This refers to the theological position of the 'Macedonians', named after Macedonius

the Christians[30] and became bishop of Tarsus in Cilicia he increased the Macedonian heresy. He also divided the natures and their individual properties and operations[31] in Christ, (24b2) and he reckoned Christ a human being, created, made, mortal, sharing in our nature,[32] and a son by grace.[33] He followed after Paul of Samosata, his master.

Theodore of Mopsuestia[34] in Cilicia succeeded Diodore. This man interpreted[35] all the books of the Old and New (Testaments), and in all his interpretations[36] and homilies[37] he demonstrates the Jewish opinion he holds about Christ, as Diodore and Paul, his masters.[38] These (ideas), which (derive) from Simon the Sorcerer, Paul, and Diodore, he increased and confirmed. He reckoned Christ a human being, created, made, mortal, sharing in our

---

I, the Arian bishop of Constantinople (342–46, 351–60, d. after 360), against whom Nicene Christians rallied in the late fourth century. The Macedonians did not understand the Holy Spirit to be coequal with the Father and the Son. Simeon's claim about Diodore's connection to the Macedonians is false since he too was an anti-Arian. Furthermore, any connection between the Antiochene fathers and the Macedonians is spurious since Theodore of Mopsuestia composed two books against the Macedonians, while Theodoret mentions composing treatises against them (*Epist.* cxvi [PG 83]). Cyril of Alexandria accuses Diodore of being a Macedonian: P. E. Pusey, 'Cyril of Alexandria, Against Diodore of Tarsus and Theodore of Mopsuestia (fragments of book 1)', *Library of the Fathers of the Church* 47 (1881): 321 n. 1.

30 Syr. *ettalmad*. This is a standard Syriac idiom for conversion to Christianity. It fits with a broader tendency to understand Christianity in pedagogical terms. See Becker, *Fear of God*, 31–38. It is not clear whether the use of the term here is supposed to refer to Diodore converting to Christianity. Simeon may be trying to make sense of how a heretic could have become bishop.

31 See note 27 above.

32 Lit. 'son of our nature'. This is equivalent to the Greek *homooúsios hēmîn*, 'consubstantial with us' (*Nestorian Chistological Texts*, 126.7 [72.19]). This is an odd Christological formulation for Simeon to critique since it is associated with some Miaphysite statements and appears even in the *Henoticon* (Grillmeier and Hainthaler, *Jesus der Christus*, 269).

33 See note 26 above.

34 Theodore of Mopsuestia (350–428) was rapidly becoming *the* theological and exegetical authority among the East Syrians in the sixth century. See the following note.

35 Syr. *pashsheq* is the same word used positively of Theodore in East-Syrian sources. He is commonly referred to as the 'interpreter' (*mphashshqānā*). See, for example, note LA 36.

36 Syr. *pushshāqē*.

37 Syr. *mēmrē*.

38 In the Acts of the Fifth Ecumenical Council of 553 we read: 'As, however, the heretics are resolved to defend Theodore of Mopsuestia and Nestorius with their impieties, and maintain that that letter of Ibas was received by the Synod of Chalcedon, so do we exhort you to direct your attention to the impious writings of Theodore, and especially to his Jewish Creed which was brought forward at Ephesus and Chalcedon, and anathematized by each synod with those who had so held or did so hold.' *Extracts from the Acts, Session* I (NPNF vol. XIV, 303).

nature, a son by grace, and a temple of the eternal Son,[39] and (he said,) 'He is not the son of God by nature but by grace',[40] along with the rest of his blasphemies, with which all of his homilies and interpretations are filled.

[349] Theodore was succeeded by Nestorius,[41] this man who had been ordained as presbyter in the church of the city of Antioch the Great, and afterwards was bishop of Constantinople. (25a1) He was from the city of Germanicia.[42] He cunningly seized for himself leadership of the wicked heresy of his masters, these men who were mentioned above, so that all those followers of his heresy might be called by his name, like Marcion,[43] by whose name the Marcionites are called, and like Eutyches,[44] by whose name the Eutychians are called.[45] Because of this that Nestorius, the enemy of righteousness, openly blasphemed in the church of Constantinople. These things which are from Simon the Sorcerer, Ebion, Artemon, Paul of Samosata, Diodore, and Theodore, the masters of Nestorius, were secretly passed on between them until that time. In his ostentation he took for himself the leadership of the heresy and he entered and stood in the church before all the people and openly blasphemed, saying: 'Let Mary not be glorified,

39 Syr. *hayklā da-brā mtomāyā*. Cf. Theodore of Mopsuestia, *Commentary on the Nicene Creed*, 200 (84). Such temple language is not uncommon in East-Syrian sources, e.g. Narsai, *Metrical Homilies*, I.115 (p. 44) and *Nestorian Christological Texts*, 11.22 (10.21).

40 Theodore of Mopsuestia, *Commentary on the Nicene Creed*, 208 (91) (which is also quoted in the Acts of the Fifth Ecumenical Council, as Mingana notes).

41 Nestorius (d. 451) was bishop of Constantinople from 428 until he was deposed by the Council of Ephesus in 431, after which he spent the rest of his life in exile. His actual theological positions have been disputed by contemporary scholars, but the association of his person with the Church of the East led to their enemies referring to them as 'Nestorians'. By the 540s his autobiographical self-defence, known as the *Bazaar of Heracleides*, was translated into Syriac, the language in which it is extant. For the English translation, see Nestorius, *The Bazaar of Heracleides*, trans. G. R. Driver and L. Hodgson (Oxford: Clarendon Press, 1925). On the reception of Nestorius into Syriac, see Abramowski, *Untersuchungen zum Liber Heraclides des Nestorius*.

42 Modern (Kahraman)Marash in south-eastern Turkey. Germanic(e)ia, a city west of Samosata, was in Syria Euphratensis and subject to the patriarchate of Antioch.

43 Marcion (d. c. 154), the founder of the dualistic form of Christianity which bore his name, was perhaps the most common heresiological whipping boy. Marcionism continued in Syria through the fifth century, and perhaps later.

44 Eutyches (fl. 450) is generally associated with a radical emphasis on the unitary nature of the incarnate word. His theology as well as his person served as a focal point of dispute at the councils of the mid-fifth century, culminating in his condemnation at Chalcedon in 451. What his precise theological views were is unclear.

45 That heresiarchs vainly want to change the name of the Church to include their own name appears, for example, in Eusebius, *Ecclesiastical History* 3.28 for Cerinthus.

because she did not give birth to God but rather a human being, created, made, mortal, and sharing in our nature', 'By grace only is he worthy of being called the son of God', and 'Because of his affinity with mortals Jesus is the son of God',[46] along with the rest of the many blasphemies (25a2) on account of which he was anathematized in the city of Ephesus by the holy fathers from intercourse with all the holy church of God, he and his masters, who were mentioned above.[47] (They anathematized) their faith and everyone who agrees with him or them. From that time to the present their name has been called 'Nestorians'.

[350] Theodoret of Cyrrhus[48] succeeded Nestorius. This Theodoret in his zeal on behalf of Nestorius made a wicked statement against these holy fathers who at Ephesus had anathematized Nestorius, his master.[49] Ibas[50] succeeded Nestorius. Along with the rest of all his blasphemies, which agree in everything with his masters, these ones who were mentioned above, this Ibas further blasphemed in one of his homilies[51] and spoke thus: 'I, Ibas, do not envy Christ who became God, since he was called God because he was a human being like me and shared in my nature'.[52] Because of this Ibas was anathematized, as was Theodoret of Cyrrhus, along with their companions

46 Cf. F. Nau, ed., Jean Rufus, *Plérophories*, PO 8 (1912): 12.4–6. See also Grillmeier and Hainthaler, *Jesus der Christus*, 270.

47 Nestorius's position regarding the application of the title 'Theotokos' ('Bearer of God') to Mary was condemned at the Council of Ephesus of 431.

48 Theodoret of Cyrrhus (393–460 [or 457/8 or 466]), was an important supporter of the Antiochene position in the mid-fifth century and remained a controversial figure into the sixth century. His works against Cyril of Alexandria were part of the so-called Three Chapters, those works condemned by Justinian in 543–44 in an attempt to reach a rapprochement with the Miaphysites. Simeon's reference to Theodoret's 'wicked statement' is part of the Miaphysite effort to build support for this very condemnation.

49 Simeon conveniently does not mention the Council of Chalcedon in 451.

50 Syr. *Hībā*. Ibas of Edessa (d. 457), who served as Bishop of Edessa (435–49 and 451–57), was, like Theodoret, condemned at the Robber Council of 449 and exonerated at the Council of Chalcedon. Also like Theodoret his person became a sticking point between Miaphysites and Chalcedonians in the sixth century. On Ibas in general and the charges against him, see Doran, *Stewards of the Poor*, 109–32. Also, see Price and Gaddis, *The Acts of the Council of Chalcedon*, 2:265–73.

51 Syr. *mēmrē*.

52 Robert Doran, *Stewards of the Poor*, 125–30, addresses three variants of this same saying attributed to Ibas, as they appear in the council acts of the mid-fifth century. See also Price and Gaddis, *The Acts of the Council of Chalcedon*, 2:266–67, esp. n. 6. However, the authors of these volumes do not seem to be aware of this particular version, which is fuller than the others and has probably been extended by Simeon. See Grillmeier and Hainthaler, *Jesus der Christus*, 270, n. 55.

and everyone who agrees with them.[53] Someone named Māri from Bēt Hardashir[54] succeeded Ibas.[55] From there the land of the Persians began to be harmed (25b1) by Nestorianism through the letters of Ibas, the interpretations of homilies, and the commentaries of his masters.[56]

The School of the Persians

[351] After Māri, a presbyter from Edessa named Māron Elitā[57] succeeded Ibas. He was a scribe[58] of the (a) school of (the) Persians, which was in the city of Edessa at that time.[59] There were in the school of Edessa at that time

53 This is a reference to the Second Council of Ephesus in 449.

54 It is not clear who this Māri is. His connections to the East may be in doubt. It is possible that Simeon is confusing his career with his mere origins. See Michel van Esbroeck, 'Who is Mari, the Addressee of Ibas' Letter?', *JTS* 38 (1987): 129–35. Van Esbroeck concludes: 'Mari the Persian was archimandrite of the convent of the *Akoimetoi* on the Asiatic shore of the Bosphorus 15 miles north of Constantinople' (129). See also Becker, *Fear of God*, 48–49, 54, 57–58. Bēt Hardashir is Rewardashir in Fars, on which see Fiey 'Diocèses syriens orientaux du Golfe Persique', 179–94.

55 The connection between these two figures is being made based upon Ibas's *Letter to Mari*, which became one of the Three Chapters. Cf. A. d'Alès, 'La lettre d'Ibas à Marès le Persan', *Recherches de science religieuse* 22 (1952): 5–25 and Doran, *Stewards of the Poor*, 111. For a translation of the text of the letter, see Doran, *Stewards of the Poor*, 169–73 and Price and Gaddis, *The Acts of the Council of Chalcedon*, 2:295–98.

56 Simeon may be expanding upon the tradition that the *Letter to Mari* was sent to the East. We know little of Ibas's own literary production, though he is associated with the translation of Antiochene works from Greek into Syriac in mid-fifth-century Edessa (although the evidence for this is thinner than scholars usually acknowledge). The 'interpretations of homilies' (*pushshāqē d-mēmrē*) can also be 'translations of his homilies'. Syr. *turgāmē*, rendered here as 'commentaries', can also mean 'translations'.

57 On his identity and name, Assemani (n. 1) suggests that this is the Maras, presbyter of Edessa, who participated in Ibas's condemnation at the Council of Antioch of 448 and the Council of Tyre-Berytus of 449, but this is unlikely since this Maras is one of those who attributed the statement of questionable orthodoxy, quoted above (see note 52 above), to Ibas (Price and Gaddis, *The Acts of the Council of Chalcedon*, 2:287. See also Vööbus, *History*, 12.)

58 Syr. *sāphrā*. This is not a commonly attested office or title in the few sources we have for the 'School of the Persians'.

59 This is one of the few actual references to the so-called 'School of the Persians in Edessa'. However, it is not certain we should translate the Syriac (*eskolā* [the final *ā* should be *ē*] *d-pārsāyē d-it [h]wā b-urhāy*) as referring to a formal institution. We find the same ambiguity, for example, in Jacob of Sarug's statement in Letter 14: 'there was in the city a school of Persians (*eskolē d-pārsāyē*) who held the teaching of the foolish Diodore with much love', 58.21–59.8. See Becker, *Fear of God*, 52.

Persians. These are some of them:[60] Acacius the Aramean,[61] who is[62] called in that school 'The Choker of Coins';[63] Barṣaumā,[64] [352] servant of Mārā of Qardu,[65] who was called 'The Swimmer among the Nests'; Ma'nā of Bēt Hardashir,[66] who was called 'The Drinker of Ash'; 'Abshoṭā of the city of Nineveh,[67] who is called a name which it is improper for us to write; John of Bēt Garmai,[68] who was called 'The Suckling Pig'; Mikā,[69] who is called

60 Syr. *w-hāwēn (h)waw b-eskolā d-urhāy b-zabnā d-pārsāyē d-itayhon menhon hālēn.* Assemani translates: 'In illa autem Schola commorabantur, quum Persae ibidem literis vacarent: quos inter . . .' The original Syriac may suggest that Simeon did not understand all of the members of the school to be Persian.

61 Acacius, Syr. *Aqāq*, Catholicos of the Church of the East (484–95/6), was from Bēt Arāmāyē, that region of Mesopotamia running from Seleucia-Ctesiphon south to the swamp region (Fiey, *L'Assyrie Chrétienne*, III.147–261). The council he called at Seleucia in 486 was attended by three figures mentioned in the following text: John of Bēt Sāri in Bēt Garmai, Mikā of Lāshom in Bēt Garmai, and Pāpā from Bēt Lāpāṭ (*Synodicon Orientale*, 59–60; in general, see ibid. 53–60; trans. 299–307; McCullough, *Short History*, 132–33).

62 It is not clear how much is to be made of the absence of the perfect form of the verb 'to be' (*hwā*) with some of the participles in the following list. If this is significant, then Simeon is specifically stating which of the following are deceased and which still alive.

63 Although it is difficult to determine the exact meaning of each of the various sobriquets Simeon attributes to the following figures, it is nevertheless clear that they are insulting. Further geographical information is provided in the altered version of this list on pp. 353–54 below.

64 On Barṣaumā, see note LN 65. He is often criticized in West-Syrian sources.

65 On this reference and the polemical attribution of servitude to Barṣaumā, see Gero, *Barsauma*, 26. Qardu or Bēt Qardu, is the Kurdish region north and east of the Tigris and north of Bēt Zabdai (the region south of modern Siirt). See Fiey, *Nisibe*, 161–84; Fiey, *L'Assyrie Chrétienne*, I.216–17; Fiey, *Pour un Oriens Christianus Novus*, 120.

66 Ma'nā of Rewardashir, also mentioned below in the *Cause* (381, 384), was an associate of Barṣaumā, but may have turned on him (Gero, *Barsauma*, 43 n. 96). Judging from the number of references to him in the *Synodicon Orientale* and the *Chronicle of Siirt*, he was a significant figure in the Church in the late fifth century. A number of original works and translations are attributed to him in the sources. Baumstark, *Geschichte*, 105–06, 348. See also Fiey, 'Diocèses syriens orientaux du Golfe Persique', 183. As Baumstark points out (105 n. 4), he is inaccurately identified with the Catholicos of 420 CE (e.g. Wright, *History*, 62–63).

67 Nothing is known of him. On Nineveh at this time, see Fiey, *Pour un Oriens Christianus Novus*, 115–16, Fiey, *L'Assyrie Chrétienne*, II: 343–49, and Chase Robinson, *Empire and Elites after the Muslim Conquest: The Transformation of Northern Mesopotamia* (Cambridge: Cambridge University Press, 2000), 66–72.

68 John of Bēt Sāri, according to the text below. He was one of the signatories at the Council of Bēt Lāpāṭ of 484 (Fiey, *L'Assyrie Chrétienne*, III.18–19).

69 Short for Mikā'ēl. Below we are told that he was from Lāshom in Bēt Garmai (Fiey, *L'Assyrie Chrétienne*, III.54–60; on him see 55–56).

'Dagon';[70] Paul, son of Qaqay, from the town[71] which is in Khuzistān,[72] who is called 'The Maker of Beans';[73] Abraham the Mede,[74] who was called 'The Heater of Baths';[75] Narsai the Leprous one;[76] and Ezalyā from the monastery of Kephar Māri.[77] These ones along with the rest of their companions were (with) one stubborn will (25b2) followers of the opinion of Ibas.[78]

But there were others who did not listen to Ibas, whose names are written here: Mār Pāpā[79] from Bēt Lāpāṭ,[80] the city [353] of the Khuzites; Mār

70 The ancient Near Eastern God demonized by the Israelites. See, for example, David Noel Freedman et al., *The Anchor Bible Dictionary* (New York: Doubleday, 1992), II: 1–2. It is unlikely that this reference is independent of the biblical condemnation of Dagon.

71 Syr. *karkā*. From the reference to Paul below, we can infer that this 'town' refers to Karkā d-Lēdān, a city built by Shapur II. See J.-M. Fiey, 'L'Elam, la première des métropoles ecclésiastiques syriennes orientales (*suite*)', *PdO* I (1970): 123–30 (repr. in *Communautés syriaques*, chap. IIIb). It is possible that the text is corrupt here and 'd-Lēdān' has dropped out.

72 Syr. *Bēt Huzāyē*. On Christianity in Khuzistān in general, see J.-M. Fiey, 'L'Elam, la première des métropoles ecclésiastiques syriennes orientales', *Melto* 5 (1969): 221–67 (repr. in *Communautés syriaques*, chap. IIIa) and and W. Schwaigert, *Das Christentum in Huzistan im Rahmen der frühen Kirchengeschichte Persiens bis zur Synode von Seleukeia-Ktesiphon im Jahre 410* (PhD thesis: Marburg-Lahn, 1989).

73 Presumably this refers to a menial and thus degrading form of labour. Cf. Löw, *Aramäische Pflanzennamen*, no. 173.

74 On Christians in Media, see Fiey, 'Médie Chrétienne'.

75 See note 73.

76 Simeon provides less information concerning Narsai, perhaps because he assumes his audience will know who this important figure in the Church of the East is. Narsai's enemy in the 'Life of Narsai' is referred to as leprous (see note LN 103). See Gero, *Barṣauma*, 60–61 n. 4.

77 Nothing is known of him. Kephar Māri is in Bēt Zabdai, the region on the west side of the Tigris, south and west of Cizre (Gazira ibn 'Umar). Fiey, *Nisibe*, 161–79, esp. 176; Fiey, *Pour un Oriens Christianus Novus*, 68–69. On Narsai's stay at a monastery there, see p. 596 below in the 'Life of Narsai'.

78 Syr. *bnay tar'itēh d-ihibā*, lit. 'sons of the mind of Ibas'.

79 Simeon uses the Syriac term of respect, *Mār(y)*, for these figures who are for him orthodox authorities.

80 Jundishapur, a city in Khuzistān, an important early centre of Christianity in Persia and famous later for its supposed medical school. In general, see Fiey, *Pour un Oriens Christianus Novus*, 83–85 as well as the material on Khuzistān in general in note 72 above. On East-Syrian study there, see W. Schweigert, 'Die Theologenschule von Bēt Lāpāt – Ğundaisābur. Ein Beitrag zur nestorianischen Schulgeschichte', *Zeitschrift der Deutschen Morgenländischen Gesellschaft, Suppl. 4: XX. Deutscher Orientalistentag 1977 in Erlangen* (Wiesbaden, 1980), 185–87. On the question of medical study there, see most recently G. J. Reinink, 'Theology and Medicine in Jundishapur: Cultural Change in the Nestorian School Tradition', in *Learned Antiquity: Scholarship and Society in the Near-East, the Greco-Roman world, and the Early Medieval West*, ed. Alaisdair A. MacDonald, Michael W. Twomey, and Gerrit J. Reinink (Louvain: Peeters, 2003), 163–74 and Becker, *Fear of God*, 94–95.

Aksenāyā[81] from Taḥāl, which is in Bēt Garmai;[82] his brother whose name was Addai; Mār Barḥadbeshabbā of Qardu,[83] who was later archimandrite[84] in the monastery of 'Ayn Qennē;[85] and Mār Benjamin of Bēt Āramāyē, who was later archimandrite in Qritā of the monastery of the school,[86] which is under the jurisdiction of the 'Umri,[87] and others with them did not agree with the will of Ibas.

After the death of Ibas all the Persians were expelled[88] from Edessa with the rest of the Edessene writers who were in agreement with them, and through the diligence of the blessed Mār Cyrus,[89] Bishop of Edessa, and by the commandment of Zeno,[90] the king of the Romans, the school in which the Persians were learning in Edessa was uprooted[91] and in its place a church

81 This is the great West Syrian, Philoxenus of Mabbug (d. 523). On the relevance of this passage to his biography, see Halleux, *Philoxène de Mabbog*, 12–13.

82 On this town, see Fiey, *L'Assyrie Chrétienne*, III.133–36.

83 On Qardu, see note 65 above. Nothing is known of this Barḥadbeshabbā.

84 Syr. *rēshdayrā*, lit. 'head of the monastery'.

85 It is not clear where this is.

86 Syr. *b-qritā d-dayrā d-eskolā* [or: -*ē*]. This phrase is unclear and the text may be corrupt, especially since *qritā* could simply mean 'village'. Furthermore, 'monastery of the school' is unclear, in contrast to 'school of the monastery'. Cf. Fiey, *L'Assyrie Chrétienne*, III.208.

87 Assemani's Syriac text does not differentiate between the letter *dalath* and *resh* in this word (*'wmdyn* or *'wmryn* with seyame). However, his Latin rendering ('Umrinorum', 'of the 'Umri') implies the latter. Perhaps he understood the diacritical mark to have been subsumed into the seyame, although in both his text and in the manuscript the seyame is not over the *resh*. If the letter should be read as a *resh*, then see Fiey, *Nisibe*, 57, 227. The *mim* is awkwardly set close upon the *waw*. If there was a confusion between these two letters in the Ms the original reading could be *'mwdyn*. There was a site 'Ammudin (Modern 'Amuda in northern Syria), not far from Dara, the Roman fortress town on the border with the Sasanians, between modern Mardin and Nisibis (cf. Pseudo-Joshua the Stylite, *Chronicle*, 54). See also John bar 'Amrāyē below in the 'Life of Narsai' (p. 613 and note LN 170).

88 Syr. *etṭred*(*w*). This term shows up in several of the sources for the closure of the School of the Persians. Cf. Becker, *Fear of God*, 75.

89 Syr. Qurā. Cf. Vööbus, *History*, 32, 37, 39–47. He also appears in the 'Life of Narsai' (see note LN 89).

90 The emperor Zeno (474–75, 476–91) aimed to resolve the ongoing post-Chalcedonian Christological controversy by issuing his *Henoticon* (482 CE), which avoided an explicit Christological position, while condemning Eutyches and Nestorius and approving the twelve anathemas of Cyril of Alexandria. On the relationship of this to the closure of the School of the Persians, see Becker, *Fear of God*, 44, 75. See also the positive view of Zeno in Philoxenus of Mabbug's *Letter to Zeno* in Philoxenus, *Three Letters*, 163–73 (trans. 118–27).

91 Syr. *et'aqrat*. This term shows up in several of the sources for the closure of the School of the Persians. See note CS 48.

in the name of mistress Mary the *Theotokos*[92] was built.[93]

These ones who were expelled from Edessa went down to Persia and (26a1) some of them became bishops in the cities of the Persians, that is,[94] Acacius of Bēt Ārāmāyē; Barṣaumā in Nisibis; Ma'nā of Bēt Hartshir; John in the town of Bēt Sāri, which is in Bēt Garmai; Mikā in Lāshom, [354] which is in Bēt Garmai; Paul, son of Qaqay, in the town of Lēdān in Khuzistān; Pusai, son of Qurṭi, in Shushṭar, the city of the Khuzites;[95] Abraham of Media; Narsai the Leprous was a teacher in Nisibis.[96]

The Apostasy of the Khuzites and the Persians from the True Faith of the Fathers

When the Khuzites and the Persians inquired into[97] ... the teachings of Nestorius and Theodore, as he received them from Ibas,[98] they made different assemblies in Persia, first at Bēt Lāpāṭ, the metropolitan city of the Khuzites.[99] This was in the twenty-seventh year of Peroz, King of Kings,[100]

92 Syr. *yāldat alāhā*. This is the controversial title rejected by the East Syrians and others who thought that, when it was used alone, it compromised the human portion of the incarnation.

93 This event may be compared to the closure of the synagogue of Edessa by Rabbula (d. 435/5 CE) (*Chronicle of Edessa*, 6.21–25).

94 This follows the same order as the list provided on pp. 351–52 above, but 'Abshoṭā and Ezalyā are missing and Pusai has been added.

95 On this city, see J.-M. Fiey, 'L'Elam, la première des métropoles ecclésiastiques syriennes orientales (*suite*)', *PdO* I (1970): 134–40 (repr. in *Communautés syriaques*, chap. IIIb).

96 Assemani misleadingly translates this: 'Narses vero Leprosus Nisibi scholam instituit'. Cf. Garsoïan *L'église arménienne*, 454: 'et quant à Narses de Lépreux, il établit une école à Nisibe'.

97 The idiom Syr. *bā'ēn b-* is unclear. Assemani suggests: 'wanted to confirm' (quum ... confirmare vellent). The text may be corrupt since the Ms has a lacuna, suggesting that either the scribe did not think it was correct or that the Vorlage was damaged.

98 The translation of this phrase may depend on the prior phrase, which is corrupt. Assemani translates it as, 'the doctrine transmitted to them by Ibas' (*traditam sibi ab Iba*). He reads the passive participle, *mqabbal*, and provides the necessary diacritical mark below the word, but the Ms has a dot above the word, suggesting it should be read as the active form: *mqabbel*.

99 On East-Syrian church councils, see Brock, 'The Christology of the Church of the East in the Synods of the Fifth to Early Seventh Centuries'. The Council of 484 called together by Barṣaumā was in part to condemn the rule of the Catholicos Babowai (*Synodicon Orientale*, 61, 211; Braun, *Das Buch der Synhados*, 74–83; Gero, *Barṣauma*, 3, 41–50; 73–88; McCullough, *Short History*, 131–32).

100 Peroz I (459–84).

and again in Seleucia and in Ctesiphon, cities of Bēt Ārāmāyē,[101] and again in Bēt 'Edrai, the town under the jurisdiction of Bēt Nuhādrā.[102]

The Orthodox Faith

They established canons of a new faith, different from the ones they had, and they separated themselves from the true faith of the holy fathers, which (26a2) they received from the Holy Apostles, which was announced through the Holy Spirit at the city of Nicaea by the 318 bishops with Constantine, the faithful (and) true[103] king of the Romans.[104] One hundred [355] and fifty sacred and holy bishops, who were in Constantinople with the Emperor Theodosius the Great, agreed (with this statement of faith),[105] (as did) the 253 bishops in the city of Ephesus with the Emperor Theodosius the Younger.[106] Also 495 bishops of Alexandria the Great and Antioch in Syria, and of the Cappadocians and of the Galatians with the Emperor Zeno agreed to it and in turn confirmed it in the book which is called the *Henoticon*.[107] They agreed and confirmed[108] at the time of Bishop Mārutā,[109] who had been

101 The Council of Acacius in 486 and the Council of Bābai in 497 CE (*Synodicon Orientale*, 53–60, 62–68; Braun, *Das Buch der Synhados*, 59–73, 83–92; McCullough, *Short History*, 132–34).

102 Little is known of this council of 485 which took place in a town near Alqosh, on the road to Nisibis. The vocalization of 'Edrai (*'dry*) is uncertain. See Gero, *Barṣauma*, 50–51.

103 See note 22 above.

104 The Council of Nicaea of 325, which was convened by the emperor Constantine (306–37).

105 Syr. *qesar* ('Caesar') throughout this passage is rendered as 'Emperor'. Theodosius the Great (379–95) called the First Council of Constantinople in 381, the second of the Ecumenical Councils, in an attempt to reassert Nicene Orthodoxy.

106 Theodosius II (408–50) convened the Council of Ephesus of 431, the third of the Ecumenical Councils, in order to repudiate Nestorius's criticism of calling Mary 'Theotokos' ('the bearer of God').

107 See note 90 above. Again, it is noteworthy that Simeon does not mention the Council of Chalcedon of 451, the decisions of which Miaphysites such as himself had been trying to overturn for decades.

108 These words, which are plural in the manuscript, are singular in Assemani's text, yet he translates them as plurals. The subject is vague.

109 Mārutā of Maypherqaṭ (Martyropolis), east of Diyarbakir (Amida), d. c. 520. For the canons agreed upon in 410, see Arthur Vööbus, *The Canons Ascribed to Maruta of Maipherqat and Related Sources* (CSCO 439–40; Louvain: Peeters, 1982). In general, see Baumstark, *Geschichte*, 53–55, or for a recent discussion of his career, Elizabeth Key Fowden, *The Barbarian Plain: Saint Sergius between Rome and Iran* (Berkeley: University of California Press, 1999), 52–59.

sent on an embassy by the Emperor, king of the Romans,[110] to Yazdegird,[111] King of Kings, in the eleventh year of his reign, with 40 bishops who were under the jurisdiction [356] of the Persians.[112] Moreover, both 33 bishops of the land of Gurzan[113] with their own kings and leaders and 32 bishops of Greater Armenia (26b1) of the Persians with their own *marzbāns*[114] recently agreed to and confirmed these things[115] with the rest of the Orthodox bishops and Christian kings from Constantine the faithful king to blessed Emperor Anastasius, living of soul.[116]

Anathemas against Those with Dissenting Views

Therefore all of these bishops anathematized, each in his own time, everyone who dares to write, teach, or transmit a faith other than this one written above,[117] which all the holy Orthodox churches in every place maintain and believe. All the Persians maintained this until the twenty-seventh year[118] when the bishops of the Persians transgressed the anathema of all the bishops and kings, which were written above, and established a faith different from theirs, one which introduces a quaternity instead of a trinity, one which confesses the Father, the Son, and the Holy Spirit, and Christ in two natures.[119]

110 Arcadius, 395–408 CE.

111 Yazdegird reined from 399 to 421.

112 At the Council of Seleucia-Ctesiphon of 410 CE the Church of the East formally accepted the canons of the Council of Nicaea.

113 One of several names for eastern Iberia (Georgia).

114 Syr. *marzbānē*, from the Persian title meaning 'Warden of the Marches'. This was a Sasanian military governor of the frontier provinces. See Philippe Gignoux, 'L'Organisation Administrative Sasanide: le cas du *marzban*', *Jerusalem Studies in Arabic and Islam* 4 (1984): 1–29.

115 This is a reference to the first Council of Dvin (in Armenia) of 505/6. See, e.g., Garsoïan, *L'église arménienne*, *passim*. Garsoïan includes her French translation of Simeon's letter in an appendix to her volume primarily because of this reference to the council.

116 Anastasius 491–518 CE. Assemani (356 n. 1) notes that we can derive from this reference a relative date for the letter since Anastasius is still alive. However, the Syriac expression *ḥay naphshā* is ambiguous since it can mean that Anastasius is still alive at the time of the composition of the letter or it can simply refer to the soteriological condition of his post-mortem soul.

117 Unless he means the preceding passage, it is not clear to what Simeon refers. This may be a reference to a portion of the document now lost, or perhaps another text to which it was appended.

118 I.e. of the reign of the Sasanian king Peroz.

119 This refers to the Council of Bēt Lāpāṭ of 484 CE, mentioned above. The Antiochene emphasis on the duality of natures within the incarnation troubled the Miaphysites, who emphasized the unity of natures within Christ.

Because of this we separated ourselves from the communion of the Nestorians from the twenty-seventh year of Peroz the king until today and we anathematized them, and we also anathematize them and Simon the Sorcerer, their first master, (26b2) Ebion, Artemon, Paul of Samosata, Diodore, [357] Theodore, Nestorius, Theodoret, Ibas, and all those who have followed in their footsteps and have stood against the truth. With them also those like them we anathematize, Mani, Marcion, Eutyches, Arius, Apollinaris,[120] and their teaching and everyone who has thought or thinks like them.

Again we fully anathematize anyone who has come with letter, council (acts), homilies,[121] liturgical poetry,[122] responsa, the making of offerings,[123] the sanctification of water,[124] or the anointing of baptism, (and) dared[125] to say that the perfect God took from us a perfect human being as a permanent connection and habitation;[126] anyone who distinguishes and attributes divine (properties) to God, the eternal Son, and human (properties) and passions and death to Jesus, the human being, the son of grace, and reckons two sons, one by nature, the other by grace; and anyone who said or says that there are two sons with their own individual properties and operations[127] in Christ after the true and ineffable union (27a1) which truly came into being from two natures.

[358] We also anathematize the faith and canons and anything which came about from Acacius, Barṣaumā, Narsai, and his heretical companions, and all who agreed or agrees with them. Again we anathematize Māri of

120 Apollinaris of Laodicea (c. 315–92) was an anti-Arian bishop and writer whose emphasis on the singular nature of the '*Logos* made flesh' led to the condemnation of his person and Apollinarianism in general, even by later Miaphysites, with whom his thought had certain affinities.

121 Syr. *mēmrē*.

122 Syr. *madrāshē* are stanzaic liturgical poems.

123 I.e. the *anaphora* portion of the liturgy.

124 I.e. for baptism.

125 The original has an asyndeton. Furthermore, 'has come' (*'etaw*) is in the plural, but 'they dared' (*'amraḥ*) is in the singular.

126 Syr. *naqqiphutā wa'muryā*. Syr. *naqqiphutā* corresponds to Gr. *sunápheia*, 'conjunction'. The incarnation as a linking of two entities or as a form of 'residence' or 'inhabitation' (*'muryā*) was a cause of anxiety for those who wanted to emphasize the unity that occurred within it. Cf. 'And he was united in one unity and conjunction, the temple and its inhabitant, the taker and the taken, the perfecter and the perfected; man and God in the one inseparable union, of one prosopon, of one Lord Jesus Christ, the Son of God – yesterday, today and for ever', *Nestorian Christological Texts*, 11.21–12.3 (10.20–24).

127 See note 27 above.

Tahāl,[128] the master of Bābai the Catholicos,[129] since in the days of this Bābai that Māri appeared, the teacher of the heresy of the followers[130] of Paul of Samosata and of Diodore in Bēt Ārāmāyē. Bābai the Catholicos, son of Hormizd, who was a scribe of Zabargan the *marzbān*[131] of Bēt Ārāmāyē, received teaching from him. Whoever does not confess that Mary is the *Theotokos*[132] may he be anathematized.

128 As Assemani notes (n. 1), this is probably not the same Māri as the one mentioned above, the addressee of Ibas's controversial letter. Appropriate to the possible pedagogical meaning of 'master' (Syr. *rabbā*), a later source states that he was a 'teacher' (Syr. *mallphānā* [in Arabic]), and furthermore that he was excommunicated by Bābai's successor, Shilā (505–521/2) (*Chronicle of Siirt* 2.1.136). See also Fiey, *L'Assyrie Chrétienne*, III.134.

129 Catholicos Bābai (497–502/3). Baumstark, *Geschichte*, 113; McCullough, *Short History*, 133–34. This reference may be used to date the text as either at the time of or just after the death of Bābai.

130 Syr. *bēt*, lit. 'house of'.

131 Syr. *marzbānā*. See note 114 above. Cf. Mār Abā's early career as scribe before his conversion to Christianity, *Life of Abā*, 210.

132 See note 92 above.

BARḤADBESHABBĀ, *ECCLESIASTICAL HISTORY*

INTRODUCTION

The so-called *Ecclesiastical History* of Barḥadbeshabbā is extant in only one manuscript, British Library Or. 6714, which François Nau, who edited the text and translated it into French, dates to the ninth or tenth century.[1] It refers to its author as 'Mār Barḥadbeshabbā, presbyter and head of the interpreters (*bādoqē*) of the holy school of the city of Nisibis'.[2] The end of the manuscript refers to him as 'Mār Barḥadbeshabbā 'Arbāyā, presbyter and interpreter'.[3] The title the text receives in the manuscript is: 'The History of the Holy Fathers who were Persecuted for the Faith'.[4] Based upon the supposition that it is identical to the text referred to as the 'Ecclesiastical (History)' in 'Abdisho' bar Berikā of Nisibis's fourteenth-century poetical bibliography of Syriac writers in the chapter on Barḥadbeshabbā 'Arbāyā, Nau and those after him have referred to it as the *Ecclesiastical History*.[5]

That 'Ecclesiastical' (Syr. *eqlesasṭiqē* [*'qlssṭyqy*][6] from Gr. *ekklēsiastikós*) alone could be used for 'Ecclesiastical History' suggests that this was understood as a specific genre.[7] For example, Isho'denaḥ of Basra in his late eighth- or early ninth- century *Book of Chastity* uses the same Syriac rendering of the Greek word *ekklēsiastikós* as an abbreviated term for the genre, when he refers to Gregory of Nisibis's late sixth-century 'Ecclesiastical (History)', which is no longer extant.[8] Already by the mid-fifth century, Eusebius's *Ecclesiastical History* had been translated into Syriac.[9] As in

1 Barhadbeshabba, *La second partie de l'histoire ecclésiastique*, 494.

2 Ibid. 495.

3 Ibid. 631.

4 Syr. *tash'itā d-abāhātā qaddishē d-etrdeph*(*w*) *meṭṭul shrārā*

5 *Bibliotheca Orientalis* III.1.169.

6 More commonly *eqlesyasṭiqē* (*'qlsysṭyqy*).

7 Brock, 'Syriac Historical Writing', 21–22.

8 Isho'denah, *Le Livre de la Chasteté*, ed. and trans. J.-B. Chabot (Rome, 1896) (also in *Mélanges d'archéologie et d'histoire* 16 [Paris, 1896]: 225–91), # 56.

9 The older of the two manuscripts of the *Ecclesiastical History* is dated to 462/3 CE (St.

Greek Patristic and other Christian literatures, it had a guiding influence on Syriac historiography.

Because only the last two chapters of the *Ecclesiastical History* have been translated in this volume, the structure and content of the text as a whole should be addressed at least briefly here. This will provide a literary context for Chapters 31 ('Life of Narsai') and 32 ('Life of Abraham of Bēt Rabban') and clarify the broader tendencies of a text of which these two chapters are only a small portion. The *Ecclesiastical History* begins with a preface,[10] which I reproduce in full since its programmatic nature reveals the author's explicit aims in composition.

> Although I have been hindered by many things from attempting to gather together the stories[11] of the holy fathers and from demonstrating the ways of their slanderers – (that is,) first (by) ignorance, second youth, and third lack of training, and, more than all these, the evil times which continually trouble the mind and deprive and remove it from learning; nevertheless, affection and love for the way of life[12] of the fathers have overcome all these things. Because of this I have approached this account.[13] For since few are those who come upon the many long accounts by which the glory of the holy ones is known, I myself have endeavoured therefore (to set down) not only chapters but also if there is a speech in the accounts of others, by which the prosperous diligence of the fathers is known, I endeavour to set it here that from this they may be a mirror for others, who may glance at them and emulate their excellence. Like statues and images of kings which are adorned with choice materials and pigments, in this way also we ourselves paint an image of their deeds, by which a prototype of their excellence is known. Just as wayfarers first investigate marks and signposts and then begin their journey, thus it is right also for us first to briefly trace out the chapter headings through which our speech will run, so that when whoever is reading comes upon them they will learn the whole purpose[14] of the story.[15]

Petersburg Codex). See the edition of Wright and McLean in the bibliography. The manuscript of Eusebius's *On the Theophania* dates to 411 (British Library Add. 12150). Neither of these are autographs.

10 The Syriac word for 'preface' used here is *mappaq b-ruḥā*, which can also mean 'apology'. It in fact shows up regularly in the *Ecclesiastical History* with the latter meaning. cf. Riad, *Studies in the Syriac Preface*, 111.

11 Syr. *tash'yātā*, or 'histories'.

12 Syr. *dubbārayhon*, or 'their deeds'.

13 Syr. *maktbānutā*.

14 Syr. *nishā* often serves as the Syriac equivalent of Gr. *skopós*. See Riad, *Studies in the Syriac Preface*, 58–59.

15 Barhadbeshabba, *La second partie de l'histoire ecclésiastique*, 496–97. On the various parts of the Syriac preface, see Riad, *Studies in the Syriac Preface*, 179–231; on the modesty expressed here, see ibid. 197–202, esp. 200.

As the author states, a chapter summary is provided after the preface. This is reproduced below because it gives a sense of the work's main themes and, as it seems to have been composed by the author himself, is especially useful for seeing how the text coheres as a whole.

I. [497.3] The first chapter, in which it is right for us to let it be known how Satan was able from the very beginning to oppose the Church and what were the tricks that he taught the errant ones.[16]

II. What were the heresies that he tore out from the church and what is the opinion of each one of them and which ones have corrupted the scriptures and which ones have not.

III. On Arius the heretic and from what opinion he came to this error. Concerning the great liberty which Alexander and his companions possessed against him. What was the cause of the council (of Nicaea).

IV. The letter of the king who ordered that they come to the council at Nicaea in Bithynia.

V. The apology of Simeon bar Ṣabba'ē. How many bishops gathered together. Concerning the liberty which the true ones possessed.

VI. The matters that the council addressed when it came together. What evils they did and did not endure from the Arians.

VII. Concerning the plan which Arius wanted to enact against the Church after he was first anathematized. What punishment he received from God through the prayer of Alexander of Constantinople.

VIII. [498] The story of the way of life of the holy ones, Eustathius and Meletius, bishops of Antioch. What were the evils which they endured from Eusebius and those who shared his opinion, wicked Arians.

IX. The story of the friend of God, Athanasius, bishop of Alexandria. How many evils he endured from the Arians.

X. What evils George the Arian made the faithful in Alexandria endure. On the form of his death.

XI. Concerning the wicked Eudoxius the Arian. Concerning the evils he made the faithful endure.

XII. The story of the way of life of Gregory the wonder worker, bishop of Neocaesarea.

XIII. Concerning Aetius the wicked. Concerning the evil of his mind.

XIV. Concerning Eunomius the Arian. Concerning his teaching.

16 Lit. 'sons of error'.

XV. The story of the holy Basil, bishop of Caesarea.
XVI. The story of the way of life of Flavian, bishop of Antioch
XVII. The story of the way of life of the glorious Diodore, bishop of Tarsus. Concerning his perseverance in the truth.
XVIII. The story of the way of life of John, bishop of Constantinople. Whence he came. Concerning his perseverance in the fear of God.
XIX. [499] The story of the way of life of the holy Theodore, bishop of Mopsuestia. What praiseworthy things he did in his episcopacy.
XX. The story of the friend of God, Mār Nestorius, bishop of Constantinople. Whence he came. From whom he received his learning of scripture. What praiseworthy thing the zealous one did in his episcopacy.
XXI. Apology against the reproofs of the wicked Cyril, from which the glorious deeds of the holy Nestorius and the excellence of his way of life will be known.
XXII. From what causes did a dispute arise between Cyril and Nestorius.
XXIII. What was done at Ephesus by Cyril and those with him before the arrival of (the bishop of) Antioch.
XXIV. What was done against the rash boldness of Cyril and Memnon of Ephesus after the arrival of John.
XXV. What that person who had been sent by the king did after his arrival.
XXVI. Not only did the see of Alexandria attack Nestorius but also the bishops who preceded him.
XXVII. What are the things that were done afterwards by that (bishop) of Antioch. What was the cause of his desertion of the truth.
XXVIII. A portion from a letter of the council which was written to the king on account of the slander of Nestorius.
XXIX. What zeal the council of the East demonstrated against the frenzy of Cyril, when he sent those who were with Maximinus that they might compel them to anathematize those who were with Diodore and Theodore. What they wrote to Proclus and the king.
XXX. What the Egyptian wanted to do against Nestorius, even in his exile. What glorious deeds that holy one performed in his exile.
XXXI. The story of the way of life of Mār Narsai, the presbyter and teacher.
XXXII. The story of the glorious deeds of Mār Abraham, the presbyter and teacher.[17]

17 Barhadbeshabba, *La second partie de l'histoire ecclésiastique*, 497–99.

The author begins the first chapter by inquiring into the 'cause' (Syr. *'elltā*) of the slander that is cast upon the fathers and teachers of the Church. In the beginning the Apostles, after receiving the grace of the Holy Spirit, made disciples among the nations.[18] They preached in the name of the Trinity but did not concern themselves with 'exactitude and the propounding of laws'.[19] The weakness of their 'students'[20] did not allow them to grapple with the exact truth. At the same time, Satan grew disturbed by the rapid growth of the Church, a development that was diminishing his own kingdom. In response, he incited pagan priests and diviners to attack the Church, but this was to no avail.

What follows is one of the more bizarre passages in the *Ecclesiastical History*.[21] In what is clearly a conflation of several traditions, including a confusion between Helen the mother of Constantine and Helen of Troy, the text describes how Satan's assault upon the Church was put to a stop by Helen, a woman from Mesopotamia who exceeded all women in beauty. This woman was converted to Christianity by Barsamyā, bishop of Edessa, and was then well-trained in the reading of scripture.[22] Valentinian, an imperial steward, eventually comes to see the woman of fabled beauty, wanting to legally wed her. When he becomes emperor, Helen shows full support for the Church. At this Satan realizes that he has failed and therefore develops a new form of attack: 'he cast schisms and divisions and he made commotions and dissensions by the mass of heresies he introduced into the Church'.[23] By this means he causes many to fall and chaos descends upon the Church.

The second chapter then describes 14 different heresies. This list, which seems to be taken as a whole from one of the author's sources, depicts the heresies that existed prior to the fourth century.[24] The chapter concludes with

18 Syr. *ntalmdun* (Barhadbeshabba, *La première partie de l'histoire*, 182.8).

19 Ibid. 182.10.

20 Syr. *yālophē*, ibid. 182.11.

21 Ibid. 184.6–185.2.

22 Note the connection between the Martyrdom of Barsamyā and Sharbēl and the *Doctrina Addai*, which contains the story of Protonike's discovery of the cross (instead of Helen). See, e.g., Jan Willem Drijvers, 'The Protonike Legend, The Doctrina Addai and Bishop Rabbula of Edessa', *Vigiliae Christianae* 51 (1997): 298–315.

23 Barhadbeshabba, *La première partie de l'histoire*, 185.4–5.

24 'Sabbatians, Simonists, Marcionites, Borborites, Daisanites, Manichaeans, Paul of Samosata, Audians, Quqites, Montanists, Timotheans, "The Pure", Arimanites, Cyrilians or Severians' (ibid. 186–99). Of course the latter two are named after much later figures, but according to the author can be traced back to an earlier period. Nau notes at 186 n. 2 that this chapter appears elsewhere extant in Arabic.

a statement which may be understood as programmatic for the *Ecclesiastical History* as a whole.

> All these heresies and the many others cover over the Holy Church like dark clouds – by the holy men their deceit has been revealed and their gloominess dissipated. For their stings are bitter. By means of questions and responses they have been destroyed. It is not the time for us to recount the cause of every single one of them, both when and in what manner each took its origin, or who were their sources, lest we be detained from what has been set for us (or: by us) to accomplish. But this one thing it is necessary to add: although all these errant ones were students to Satan, that one who continually *works eagerly within the sons of disobedience*,[25] nevertheless more (trouble) than all of these is in these two groups – I am able to demonstrate his power in the Holy Church – the one of the Arians and Eunomians, the other of the Cyrilians and Severans. Because of this also let us turn our speech against the two of them, first against the Arians, (inquiring into) both who is their heresiarch and whence he came to this error, and then against these others.[26]

After this point, the *Ecclesiastical History* commences its more detailed history of events from the early fourth century onwards, addressing the fourth-century 'heresies', starting with that of Arius.

As is apparent from the table of contents presented above, several chapters of the *Ecclesiastical History*, including the two translated here, consist of self-contained biographies. The style of these individual units relies on Christian hagiography and many of the tropes of this genre – ultimately deriving from parallels with the life of Jesus Christ on earth – are apparent. For example, the holy men described by the text are often precocious from a young age, excelling their peers in virtue and talent. Despite the numerous enemies who attempt to obstruct them, they are ultimately successful and die enjoying recognition of their greatness. This hagiographical tone suggests that we should be especially hesitant to attribute historical value to the claims made by the text.

Furthermore, in the broader body of the work the sources of the *Ecclesiastical History* are often readily apparent. Nau notes among these Socrates Scholasticus's *Ecclesiastical History*, the *Bazaar of Heracleides* of Nestorius, and documents relating to the Council of Ephesus.[27] The text's utter dependence at times on clearly identifiable sources for the fourth and fifth centuries suggests that the East Syrians knew little of the ecclesiastical

25 Eph 2:2.

26 Barhadbeshabba, *La première partie de l'histoire*, 197.11–199.2.

27 Barhadbeshabba, *La second partie de l'histoire ecclésiastique*, 500–01.

events of the past except for what they learned from books deriving from the West. There is a change in tone and source material in the last two chapters, the two lives of Narsai and Abraham of Bēt Rabban, translated here. These two men were the heads of the School of Nisibis and the author would have had much closer contact with their writings as well as texts written by their contemporaries and could possibly have known Abraham of Bēt Rabban himself.

The following is a schematic outline of each of the two chapters translated here:

Chapter 31 ('Life of Narsai')	*Pages in the Nau Edition*
Preface	588–90
Origins, childhood, early contemplative knowledge	590–94
The youth Narsai's leadership in time of persecution	594–96
Residence at Kephar Māri in Bēt Zabdai	596
First arrival in Edessa	596–97
On Barṣaumā of Nisibis	597–98
Rabbula, first Head of the School; Narsai takes over the School	598–99
Narsai is slandered and attempts to convert him fail	599–602
Narsai's public accusation and flight	602–05
Narsai arrives at Nisibis	605–06
Barṣaumā persuades Narsai to settle in Nisibis	606–08
Satan's assault on Narsai in Nisibis	608–11
Narsai's scholastic asceticism	611
The heretical Jacob of Sarug inspires Narsai to write	612
Criticism of and trouble with the Persian authorities	612–13
Narsai is slandered again	614
The miraculous healing of a boy harassed by a demon	614–15
Conclusion	615

Chapter 32 ('Life of Abraham of Bēt Rabban')	
Early life and training under Narsai	616–17
Abraham's learning appropriate to what is required in the body	617–20
Abraham's ascetic way of life and the awe he inspired in many	620–21
His work at the School and in teaching	622–24
Enemy brothers accuse him	624–26
The wicked Jews attack Abraham	626–27
Abraham's sturdiness and defence of the Doctors of the Church	627–30
Conclusion	630–31

LIFE OF NARSAI: TRANSLATION AND NOTES

Chapter 31. The story of that one who has passed to the house of the holy ones,[1] the blessed Mār Narsai, whence he came and what sort was his teaching.[2]

Preface

[588] Since we have reached this point with the help of God we should not pass by as something extraneous[3] the story of the virtue of our own Persian fathers; I am speaking of Mār Narsai and Mār Abraham, the blessed ones. For although we are not capable of plaiting crowns for their way of life[4] nor of weaving a coat full of the beauties of their virtues, nevertheless, although in prosaic speech, let us make remembrance of their glorious deeds among their companions, lest we be found to be ones who reject their glittering beauties.[5] We first will tell the story of the way of life of that one who has passed to the house of the holy ones, Mār Narsai. We will then include[6] that of Mār Abraham, his student. For there is a custom among men that whenever those dear to them or those who reared them pass away, because of the eager longing of love for them and the remembrance of their beauties, by means of choice pigments or with materials glittering [589] with beauty, they paint an image of their loved ones and possess them as likenesses which

1 The 'house' or 'place of the holy ones' (Syr. *bēt qaddishē*) can be the physical structure or locus where the remains of holy men are kept. This then may suggest that there was such a sacred building or location at the School of Nisibis dedicated to the fathers of the School who had passed away.

2 Some of the information provided by this text can be found in an abbreviated form in the later *Chronicle of Siirt* 2.1.115–17, 136–37.

3 The Syr. *barrāytā* is Nau's emendation for *bsh'ṭ'*.

4 The Syr. *dubbārē*, which can commonly mean 'custom' or 'manner', often has a technical meaning of 'discipline' or 'ascetic practice' and even serves as the opposite of 'theory' in the philosophical and monastic dichotomy of theory/practice. On this whole phrase, see Riad, *Studies in the Syriac Preface*, 209.

5 It is a commonplace to preface works of praise with comparisons to the different plastic arts. The author also apologizes that his work is not in poetry, but is rather 'in prosaic speech' (*b-melltā shḥimtā*). This is in part rhetorical convention, but there are a number of examples of praise in Syriac poetry from the late fourth century onwards (e.g. the *madrashē* of Balai on Acacius, bishop of Beroea in *S. Ephraemi siri, Rabbulae episcopi Edesseni, Balaei aliorumque opera selecta*, ed. Julian Joseph Overbeck [Oxford: Clarendon Press, 1865], 259–69). On the author speaking about his own work in general in the preface, see Riad, *Studies in the Syriac Preface*, 218–30, esp. 221 and 230.

6 There is a metathesis of *mpqynn* for *mqpynn*. This may be in the manuscript, but since it is not noted by Nau it is more likely a mistake in the printed edition of the text.

according to the shape of their features are akin to them.[7] By the similarity of the resemblance to them, the grief of those who love them is soothed and the seething of their minds is cooled from thoughts about them. Thus let us also, in place of dead images and silent likenesses, adorn our tongue and sanctify our lips so that by our speech we can paint upon the minds of the lovers of truth a praiseworthy image of the way of life of the glorious one, and as a polished likeness of beauty let us plait a crown of his beauties so that, after the discerning power of the sense of hearing contemplates it and presses the harmony of its loftiness within its mind,[8] it (i.e. the crown) may be a peaceful haven for the earnest desire of love for him. For if we were to paint a fixed image, it would doubtless be easier for us to do this, because the vision of the eyes serves the natural constitution of his likeness and the harmony of his features. With craftsmanship it is easy for someone to take the different particulars of the subject in his mind, and he draws them first with simple lines.[9] Then he adorns them with pigments that are able to demonstrate certain similarities to his likeness.[10] But we paint not an image which is visible nor do we draw a fixed likeness, but rather a simple image which is not visible and a likeness [590] which transcends the senses of the body. This intellectual commander of the army is searched out with the knowledge of the soul and is grasped with the eyes of the mind. In addition to this, it is not easy for us to contemplate the virtue of the diligent ones due to the heaviness of the body.[11] But love for the holy one goes beyond all

7 The author now switches his approach by suggesting that he will, in fact, produce beautiful plastic arts in honour of his subject. However, this will be through words which form representations in the mind. Although it derives from Classical rhetorical practice, the analogy between writing and painting images became a commonplace in Syriac literature, especially in the prologue to Syriac texts. The analogy to images of the dead may reflect local practice, similar to the mosaic and sculptural images of the dead we find in Edessa and Palmyra respectively, but this analogy may here also derive from Classical practice as mediated through Greek texts. The metaphorical use of painting and image making also follows the logic of the Greek psychology and epistemology that had come into the School of Nisibis by this time: knowledge was understood as representative. See note CS 142.

8 The preceding line is difficult. I have not followed the manuscript which vocalizes *ṭb‘* as the perfect form, *ṭba‘*. Instead I take it as a participle, *ṭāba‘*, translated as 'presses', so that it can be parallel with the participle, *maṣed* ('contemplates').

9 The 'simple lines' could also be rendered as 'dark lines'. In either case this phrase seems to refer to the practice of drawing an outline sketch before the colour is added to a painting.

10 Lit. 'certain likenesses of his likeness'.

11 This reflects the physiological understanding which lies behind much late antique ascetic discourse. The purpose of ascetic practice was to lighten and dry out the body, making it less of a hindrance to the soul, which it regularly led astray. Cf. Shaw, *The Burden of the Flesh*.

these things and kindles our mind that we might repeat some of his glorious deeds, even if only a few.

Origins, Childhood, Early Contemplative Knowledge

Now this man of God was from the land of M'altā and the name of his town was 'Ayn Dulbā.[12] From the time of his youth his thought stirred him to be grown with the irrigation of the divine scriptures. Although in the time of youth the orders of rationality are mixed up, as the saying of the wise one who said: *Youth and ignorance are vanity*;[13] *the child believes every word*[14] because of the desire of the body and the heat of its temperature;[15] nonetheless this holy one immediately let it be known what would come from him once he reached full stature, and just as a praiseworthy plant, when from the beginning of its growth it hastens to bring forth lovely shoots, while in this through its prior abundance it hints at another change to the workers who tend to it, thus also this holy one did, since in the time when the thought of many is moved by youthful onrushes to stray after empty things by which youth is enticed to transgress [591] the paths of the vineyard, he, however, departed immediately from all the fierce onrushes of weak childhood, while he distanced himself from delicate ornaments and from desirable enticements as well as all earthly distraction. He was continually going about wholly in the sphere of virtue, as the blessed Timothy.[16] For he had along with the possession of virtue also care for the divine teaching, according to the word of the psalmist: *While he was continually meditating upon the law of the Lord*,[17] and like that one who was saying this with the blessed David:

12 Modern *Deleb*, Fiey, *Assyrie Chrétienne* II.685–86 (see map on p. 704). 'The source/spring of plane trees'; the *Chronicle of Siirt* gives the same location (2.2.114). Ma'altā (Fiey, *Assyrie Chrétienne* II.675–81, also see I.213–15), referred to as the region of the village, is now a separate town. Both are north-west of Dohuk in Iraqi Kurdistan.

13 Eccl 11:10 (12:1).

14 Prov 14:15.

15 The author here medicalizes the traditional proverbial wisdom of scripture. The 'heat of its temperature' (*ḥammimutā d-muzzāgāh*) derives from Greek medical science. Greek physiology was integrated into the Christian ascetic notion of the body, e.g., Shaw, *The Burden of the Flesh*, 79–128.

16 The source of this striking expression, 'sphere of virtue' (Syr. *giglā da-myattrutā*), is unclear.

17 Ps 1:2. The use of this quotation and the following one is typical of the East Syrians' positive emphasis on God's law, in contrast to the more common denigration of the law found in both East-Syrian and other Christian literature, particularly as part of an anti-Jewish rhetorical strategy.

How I loved your law and all the day it is the object of my reflection.[18]

After these (characteristics), modesty came in the likeness of a praiseworthy icon, which is akin to the true prototype.[19] After he joined himself to the hard yoke of fasting from the very beginning, he possessed for some time chastity, pleasantness, and humility, through the spurning of desires, while he continually worked in the spiritual field. Because in everything he understood and in the manner of a student received (the lesson)[20] that the things which are in the flesh are unable to please God, since the mind which is in the flesh is an enmity unto God, but the mind of the spirit gives life and peace;[21] on account of this he disregarded all the objects of desire and he took care to complete the free will of his [592] intellectual soul.[22] Because our soul is adorned in this temporal life with two faculties, that is, by intellectual thought and the passive portion,[23] and by that former portion contemplative knowledge rushes to do whatever it has the capacity naturally to receive in its exaltedness,[24] by this second passive portion it gives birth to two other faculties whose nature is to be moved passively.[25] Sometimes it uses them

18 Ps 119:97.

19 The terms 'icon' (Syr. from *yuqnā*, from Gr. *eikṓn*) and 'prototype' (Syr. *tape(n)kā*, of Persian origin) appear also in the *Cause*, and reflect the basic Platonic concept of mimesis employed within the text. Here Narsai's modesty is an 'image' or 'icon' of the 'prototype', that is, the ideal modesty, which like all virtues belongs to God.

20 This seems to be a technical usage of the word. The Syriac *qabbel* usually takes an explicit, or at least implicit, direct object.

21 This distinction between the two types of mind derives from Rom 8:5–8. However, as in other passages the physical body's hindrance in spiritual matters is emphasized in a manner which reflects the Greek medical body.

22 The 'intellectual soul' (Syr. *naphshā yaddu'tānitā*) refers to that portion of the soul characterized as rational and active by both the Neoplatonists and Evagrius of Pontus. Such a distinction was made because the soul was understood also to have a simple vegetative and passive portion.

23 The 'passive portion' (Syr. *mnātā ḥāshoshtānā*) of the soul. Greek words derived from the verb *páschein* ('to suffer') are expressed in Syriac often with the root ḥ-sh-sh, e.g. *hāshoshtā* ('passive') and *ḥāshoshā'it* ('passively') in the following passage. The Syr. *mnātā* is Nau's emendation for the manuscript's *melltā* ('word').

24 This is an awkward, difficult clause. The phrase 'contemplative knowledge' (lit. 'knowledge of contemplation'; Syr. *ida'tā d-ta'āwriya*, from Gr. *theōríā*) refers to the knowledge acquired in Evagrian contemplation. On *theōríā* in Syriac, see, for example, Brock, 'Some Uses of the Term Theoria in the Writings of Isaac of Nineveh'.

25 As in the *Cause*, we find here a psychology that divides the soul into active and passive portions. This distinction, which is originally Aristotelian, was mediated to the Church of the East through both the Neoplatonism of the Evagrian corpus and the Aristotelianism of the later Neoplatonic commentators on Aristotle.

in an ordered manner[26] and sometimes outside of the truth according to the governance of its freewill. He took care to change his steps according to its first cause,[27] because, whenever it uses them immoderately and wickedly like a wild animal, it falls completely from the rank of its nature.[28] Whenever it is empowered to work with these things justly and prudently according to the truth of its freewill, it goes beyond everything which is in opposition to (its) constitution[29] and the fleshly tumult, while cooling off with its pure luminous clarity[30] the whole flame kindled by objects of desire[31] and overcoming with intellectual power all the evil troops of pride, anger, and canine impudence, as the divine Paul outlines: *Now therefore I am in my mind a slave of the law of God. I am in my flesh a slave of the law of sin. There is nothing which I want that I do. But evil, which I hate* [593], *that is what I do*,[32] by this making known that some things are of the body, others are of the soul. The one, because of the opposition of its constitution and the necessity and longing of its need, is continually attracted to what is opposed to it. The other, because of its subtlety and the simplicity of its substance,[33] is liberated from this necessity[34] of the body and continually meditates with its subtle intellect that it might perform the things which that essence, rich in blessings,[35] takes pleasure in, while distributing equally with righteousness and justice and dividing the movements of these things for whatever serves for its ascent. From this it is known that all practice and the life of

26 Or 'in a proper manner', lit. 'according to (its) order' or 'according to (its) rank' (Syr. *ṭaksis*, from Gr. *táxis*). This may not be simply an idiomatic phrase, but rather a specific reference to the 'rank' that each species has in creation. See note CS 56 regarding a similar usage.

27 I.e. the soul's first cause or origin (Syr. *'elltāh qadmāytā*).

28 Lit. 'from all the rank of its nature'. Again, the word here derives from Greek *táxis* and may be translated variously.

29 Syr. *saqublāyutā d-muzzāgā*. As elsewhere in this portion of the text, the language is clearly Evagrian in origin. Cf. Evagrius of Pontus, *Kephalaia Gnostica*, 1.2 (pp. 16–17).

30 Syr. *shaphyutāh dkitā*. Syr. *shaphyutā* , translated here as 'luminous clarity', comes from a root meaning 'limpid' or 'clear', but is commonly used with a specialized meaning in Syriac spiritual literature for the clarity one finds in a higher experiential state. It is the source for the title of Sebastian Brock's book on Ephrem, *The Luminous Eye: The Spiritual World Vision of St. Ephrem*. See pp. 71–79 therein for a discussion of the term.

31 Lit. 'flame of combustion of objects of desire'.

32 Rom 7:15.

33 'Sublety' (*qaṭṭinutā*) and 'simplicity' (*pshiṭutā*) are attributes of the immaterial, spiritual realm. Non-material entities do not have parts and are therefore simple (cf. Gr. *haploûs*). See note CS 63.

34 Syr. *ananqē*, from Gr. *anánkē*

35 Syr. *mārat ṭubē*, lit. 'mistress of good things'. This expression is also used for the divine essence in the *Cause*, for example, on p. 335 and p. 379.

performing the commandments polish[36] the passive portion of the soul, that is, the movements and the two faculties of anger and desire,[37] while hindering them from being moved by these things to go out from whatever limits for us the necessities of life in the world. The practice of divine contemplation,[38] the other portion of the soul, which is foremost and exalted, is entrusted with the straining – I refer to the intellectual thought and the discerning mind.[39] For they also often give movements which are contrary to nature, not only effective and active ones, but also true and knowing ones. Whenever it abandons [594] the true knowledge of natures[40] and is led by compulsion, as if by an onrush, towards the desire belonging to mendacious error, it too goes in a crooked path and is moved by the ambushing onrush to incline towards that which is the opposite of discernment.

Because this holy one knew that true contemplation of the spirit[41] draws and raises up (the mind) from this depth of error and from the chasm of falsehood to the height of truth, while it alone can purify it from all the filth of deceit; on account of this he disregarded all the objects of bodily desire typical of youth and began to increase the pure faculties of his soul with the spiritual milk of the fear of God, according to the life of contemplation, as the Lord's word instructs us: *Seek for yourselves first the kingdom of God and his righteousness, and all these things will be added unto you*,[42] because *the fear of God is the beginning of wisdom*,[43] according to the prophetic

36 Note the prior tradition of using the language of purification, cleansing, and polishing to address the relation to self and soul in Ephrem, e.g., Edmund Beck, *Des Heiligen Ephraem des Syrers Hymnen de Ieiunio* (CSCO 246; Louvain: Secrétariat du CorpusSCO, 1964), 1–5 (Hymn 1). This prior tradition is rendered here in Greek philosophical terms.

37 'Anger' (Syr. *ḥemtā*) and 'desire' (Syr. *regtā*) are equivalent to the *thumós* and the *epithumíā* of Platonic psychology. These two 'faculties' (Syr. *ḥaylē*, Gr. *dunámeis*), along with their various 'movements' (Syr. *zaw'ē*, Gr. *kinḗseis*), make up the passive portion of the soul.

38 Syr. *ta'āwriya*, from Gr. *theōríā*. 'Divine *theōríā* … seems to be not of Evagrian, but of Dionysian origin, though it also occurs in the Syriac translation of the Lausiac History' (Brock, 'Some Uses of the Term Theoria in the Writings of Isaac of Nineveh', 412).

39 The metaphor of 'straining' and 'purification' appears also in the *Cause* (see notes CS 129 and CS 130). Again, we have a combination of Evagrian and later Neoplatonic psychology. For a discussion addressing *thumós* and *epithumíā*, that is, the passive portions of the soul, and the purification of the soul, see, e.g., Philoponus, *In de Anima*, 18.8–19.

40 This reading removes the awkward *seyame* (pluralizing diacritical mark) from the word 'true'.

41 This is an Evagrian expression. For example, see Isaac of Nineveh, *Second Part*, 23 n. 5 (versio).

42 Mt 6:33. Note the use of this verse by Evagrius (Sinkewicz, *Evagrius of Pontus*, 6, 196) and Isaac of Nineveh (*Second Part*, 68 [78–79] [14.37])

43 Ps 111:10.

word. Also this holy one when he was seven years old went to the school[44] for youths, and from the fervour of his love and the speedy movements[45] of his soul, in nine months' time he memorized the whole Psalter.[46]

The Youth Narsai's Leadership in Time of Persecution

But after a short time by Satan's instigation paganism was put into motion against the truth.[47] [595] The Magi, the wise men of Persia, heard about this school and they came (to see) if it was possible for them either to make the youths deny what is true or to remove them from their prior opinion. The teacher at that time, strengthened by the grace of the spirit, led the school away and went and hid on a mountain, like those holy ones from the time of Elijah,[48] and they did not fear the sword. These true ones were neither hindered nor overwhelmed by the torments, but they were there until the gloom of the persecutors passed. During this whole storm Mār Narsai was encouraging his peers[49] to learn and take care for the fear of God, as the blessed Daniel (did) his companions, in that at that time he was saying: Love for your law is *greater than gold and greater than precious stones*,[50] and sometimes, *Your words are sweet to my palate more than honey to the mouth*,[51] and at other times, *Do not fear those who kill the body. They are unable to kill the soul. Fear rather whoever is able to destroy the soul and*

44 Syr. *eskolē*, from Gr. *scholḗ*.

45 Those with a quick intellect are described as having 'speedy movements' in their mind or soul. Cf. the description of the angels on p. 349 of the *Cause*.

46 Lit. 'he repeated David'. The Syriac verb 'repeat' (*tnā*) can have a similar meaning as the cognate Rabbinic term, which is also used in pedagogical contexts. The Psalter, which was the text studied for elementary literacy in part because of its liturgical significance, is regularly referred to as simply 'David' after its pseudonymous author.

47 It is reasonable to question the authenticity of the following account. Furthermore, the persecution does not help to date Narsai's youth, since there were a number of outbreaks of persecution in the fifth century, under Yazdegird I (399–420), Bahram V (421–39), Yazdegird II (439–57), and Peroz (459–84). Even if Narsai's youth was affected by persecution, the story of the 'school for youths' being taken into the wilderness and the child Narsai consoling and encouraging them in their exile seems far-fetched. Furthermore, how would the author of this text have known about these events?

48 1 Kgs 19:1–18 describes Elijah's flight to Mt Horeb.

49 Dan 1:10 lit. 'sons of his tooth'.

50 Ps 19:10 (11). Theodoret, *Commentary on the Psalms, Psalms 1–72* (trans. Robert C. Hill; Washington, DC: Catholic University Press, 2000), 133–38 (PG 80.898–1000) on Psalm 19 addresses the positive understanding of the law typical of Antiochene theology and exegesis.

51 Ps 119:103.

the body in Gehenna,[52] according to the word of the Lord. The holy one was in this school for a period of nine years. He even exceeded his master in instruction. For who would not wonder at this successful athlete and second Daniel, [596] who despised all objects of desire! For the threats of the judge did not frighten him, nor again did worldly incentives lead him astray from his love of Jesus.

Residence at Kephar Māri in Bēt Zabdai

Later after he was bereft of his upbringing since his parents had left this world early, he heard about the brother of his father whose name was Emmanuel,[53] who was the head of a monastery in the region of Bēt Zabdai in the monastery called Kephar Māri.[54] They say that he came to that place after he was instructed at the School of Edessa.[55] He made the monastery abound with a great assembly of brothers and he created a school there.[56] Because of his training and the sturdiness of his ways and his care for the truth, he was made a priest[57] of all the countryside and finally was commissioned to lead the church of Amida.[58] He arose and came to him, and after Emmanuel found and recognized him and also learned from testing him that he was more illuminated in learning than the teachers and brothers who

52 Mt 10:28.

53 Nothing else is known of Emmanuel. However, the course of his career demonstrates the porousness of the boundaries between Rome and Persia. Presumably, like Narsai, he came from Persia, but then went to Edessa, returned to Persia to the monastery of Kephar Māri, and finally died as bishop of Diyarbakir, again in Roman territory.

54 See note SL 77. Simeon includes an Ezalyā from the monastery of Kephar Māri in his list of members of the School of the Persians in Edessa (*Epistle* 352).

55 Nau here translates *eskolē* with a *seyame* (pluralizing diacritical mark) as a plural, but ignores the *seyame* elsewhere in the manuscript. It is more likely that all instances are simply cases where it is used to express the long e (ē) sound at the end of a singular word.

56 This may be an anachronism, since it resembles the standard practice of the mid-sixth century onwards as it is represented by other sources (see Becker, *Fear of God*, 161–62).

57 Syr. *peryādewṭā* from the Gr. *periodeutḗs*. This is a priest who serves as the bishop's representative in the countryside, visiting villages and monasteries.

58 Amed/Amid/Amida is modern Diyarbakir, which sits on the left bank of the upper Tigris and is today a major city in south-eastern Turkey. Much of the Christian community of Nisibis moved to Diyarbakir in 363 after Jovian ceded five transtigritine provinces to the Sasanians; Ammianus Marcellinus, *Res Gestae*, ed. and trans. J.C. Rolfe, I-III (Cambridge, MA; London, 1935–40), 25.7.9–11. The best sources for Christianity in the city in the fifth and sixth centuries are the lives of local holy men found in John of Ephesus's *Lives of the Eastern Saints*. See also Harvey, *Asceticism and Society in Crisis: John of Ephesus and 'The Lives of the Eastern Saints'*, much of which concerns John of Ephesus's description of the holymen of Diyarbakir.

were there, he along with the whole community asked him to instruct them in how to read a manuscript.[59]

First Arrival in Edessa

After he consented and was with them one winter, he heard about the assembly which is in Edessa. He left and departed for there, and after he went and found the assembly which was flourishing with spiritual intercourse and instruction in the scriptures, he was there ten years. When his uncle heard about his learning, he sent an anathema after him[60] and brought him and convinced him to join [597] him and benefit the brothers who were there. After he consented to this, about three hundred brothers assembled around him within a brief period. Due to the love of learning he possessed and perhaps because of an unknown (reason),[61] he left after some time and secretly departed for Edessa again. He was there ten more years. When that holy one (i.e. Emmanuel) knew that the time of his death was already near, he sent an anathema after him a second time, harsh with great entreaties, and he brought him from Edessa and entrusted to him the whole assembly of the monastery.[62] A little later he rested (i.e. died) and after this he (i.e. Narsai) was there one year, nourishing all the brothers who were there in bodily as well as spiritual things, while he was painting before them a beautiful likeness in himself,[63] according to the apostolic word, *with all good works*.[64]

59 Or 'portion', i.e. of a manuscript or lection. This is an appropriate form of hagiographical precociousness for a text composed in Nisibis since it is a typical practice at an East-Syrian school (cf. Thomas of Marga, *Book of the Governors* I:75.8, II.149; ibid. I:163.7–12, II: 328). The verb, the *afel* form of q-r-', is used in the 'reading lesson' at the time of creation in the *Cause* (p. 348) and also in a number of school texts to form the noun, *maqryānā* ('reader'), one of the school offices.

60 It seems that this would only have been possible if Emmanuel was already bishop of Diyarbakir. However, Diyarbakir is far from Kephar Māri, which was in Bēt Zabdai, under Persian rule and subject to the church of Nisibis.

61 This obscure line may correspond with the allusions the author makes to the criticisms that were made of Narsai. However, this line could also be rendered: 'Because of that thing which was not known (to him)', i.e. 'there was something he wanted to learn there'.

62 Again, it seems strange that Emmanuel, the bishop of Diyarbakir, could formally establish his nephew as the head of a monastery in Bēt Zabdai. It is possible that the text is vague and is referring to another monastery, one near or in Diyarbakir.

63 Or 'in his soul'.

64 Tit 2:7. The full verse is: 'In every thing show a likeness in yourself with all good works, and in your teaching may you have a sound word'; compare this to the NRSV: 'Show yourself in all respects a model of good works, and in your teaching show integrity, gravity....'

After he was there for one year, he handed the work of teaching over to one of the brothers who were there, whose name was Gabriel, and he again departed for the School of Edessa.

On Barṣaumā of Nisibis

At that time Mār Barṣaumā, the bishop of Nisibis, went to Edessa and the two of them were there together, intimates of one another.[65] Because Mār Barṣaumā was a sharp person, in little time he learned and was illuminated in the scriptures as well as their meaning more than anyone else. Grace afterwards moved him to direct his foot [598] to the city of Nisibis. After he came and was tested in his learning, he was commissioned by the bishop and all his clergy to be the homilist[66] in the church. Because of the polish of his speech he was loved in all the city, and after the bishop at that time had gone to rest, he was deemed worthy of the work of the episcopate by the whole community. After he received ordination[67] to the high priesthood, he did everything that the ecclesial canon teaches as the Christian teaching.[68] What this glorious man did in his episcopate, what harmful weeds[69] he uprooted from the Christian field, what good seed he planted in the Eastern region by means of his beautiful traditions and ecclesial canons,[70] now is not the time for us to tell, since our aim is another.[71]

65 On Barṣaumā, bishop of Nisibis at the time of the foundation of the School and a controversial figure within the Church of the East, see Gero, *Barṣauma*.

66 Syr. *mtargmānā*, lit. 'translator', but this term often refers to a type of homilist whose works were called, *turgāmē*. If this term is to be taken literally as 'translator', it may suggest that some members of the church spoke Persian and required translation during the lection and homilies.

67 Syr. *kirāṭāwnya*, from Gr. *cheirotonía*.

68 This is clearly an apology for one who was highly contested in his lifetime and 'a suspect figure in the eyes of subsequent "mainline" Nestorian tradition', Gero, *Barṣauma*, 1.

69 Syr. *zizānē*, from Gr. *zizánion*.

70 The 'traditions' (*mashlmānwātā*) may refer to the exegetical ideas he passed on, since this term is specifically used to refer to the exegesis of the School in the *Cause* (p. 382); see also Gero, *Barṣauma*, 89–90. The canons (*qānonē*) may be either those of the Council of 484 (see note SL 99) or the canons of the School of Nisibis, either the original ones, which are no longer extant, or those of 496 (Vööbus, *Statutes*, 31–32).

71 Syr. *nishā*, equivalent to Gr. *skopós*. See note 14 in the introduction to Barḥadbeshabbā's *Ecclesiastical History* above.

Rabbula, First Head of the School; Narsai takes over the School

There was an exegete then at that time in Edessa. They say about him that he was an enlightened man.[72] His name was Rabbula.[73] This man was adorned with all things, with true learning and perfect virtue in manner of life.[74] He bore all the work of the school, reading as well as elementary instruction[75] and interpretation.[76] He also had confidence in speech. After this holy one fulfilled his course, according to the will of God, [599] and rested from his labour, there was an inquiry concerning who would be suitable for the work of teaching after him. All of them equally shouted, 'Mār Narsai the presbyter is suitable, not only because of his old age,[77] his success, his work, and the elegance of his speech, but also because of his perfect and divine manner of life and his condescension towards everyone'. After they compelled him with many (entreaties), he received only the work of teaching and made for himself a reader and an elementary instructor so that it would be easier for him to work at (interpreting) the meaning of the divine scriptures.[78] He led

72 Syr. *saggi nuhrā*, lit. 'much of light'.

73 This passage has a number of parallels with the description of Cyrus in the *Cause* (pp. 382–83). The Rabbula, whom this passage seems to be mistakenly referring to, was the main antagonist of the Dyophysite cause in fifth-century Edessa! On Rabbula, see most recently Doran, *Stewards of the Poor*, 41–105, which includes a translation of his Vita. For an older, but fuller study, see Georg Günter Blum, *Rabbula von Edessa. Der Christ, der Bischof, der Theologe* (CSCO 300; Louvain: Secrétariat du CSCO, 1969). See also note CS 460. This passage, as well as an interpolation to the *Life of Alexander the Sleepless*, are the sources for the scholarly tendency to mistakenly associate him with the School of the Persians in Edessa (cf. *Life of Alexander the Sleepless*, E. de Stoop, ed., *Vie d'Alexandre l'Acémète*, lat., PO 6:5 (1911): 673.13–674.13; see comments at Daniel Caner, *Wandering, Begging Monks: Spiritual Authority and the Promotion of Monasticism in Late Antiquity* (Berkeley: University of California Press, 2002), 250.

74 The Syriac phrase, '(he) was adorned with all (things)' (*b-kolhēn mṣabbat* (*h*)*wā*), then followed by an exepegetical line referring to the specific virtues, may also be found in the *Cause* in its description of Ḥenānā of Adiabene (see *Cause* 390). This phrase may have a Greek source. In the traditional Neoplatonic introduction to Aristotle, which consists of ten sections, the sixth section asks what qualities are needed for one about to embark on the study of Aristotle. In Philoponus's commentary on the *Categories*, he states that the student (*akroātḗs*) should be '*en pâsi kekosmēmenos*' (Philoponus, *In Categorias* 6.30), which is strikingly similar to the Syriac phrase.

75 Syr. *hegyānā*, which could also be rendered 'vocalizing'.

76 For a discussion of the three categories of teaching, *qeryānā*, *hegyānā*, and *pushshāqā*, and their relationship to the three echelon system at the School of Nisibis, see, e.g., Becker, *Fear of God*, 70–71, 87–88. See Appendix III on this passage and its parallel in the *Cause*.

77 This phrase serves as a confirmation for those who would argue that Narsai lived to an uncommonly old age. Cf. Baumstark, *Geschichte*, 110.

78 See Appendix III on this passage and its parallel in the *Cause*.

the assembly for the long period of twenty years, in all things beneficial, and in that time, *there was no Satan nor evil appearance*.[79] But it is not our set purpose to describe all his glorious deeds, lest our speech burden the audience.

Narsai is Slandered and Attempts to Convert Him Fail

When Satan saw that his kingdom was already despoiled, his side brought low, and his force diminished, he then began to stir up trouble and fear by means of evil men.[80] He found as the symposiarch[81] for his error the local bishop whose name was Cyrus,[82] a man heretical and evil [600] in mind, and with a pack of thieves – I mean, his clergy – he raised sedition against him. They were saying, 'This exegete is heretical, since he agrees with the opinion of Theodore (of Mopsuestia) and Nestorius, students of Paul (of Samosata).[83] He meditates upon their writings and speaks their traditions.' After the sons of the evil one conspired to make him depart, if it was possible, from his prior opinion and to make him their ally, or to cast him from life completely, as the Jews did our Lord and the Apostles, some men came to him who showed him the outward appearance of friendship and revealed to him the deceit which was composed against him by the whole community. They advised him that if it was possible he should depart from that prior opinion. But the cause of this was envy. For they thought, 'How can a Persian man subdue Romans, this man, who is also foreign to the order of reason?'[84] They composed against him an accusation with that prior one,

79 1 Kgs 5:4. This line occurs before Solomon is about to build the temple, thus suggesting a comparison between the schools and the temple in Jerusalem.

80 Similar statements show up in other parts of the *Ecclesiastical History*, e.g., Satan's plotting against the Church in Chap. 1 (Barhadbeshabba, *La première partie de l'histoire*, 182–85).

81 Syr. *rēsh puḥrā*, lit. 'head of the banquet or company'. This term appears in the *Acts of Mār Māri*, in *Acta martyrum et sanctorum syriace*, 1.70.20ff, or Amir Harrak, trans., *The Acts of Mār Mārī* (Atlanta: Society of Biblical Literature, 2005), 42 (19)ff. See Harrak's discussion of the ancient near eastern background of the *puḥrā* at xxii–xxvi.

82 Syr. *Qurā*. On Cyrus, see note SL 89.

83 Paul of Samosata was commonly posited by the East-Syrians' enemies to be the teacher of their exegetical fathers. See note SL 20.

84 Whether this passage is historical or not, such concerns about a Persian living among the Romans would have made sense in the fifth and sixth centuries, a time when the Sasanian and Roman Empires were at war regularly. See Engelbert Winter and Beate Dignas, *Rom und das Perserreich: Zwei Weltmächte zwischen Konfrontation und Koexistenz* (Berlin: Akademie, 2001) on political and diplomatic relations between the two empires. Questioning someone's

another one, which was more evil than (the first), saying, 'His mind is with the Persians. He seeks to raise sedition within the border region and wants to stir up the kingdoms. Moreover, perhaps he would betray the city of Edessa.' Then when this holy one had heard [601] the accusations and learned[85] of this contrivance and evil artifice,[86] he prayed and said, 'Lord, your eyes are upon faith, since *faith has perished and hastened away from their mouth. Truth has perished from the earth and no one is upright among human beings. For all lay in wait in ambushes and each man hunts his brother for destruction.*'[87] Although at times they lured him with great enticements and at other times they scared him with the threat of force, the foot of his thought did not slip from the straight path of faith. Rather, he would say: *The wicked were sitting and meditating against me, but I was meditating upon your commandments.*[88]

When those who cause others to stumble[89] understood that his thinking was not going to desert his prior opinion, they asked him to do this, however, in outward form and to confess only by word of mouth that he actually agreed with their way of thinking. He then responded to them, 'This is opposed to the word of the Apostle. For thus he spoke: *In your teaching let there be for you a sound word, which is chaste and uncorrupted, and no one will despise it, since whoever stands against us will be ashamed, when he is unable to say anything hateful against us.*[90] If I do this, what is the sound word, which is adorned with teaching and the chastity of the fear of God? What will the incorruptibility gain [602] by which we appear as true before those who are against us?' After those who lead astray heard this sound

---

capacity to reason is an especially heinous insult in a context where such a capacity is considered the characteristic differentiating human beings from other animals (see the discussion of the Tree of Porphyry in Appendix II). Note the use of the word *ṭaksā* (see note CS 56).

85 The text seems to be corrupt here. The Ms has *wylpw* with a *ptāḥā* (a short *a* vowel) over the *yod*. Nau takes this as the *pa'el* form meaning, 'and they taught him' (understanding the demonstrative *hānā* to refer to Narsai). However, this should be the irregular form, *alleph* (*'lp*), with the frontal *ālaph* (') instead of the *yod* (*y*). The rendering, 'he learned', is derived by removing the final *wau* and ignoring the manuscript's *ptāḥā*. Ignoring the vowel provided by the Ms and taking the text as it is would offer 'they learned', but this does not make sense in this context. Perhaps the singular verb was accidently conflated with a following demonstrative pronoun, *hu* (*hw*).

86 Syr. *ṭeknā*, from Gr. *tékhnē*.

87 A conflation of Jer 5:3, Jer 7:28 and Mic 7:2.

88 Ps 119:23.

89 Syr. *makshalē*, or rendered passively as 'those who are caused to stumble'.

90 Tit 2:7–8. Narsai quotes from the same passage which was used above to describe him, cf. note 64.

response, they replied to him, 'Even Paul, the Lord, and the Apostles proportioned their doctrine to the weak, or have you not heard the word of Paul who said: *With everyone I became everything so that I might benefit everyone.*[91] *Bear one another's burden.*[92] For you in whom there is faith, maintain it in yourself before God and *leave room for the wrath (of God)*.'[93] When the holy one heard their crafty response he said to them: 'What shall I do regarding the Lord who said: *Whoever acknowledges me before human beings I too will acknowledge him before my father who is in heaven and whoever denies me before human beings I also will deny him before my father who is in heaven.*[94] Or regarding Paul who said: *If I were pleasing human beings up to this point, I would not be a servant to the Messiah.*[95] *One who does his will is better than a thousand who are opposed to it.*[96] For what is the benefit that I should deny the truth and make others to trust in error?'

Narsai's Public Accusation and Flight

When they knew that it was not possible for them to make him stray by these (arguments), they went with an accusation before the crowd and they passed a sentence against him of burning by fire.[97] Then one of [603] his friends, when he heard of their deceit, came quickly and informed the holy one, 'If you do not save yourself by some means tonight, they will cast you into the fire'. When the spiritual athlete had learned this, that all of them were subject at that time to Satanic error and that they had a Jezebel-like

91 1 Cor 9:22. This text does not follow that of the Peshitta. The author seems to be quoting from memory (or a faulty text) since the preposition *'am* ('with') instead of *l-* and the verb *ētar* ('I might benefit') instead of *aḥē* ('I might save') come from the preceding verses.

92 Gal 6:2.

93 Rom 12:19. This same biblical verse is quoted by Narsai below at 604.12–13.

94 Mt 10:32.

95 Gal 1:10.

96 Sir 16:3.

97 The text uses what seems to be legal language for an extralegal attempt to kill Narsai. In any case, it is doubtful that burning alive was a legal form of punishment in Edessa and the text may be engaged in the standard hagiographical practice of characterizing the saint's enemies as excessively violent and cruel. However, there seems to have been de facto carte blanche in the selection of punishments in the later Roman Empire and so any form of punishment, however gruesome, may not be so unrealistic. See, for instance, Ramsey MacMullen, 'Judicial Savagery in the Roman Empire', *Chiron* 16 (1986): 147–66 (repr. in *Changes in the Roman Empire: Essays in the Ordinary* [Princeton: Princeton University Press, 1990], 204–17), or Kathleen Coleman, 'Fatal Charades: Roman Executions Staged as Mythological Enactments', *Journal of Roman Studies* 80 (1990): 44–73.

mind,[98] he quickly arose after it had become dark, trusting in divine aid, and he departed from there.[99] When he arrived at the church of the city, he found there some Persians. He asked them if it was possible to take his books with them. For this was his whole treasure. For when they learned the cause of the affair they were very pleased (to help him) and diligently carried all his books all the way to Nisibis. The next morning there was a search in Edessa, by his friends as well as his enemies, those whose desire did not succeed. After they informed Cyrus about his manner of life and about the ordering of his thought and about his care for learning, they set up a great crowd against him (i.e. Cyrus), as if he were the cause of the affair.[100] From the cause of envy it came to this.[101] (They said,)[102] 'Perhaps something leprous clings in his mind and by this pretext he is seeking to make it stick to us'.[103] When this evil abortion heard that he had come out against the truth at the wrong time, he laid down before them [604] with oaths that he was not[104] one of these men, and that neither did he perceive that affair nor was he the cause of it, but that others led him astray, 'If I had known that it was thus as you have said, I would not have chased him from here, even if he was sick in his mind, which was marred from his being accused'. He also said, 'If there is someone who is able to bring him again, I will judge that person worthy of double honour'. After many tried and were unable to do this, adversaries began to peek out from their holes and to mock him before his friends as one who induces confusion, as haughty and headstrong,[105] since he left and secretly departed.

98 Syr. *izabelāytā*. Such a Syriac adjectival formation became common in the sixth century. On Jezebel, see 1 Kgs 21. The comparison to Jezebel is also made in Chap. 30 of the *Ecclesiastical History* on Nestorius's exile, at 580.2 to describe Cyril's attacks on Nestorius.

99 On the secret flight of saints, see Alison Goddard Elliot, *Roads to Paradise: Reading the Lives of the Early Saints* (Hanover, NH: University Press of New England, 1987), 89.

100 This sentence is unclear. Presumably 'they' refers to Narsai's friends. The syntax of the Syriac phrase rendered 'as if he were' is awkward.

101 It is possible that this sentence is part of the following quotation.

102 The following is not clearly marked as a quotation. It is only the phrase 'to us' that would explicitly suggest this.

103 Narsai was referred to as the 'leprous' by his enemies (see note SL 76). Cf. *Barhadbesabba, La première partie de l'Histoire*, 201.

104 The text has *laytēh*, lit. 'she is not', which must be a scribal error for *laytaw(hy)*, the masculine form.

105 This lines seems corrupt: *bar ḥulṭānā ba-ḥthirā ba-sphāphā*. The first term, *bar ḥultānā*, lit. 'son of mixture or commingling', may refer to someone who causes confusion. The two terms following this one have the preposition *b-* added, perhaps in analogy with the preceding object ('him', Syr. *bēh*). The former of these two terms is clear, but the latter, *s-p-p-'* (*sphāphā*, 'burning') does not fit and I have emended it to the adjectival *sappiphā*. Another reading would be to emend *ḥthirā* to a noun and to translate the *b-* with the nouns adverbially.

After the holy one heard about these men's mockery and his friends' sadness, he wrote (a letter)[106] and sent (it) to them, (saying) 'It seems to me that you have forgotten the story of Moses, for what reason he departed from Egypt,[107] and that of Jacob who came to Haran,[108] and the prophet David how at one time he departed from Saul and at another time from Abshalom, and he was not held blameworthy.[109] In the same way our Lord and Paul, his student, did this. Who would dare to blame them? For it is written thus: *Leave room for the wrath (of God)*.[110] And again: *Go, my people, and enter your chambers and close your doors before you and hide yourself for a little while until my wrath passes.*[111] Who indeed mocked and made game of[112] the prophet Jeremiah because [605] he fled and hid himself from the evil king of his time, except one who is like you?[113] Has it not been heard by you then the news of the six towns of refuge which Moses commanded the people to build as an aid to the wronged?'[114] When those impudent men heard these things, even they were ashamed and embarrassed of their own boldness.

Narsai Arrives at Nisibis

The holy one, after he arrived in Nisibis, did not enter the city. For he thought that he would perhaps be hindered from his intended goal, which was in truth what happened. But he went to the Monastery of the Persians, which

106 For a discussion that treats the following text as if it were an actual letter, see Arthur Vööbus, 'Les vestiges d'une lettre de Narsai et son importance historique', *OS* 9 (1964), 512–23. However, there is little reason to believe that an actual document is preserved here (cf. Becker, *Fear of God*, 234 n. 72).

107 This refers to Moses' initial flight from Egypt when he went to Midian (Exod 2:11–15).

108 Jacob went to Haran when he fled his brother Esau after tricking him out of his paternal blessing (Gen 28:10).

109 E.g. 1 Sam 19:8–17 and 2 Sam 15:13–31 respectively.

110 Rom 12:19. This is ironic since the same biblical verse is quoted by those trying to persuade Narsai to dissimulate at 602 above.

111 Isa 26:20.

112 The Syriac text has *'ṭṣry*, which could be rendered as 'he burst/was torn (with indignation)', but assuming the manuscript has made the common confusion of the letters *dalath* and *resh* we may emend the text to *'ṭṣdy*, vocalized as *'eṭṣari*, which makes more sense here. It is unclear what Nau thinks of this word because his translation, 'a blamé', is ambiguous.

113 Cf. Jer 36:19–26.

114 Num 35.13–14. The Syriac, *'shiqē* ('wronged'), can mean those who are oppressed in general, but the root *'-sh-q* is used in particular for making false accusations and slanders of one who is innocent. This sense may be what suggested the word to the author. The cities of asylum established by Moses according to the passage from Numbers were for accidental murderers.

lay to the east of the city.[115] For his intention was to go down to the east, that is, to the interior of Persia, in order that he might provide instruction[116] there and plant the seed of the learning of the fear of God even if (only) in a few who were there. When he was thinking to do this, three clergymen happened on the monastery and saw that the man was modest in his face and honourable and glorious in his radiant appearance, and they asked about him, who he was and what news he brought. Then after they learned the object of their question, they eagerly entered and informed Mār Barṣaumā about him. When he heard, he earnestly sent to him some men from the clergy, (saying) that if he ordered he could enter the city. After he was not persuaded to enter with them and gave as an excuse for this sometimes weariness, [606] at other times sickness, sometimes that he was a stranger, at other times that he was an unknown person, even sometimes that there was no need for him to enter, then the bishop again sent people, but this time his archdeacon and ten of the clergy as an honour to him. When they went out and entreated him in many ways that he might see his friend, he thought that perhaps it might be a mark of shame and contempt for him to not enter. So he stood and entered with them.

Barṣaumā Persuades Narsai to Settle in Nisibis

After he entered the city, Mār Barṣaumā went out to meet him with much pomp and with comely honour he led him into the church. Then they conversed with one another for a little while. After he learned the cause of his migration from there, he requested that, if he desired, he should leave off his prior design, and that which he intended to do far off would be accomplished there in proximity and by the interaction of the two of them planting the assembly of Mesopotamia, so as to offer a great benefit to both sides, to the Romans and the Persians at once.[117] Then as if to someone who was resisting, the bishop said to that holy one: 'Do not think that this deed is human, master.[118] For although they planned evil against you and completed their satanic plan,

115 Some monasteries and schools had specific ethnic identities. That Narsai would go to a monastery identified with Persians *within* the Persian realm would suggest that this one was specifically Persian (in contrast to the broader Aramaean population) and that Narsai himself, whose name is Persian, was ethnically Persian. On such ethnic associations, see, e.g., Becker, *Fear of God*, 66–67. Dillemann, *Haute Mésopotamie Orientale*, 95, mentions the settling of Persians in Nisibis after it was ceded to the Sasanians in 363 CE.

116 Syr. *ne'bed tulmādā*, lit. 'he might make instruction or discipleship'.

117 Nisibis was on the Sasanian side of the border with the Roman Empire.

118 Syr. *abun*, lit. 'our father', a term used for masters in a monastic context.

nevertheless that hidden providence, which sees everything, did not turn away from you. But it did what was expedient for the purpose of providence, just as in the time of Joseph and in the time [607] of the Apostles.[119] Just as at one time the assembly migrated from Antioch to Daphne and from there to Edessa,[120] so also now I think that it has migrated from Edessa to here because the ones who were reading[121] were not worthy.[122] For, behold, also the Apostles endeavoured much to plant the gospel in Judea. Because that rabid nation was not worthy of this lasting good, when they thought to harm them by expelling them from their midst, it rather turned out to be a benefit for the Apostles since they were not chastised along with them in Titus's punishment.[123] But by this cause they went over to the gentiles. Then they *went out to the ways and the narrow paths*. They *compelled* the gentiles *to enter* the messianic banquet.[124] Thus now also it seems to me that this has happened. Because the Romans were not worthy of receiving the truth nor of enjoying the shining rays of the light of true faith, and are going to earn[125] punishment for their sins; on account of this they incited a war against you, that you yourself would be saved like Lot from punishment, while they will be destroyed like the harmful Sodomites.[126] But you also, like the Apostles,

119 Presumably the text is referring to Joseph being taken against his will into Egypt, which it compares in the following passage to the scattering of the Apostles after the Roman repression of the Jewish Revolt (66–73 CE). According to the author, both events worked in the end according to divine providence.

120 This is obscure. The 'School of Edessa' may have been understood to be a successor of a prior school that had existed in Antioch, which first moved to Daphne, the suburb of Antioch, and then to Edessa. There is no precedent for this. It is possible that this tradition derives ultimately from the story of the transfer of St Babylas's remains to Daphne and their subsequent removal during the reign of Julian. The remains were eventually returned to Antioch, but perhaps there is a connection here to this story since there was a strong interest in the story of Julian in Edessa, such as we find in the Syriac Julian Romance, J.G.E. Hoffmann, *Iulianus der Abtrünnige* (Leiden, 1880); Hermann Gollancz, trans., *Julian the Apostate* (London: Oxford University Press, 1928).

121 I.e. studying.

122 This suggests that there were problems within the schools themselves, particularly the School of the Persians, and it differs from the reason provided earlier in the text for the closure of the School.

123 The destruction of the Temple in 70 CE. Cf. Eusebius, *Ecclesiastical History*, 3.1.

124 Cf. Lk 14:23.

125 Nau's text has *lmlp'*, which is a mistake for the manuscript's *lm'p'*, the manuscript having an *'ayin* instead of a *lāmadh*. Vocalized as *l-me'pā* this can mean 'increase, gain, collect, amass', which can take *'agrā* and *yutrānā* as a direct object (Payne Smith, *Compendious Syriac Dictionary*, 422).

126 Cf. Gen 18:16–19:29.

busy yourself and plant here the word of Orthodoxy. For if you do this, the two sides will easily benefit, since it is close enough for your students to come here [608] to you. Furthermore, Persians frequent here because of the climate of the place,[127] and because the place is bountiful in all kinds of products[128] it is easy for the brothers to live and succeed in learning scripture, especially since I myself will be a helper to you in this business. For although it happens that brave fighters are vanquished and flee from their enemies, yet whenever they do not depart to far away but reside at the side of a nearby place, this is a sign of their victory and the health of their soul. In this way also if you reside[129] here in the neighbourhood of Edessa, it will be a sign of your victory and a disgrace unto your enemies.'

After the holy one heard these words, his thought was inclined a little and he promised him that if it was possible he would do this. That Barṣaumā, as soon as he heard this, rejoiced greatly. Then he bought for the school[130] a caravansary[131] on the side of the church. Because there was a school there before, and an exegete from Kashkar[132] whose name was Simeon, a great and excellent man,[133] there was no hindrance in this matter, but the prior students[134] busied themselves with learning. In a short time brothers began to gather from all regions because of this holy one. These (deeds) of his (i.e. Barṣaumā's) glory will suffice up to this point.

127 On the climate of upper Mesopotamia, see Dillemann, *Haute Mésopotamie Orientale*, 64–67. Despite the dry heat of the summer, it is possible that some Persians visited Nisibis in the summer to avoid the even worse conditions farther south.

128 On agriculture in Nisibis and its environs in antiquity, see ibid. 68–73.

129 Lit. 'sit'. This could also be translated as 'study'.

130 Syr. *eskolē*.

131 Syr. *bēt gamlē*, lit. 'place of camels'.

132 It is doubtful that he was an 'exegete' (or interpreter, Syr. *mphashshqānā*) in the later technical sense of the term. It is more likely that Kashkar is the modern city of Wasit in southern Iraq, rather than the Kashkar in Central Asia.

133 In the *Chronicle of Siirt*'s chapter on the life of Narsai, when Narsai flees to Nisibis, he finds 'a small school' which belonged to 'Simeon of Beit Garmaï' (*al-Jarmaqāni*). In this text it is only after Narsai has set up his school that Barṣaumā becomes interested in him: *Chronicle of Siirt* 2.1.114. See also Vööbus, *History*, 50 and Gero, *Barṣauma*, 64.

134 Syr. *eskolāyē*.

Satan's Assault on Narsai in Nisibis[135]

Let us then also briefly make manifest [609] the manner of his way of life and his kind of teaching, and how Satan did not cease from his war with him, but at times openly, at other times secretly, was fighting to conquer him. For this is set before us now to demonstrate, after we first set down the pretexts by which Satan found the opportunity to cause trouble. For because a cell was given to the holy one by the side of the house of Mār Barṣaumā and everyone would throng to catch sight of him and salute him, first, because of the novelty of the matter, second, because of the modesty of his deportment, third, because of the excellence of his face, fourth, because of his condescension towards everyone, fifth, because of the abundance of his love, sixth, because of the copiousness of his teaching; on account of this, one day the wife of the bishop, whose name was Mamai,[136] when she was coming from the church and saw the great crowd that was standing there and the horses and the nobles, she was moved with great envy against this and she began to be incensed with anger, like Jezebel the instigator.[137] With great anger she entered her house, saddened and with her face darkened, like Cain the murderer.[138] After Mār Barṣaumā saw her and learned what the cause of her unhappiness was, she began to mock him and make him jealous of the holy one, saying, 'You yourself are not the bishop, but rather a subordinate! You are not honoured, but rather one who honours others. [610] But the bishop is this man, the neighbour you have made for yourself!' After he asked her what the occasion was for these words, she

135 The dispute between Narsai and Barṣaumā is also described in the later *Chronicle of Siirt* 2.1.136–37 and *Mārī, De patriarchis*, 47.20ff (see note 13 in the introduction to this volume). On this dispute, see Gero, *Barṣauma*, 68–72.

136 Barṣaumā probably married sometime after the formal legalization of clerical marriage at the Council of Bēt Lāpāṭ (Gundeshapur, the prestigious Sasanian city) in 484 (Gero, *Barsauma*, 41 n. 87). On the Council and Barṣaumā's role in it and its aftermath, see Gero, *Barṣauma*, 41–56, 73–78, 79–88. On Barṣaumā's marriage, see Gero, *Barṣauma*, 57, 68–72, 82–83. On Mamai, the variant renderings of her name, including Mamowai, and the possible Persian origin of the name, see Gero, *Barṣauma*, 57, n. 188.

137 Again, on Jezebel, see 1 Kgs 21. See 98 above for a comparison of Narsai's opponents in Edessa to Jezebel. On women as the cause of men's fall, see Kate Cooper, *The Virgin and the Bride: Idealized Womanhood in Late Antiquity* (Cambridge, MA: Harvard University Press, 1996), 17–19.

138 Gen 4:5 is similar but not verbally the same. It is not clear whether the text is making a comparison to Cain because of Mamai's envy or her deceit, two sins Cain commonly represents. See Glenthøj, *Cain and Abel in Syriac and Greek Writers*, 284–86.

said, 'You, busy yourself at actually being the bishop of Nisibis![139] Get up and look at how many nobles' horses are standing at the door of the cell of your exegete![140] You will know right away what the occasion is!' Because human nature is wont to be led after weak passions and empty counsels, as it is said, 'the jealousy of a man is (greater) than his companion',[141] on account of this he was hurt by the holy one. When the holy one came to see him, as was his custom, and he did not rejoice at his approach as he always did, after a little while he asked him what the cause of this was, and when he learned to what extent the woman was the cause of evils from the beginning until the present,[142] he left and departed, and he went out to the monastery of Kephar Māri,[143] which is in Bēt Zabdai,[144] and he produced there two *mēmrē*, one on himself, the incipit of which is: 'Poor is the time which was presented to me in the place of my sojourn; and in it short is the acquisition of the spiritual life',[145] and the other is 'Eve is the source from which life flowed to human beings; she returned the pleasant drink to the bitterness[146] of death',[147] on the wife of Mār Barṣaumā. When he read this *mēmrā* in Nisibis before the faithful and before the whole church, then the bishop felt remorse and sent for him to be brought from there. Because the

139 This line is not clear. The manuscript has *tshkr* (with a short *a* vowel added above the *t*) but the word *tkshr* (voc. *tekshar*), which is what I have translated here, has been placed in the margin. Unfortunately I am unable to check the manuscript to see if *tkshr* is in the same hand. The original word, *tshkr* (voc. *teshkar*), meaning approximately 'you dishonour', fits awkwardly with the rest of the sentence.

140 Or 'Get up and look at the door of the cell of your exegete, how many nobles' horses are standing (by it)!'

141 Eccl 4:4.

142 It is possible the author is making a generalization here about all women, in which case 'woman' should be rendered without the definite article and 'beginning' would refer to the beginning of creation and Eve's responsibility for the fallen state of human beings.

143 See note SL 77.

144 Bēt Zabdai was the region south of modern Siirt, in south-eastern Turkey.

145 Narsai, *Homiliae et Carmina*, I: 210–23. W. Macomber, 'The Manuscripts of the Metrical Homilies of Narsai', 297 (Ms. 25). See also Corrie Molenberg, 'As If From Another World: Narsai's Memra "Bad is the time"', in *All Those Nations ... Cultural Encounters within and with the Near East*, ed. H. L. J. Vanstiphout et al. (Groningen: Styx Publications, 1999), 101–08.

146 Syr. *merrat*, but the text could also be vocalized as Syr. *mārat*, 'mistress'.

147 Narsai, *Homiliae et Carmina*, II: 353–65. Macomber, 'The Manuscripts of the Metrical Homilies of Narsai', 305 (Ms. 80). See also Corrie Molenberg, 'Narsai's memra on the reproof of Eve's daughters and the <tricks and devices> they perform', *LM* 106 (1993): 65–87. Both of Molenberg's essays may miss the mark by assuming that these texts reflect historical reality, when in fact it is possible that the biographical context has been in part invented to fit the topic of each of these two *mēmrē*. This would be something akin to what we find in, for example, Suetonius's *Lives of the Poets*.

holy one knew [611] that the proximity of his cell stirred up strife between them, as soon as he arrived he bought for himself a cell in another location set close by to there, and there was for him some breathing space and quiet, and they maintained love for one another until the end.

Narsai's Scholastic Asceticism[148]

Now he would take a simple nourishment regularly of one meal, and again he would do this at evening time, or once every two days. His bed was a mat of reed and palm, his bedding a patched cloak. He would work wholly in meditation upon the liturgy[149] and meditation on the scriptures, not giving place for sleep to fall upon himself,[150] but upon a common seat[151] he would drive sleep from his brow,[152] and if it happened that he was conquered to slumber from his vigil, either he would stand and walk or he would place in his nostrils materials which excite and awake, like spicy and sour things, or hot or pleasing things, or he would lay a tome upon his face and in this way he would sleep upon his seat.[153] Often the tome would be the cause of waking him, since it would tip from its weight[154] (and fall) from his face to his hands.[155] The holy

148 See the discussion of this passage in Becker, *Fear of God*, 205.

149 Syr. *hergā d-teshmeshtā.*

150 Lit. 'his sides'.

151 This puts an emphasis on his humility and approachability, since a seat (Syr. *kursyā*) is commonly the throne of a teacher or bishop.

152 Lit. 'eyebrows'.

153 Syr. *mawtbā*. This is the same term used for the school 'session'.

154 The manuscript reading, *nt''* (voc. *nāt'ā*), which Nau presents in a footnote, seems better than his suggested emendation, *nṭ''*. It is not clear why Nau made this far more awkward emendation.

155 The notion of sleep in this passage has a clear Evagrian monastic background: 'There are certain impure demons who always sit in front of those engaged in reading and try to seize their mind, often taking pretexts from the divine scriptures themselves and ending in evil thoughts. It sometimes happens that they force them to yawn more than they are accustomed and they instill a very deep sleep quite different from usual sleep. Whereas some of the brothers have imagined that it is in accordance with an unintelligible natural reaction, I for my part have learned this by frequent observation: they touch the eyelids and the entire head, cooling it with their own body, for the bodies of the demons are very cold and like ice; and the head feels as if it is being sucked by a cupping glass with a rasping sound. They do this in order to draw to themselves the heat that lies within the cranium, and then the eyelids, relaxed by the moisture and cold, slip over the pupils of the eyes. Often in touching myself I have found my eyelids fixed like ice and my entire face numb and shivering. Natural sleep, however, normally warms bodies and renders the faces of healthy people rosy, as one can learn from experience itself.' Evagrius, *On Thoughts* 33 (trans. Sinkewicz, *Evagrius of Pontus*, 176).

one demonstrated all this diligence so that while he was fleshly and mortal he emulated the way of life of the angels.

The Heretical Jacob of Sarug Inspires Narsai to Write

[612] Now because the heretics, the sons of error, saw that with these things they were not able to overpower the holy one and stir up the Church against him as before, one of them whose name was Jacob of Sarug, who was eloquent for evil and joined closely to heresy, began to compose his heresy and error hypocritically by the way of the *mēmrē*, which he composed, since through the pleasant composition of enticing sounds he drew[156] the bulk of the people from the glorious one.[157] What then did the elect of God do? He did not even ignore this, but according to the word of the psalmist he did what he said: *With the chosen you have been chosen and with the perverse you have been crooked*.[158] But he set down the true opinion of orthodoxy in the manner[159] of *mēmrē*, fitted upon sweet tones. He combined the meaning of the scriptures according to the opinion of the holy fathers in pleasant antiphons in the likeness of the blessed David.[160] He established one *mēmrā* for each day of the year and he divided them into twelve volumes,[161] each one of which consists of two prophets; all of them adding up to twenty-four prophets.[162] He also set down another, one which concerns foul habits, which is two other prophets, aside from the other subjects which he set down according to the occasions that demanded at the time.

156 Again, Nau's emendation, *'ṭp* (voc. *'ṭaph*) 'to turn back, return' seems unnecessary next to the manuscript reading, *ntp* (voc. *ntaph*), which he provides in a footnote.

157 The Syr. *quṭnā* ('bulk of the people') could also be rendered 'congregation', which would mean that Narsai was feeling pressure specifically within his own community due to Jacob's work.

158 Ps 18:26 (17:27). See Theodoret, *Commentary on the Psalms, Psalms 1–72* (trans. Robert C. Hill; Washington, DC: Catholic University Press, 2000), 128 (PG 80.981).

159 Syr. *ba-znā mkaynā d-*, lit. 'in the fitted (or: constituted) manner of', but in rendering the English I have translated *mkaynā* as if it agrees with *mēmrē*.

160 It is not clear why 'tones' (Syr. *qinātā*) and 'antiphons' (Syr. *hphākātā*) are mentioned here since they do not belong to the *mēmrā* genre, which was apparently chanted and not musical. David was commonly understood as the psalmist.

161 We find similar statements in the *Chronicle of Siirt* (2.1.115) and 'Abdisho''s *Catalogue*, Chap. LIII (*Bibliotheca Orientalis* III.1.65).

162 Divisions of compilations seem to have been occasionally referred to as 'prophets'. See 'Abdisho''s *Catalogue*, Chap. XIX (*Bibliotheca Orientalis* III.1.31) on the works of Theodore of Mopsuestia. See also Baumstark, *Geschichte*, 110.

Criticism of and Trouble with the Persian Authorities[163]

After Satan was beaten in these things he began to stir up and agitate against him in another manner. How? For when [613] Peroz[164] went to Bēt Kaphtarāyē[165] and that which was contrary to what he expected occurred, because of the vain elation of his mind, the holy one set down this *mēmrā*, the incipit of which is this: 'Friend of human beings, who has turned human beings to knowledge of himself, turn my mind toward the teaching of the word of life'.[166] Then, because he set in it rough words which suggested the pride of his thought, seditious brothers went from among his students to Kavad,[167] while he was camped against Amida.[168] These are their names: Qaphar of Lādab from 'Ayn Addad[169] and John bar 'Amrāyē,[170] accursed men, and they pointed him out there and said to him (i.e. Kavad), 'That one who sets down these (verses) is your adversary and the enemy of your kingdom'. But then when believing people from the Khuzites[171] who were there heard this they informed the holy one about this accusation, and immediately he produced another *mēmrā*, the incipit of which is: 'Summit of the (four) quarters (of the world), turn to the order of authority'.[172] The

163 Gero, *Barṣauma*, 71–72.

164 Sasanian king, Peroz I, 459–84 CE.

165 This place is unknown. Vööbus takes this as a mistake for Bēt Qaṭrāyē (*History*, 117).

166 This *mēmrā* is no longer extant.

167 Sasanian king, 488–531 CE.

168 Syr. *Āmed* (Diyarbekir). This refers to Kawad's long and eventually successful siege of Amida in 502/3, which is described in Pseudo-Joshua the Stylite, *Chronicle*, 50–53 and Procopius, *Wars*, I.7. The broader Persian War of 502–06 is treated fully by Pseudo-Joshua the Stylite, *Chronicle*, 46–100 and Procopius, *Wars*, I.7–9.

169 Nothing is known of him. I have translated *ldby'* as 'of Lādab' (vocalized: *lādabāyā*) based upon Fiey, *Assyrie Chrétienne* III.75,136, which would place it in Bēt Garmai. According to Fiey, this could also be Lārb. 'Ayn Addad is unknown.

170 Nothing is known of him. On his ethnonym, see Fiey, *Nisibe*, 57, 227 and note SL 87. Nau notes that *'Amrāyē* is inserted in the margin.

171 This passage would suggest that the author believed Narsai to have been at the siege or at least that Kavad established Nisibis as his headquarters during the campaign, which is possible since it was the Persian city closest to Roman territory and would be the appropriate place from which to launch a campaign against Diyarbakir. However, Pseudo-Joshua and especially Procopius seem to suggest he was at the actual siege. The text could also be referring to a later period in the broader campaign when Kawad was in the area of Nisibis (for example, see Pseudo-Joshua the Stylite, *Chronicle*, 54). One also wonders what Khuzites are doing at a siege of Amida, unless they are part of the army, and if they are, this suggests that there were Christians from Khuzistan in the Sasanian military fighting against Rome, which is noteworthy in itself.

172 This *mēmrā* is no longer extant.

Khuzites translated it into the Persian tongue. When it was read before the king, because there were enticing words in it, which referred to the kingdom of Persia, the king ceased from this opinion and the accusers, as a sign of their guilt, left and departed from there in flight.

Narsai is Slandered Again

[614] Again, another matter. One time when an emissary was passing through, some men from the city made the accusation against him, 'He is an enemy of your kingdom and he spies for the Romans'. When the emissary heard these things, he promised that when he returned from Roman territory he would crucify him. When this athlete heard that he (i.e. the emissary) decided upon the death penalty for him without inquiry, he said, 'If you return safely,[173] the Lord truly does not speak in me'. After he went, completed his mission, and then arrived in Antioch, he died there according to the holy one's word. He ceased from his threat,[174] and the accusers were ashamed.

The Miraculous Healing of a Boy Harassed by a Demon

You have heard what he did against Satan. Come now and see what the hidden sign has ministered by him.[175] One day when he was coming to perform exegesis a woman was sitting in the marketplace along with her son. When the holy one was passing by, a demon threw the youth to the ground and beat him severely. Immediately his mother, crying, stood up and grabbed the feet of the glorious one and said, 'Lord help me'.[176] The athlete then said to the brother with him, 'Do not falter, since if we seek

173 There may be a pun here since what is translated as 'safely' (Syr. *ba-shlāmā*) can also mean 'in peace' – exactly how an emissary would hope to return.

174 Lit. 'he/it ceased from the threat of him', the pronominal suffix rendered either subjectively as 'his threat' or objectively as 'the threat against him' (lit. 'of him'). This phrase is awkward since the subject seems to be the emissary who was dead. The manuscript could be corrupt, in which case perhaps a *waw* fell off the verb and its third-person plural subject was 'the accusers'.

175 The 'hidden sign' (Syr. *remzā kasyā*) is divine providence which surreptitiously fulfils its will within the world (cf. Barhadbeshabba, *La second partie de l'histoire ecclésiastique*, 504.1, in the chapter on Theodore of Mopsuestia). There is a play on words in this particular passage since the anecdote itself, as is stated below, 'hints at' (Syr. *termoz*) the other virtuous and powerful acts of Narsai. The 'hidden sign' appears in earlier literature, e.g. Narsai, *Metrical Homilies*, I.323 (p. 56).

176 This story seems modelled on similar entreaties in the Gospels, cf. Mk 7:25.

from the Lord about this (matter) with a clear intention, he will work by our hands even things greater than these, as he said: *Everything that you seek in prayer and you believe, you will receive*'.[177] After this he gave a command to the brothers [615] who were with him and they presented their prayer in the middle of the marketplace and they chanted[178] a psalm over him. After he prayed he set his hand upon him and traced between his eyes the outline of the cross. Immediately the demon[179] fled from him, and he did not throw him down again. This affair suffices for us to hint at also the other things which occurred and have not been set down here.

Conclusion

These are the glorious deeds of the holy one. This is the manner of his teaching and the order of his way of life, he who from his youth to his old age led the assembly of Nisibis forty years,[180] the one of Edessa twenty,[181] and the one of the monastery six years. He was buried in a good old age with all the holy ones, those of the same faith as him. Henceforth a crown of righteousness is preserved for him, which the Lord will bestow upon him on that day.[182] To Him and to his Father and to the Holy Spirit honour and glory for ever and ever. Amen.

177 Mt 21:22.

178 Syr. *shammesh*(*w*). This word literally means 'to serve' but it is used for the performance of the liturgy.

179 The word for demon (Syr. *daywā*) is different from the one used above (Syr. *shē'dā*).

180 From this Vööbus argues for two dates of exodus from Edessa, the first when Narsai left, for which event Vööbus understood the present text to be a description, and the second in 489, referred to in most of the other sources (*History*, 33–47). The presupposition in this is that Narsai did not live until 529, the necessary date of death if he led the School for forty years *and* left Edessa in 489. Vööbus, however, assumes that forty years represents an accurate calculation and not a typological number. Several Israelite figures' careers lasted forty years: Eli, David, Solomon, Jehoash, and Moses, who led the people in the wilderness for this amount of time. If Vööbus is correct, then Narsai lived to an extremely old age, since he is referred to above as already old when he took over the school in Edessa (p. 599 and note 77). The sources disagree on the length of his tenure of office. For example, the *Chronicle of Siirt* (2.1.115) also states that it was forty years, while the *Cause* gives forty-five (see note CS 394). Later sources give even more variations (Vööbus, *History*, 118–21).

181 This number could also be typological. For example, Samson judged for twenty years before he was betrayed, Judg 15:20.

182 2 Tim 4:8; Jas 1:12.

LIFE OF ABRAHAM OF BĒT RABBAN: TRANSLATION AND NOTES

Chapter 32: The story of the way of life of Mār Abraham, the presbyter and exegete of the divine scriptures[1]

Early Life and Training under Narsai

[616] Now this spiritual athlete was also from the land of M'altā.[2] For he was a kinsman of Mār Narsai and of the same stock as well as from the same village.[3] The name of his father was Bar Sāhdē.[4] After he reached fifteen years of age, he was moved by divine instigation to let go of and abandon all the desirable things of this world and to concern himself with spiritual labour. When he heard about Mār Narsai, where he was and what his work was, he asked his father that they (i.e. his family) might conduct him to him. Then after his father was persuaded and brought him to Nisibis and Mār Narsai was informed about him, that he was his kinsman, he asked what his name was. His father said, 'Narsai, like your own name'. Immediately he changed his name and called him Abraham and said, 'There should not be two Narsais in one cell'. As it seems to me, by prophecy this [617] happened, since just as Abraham became 'father of many nations'[5] by changing his name, so also it was established that he would be so for all of Persia by a spiritual birth. After he was there a short time and he was tested, progressing from day to day in the learning of the fear of God and in the fervour of his love,[6] he manifested great care for learning. Furthermore, his master showed special concern for him and in little time he surpassed many, those of the same age as him, in his training. In his conduct he was so (excellent) that

1 On Abraham, see Baumstark, *Geschichte*, 115; on him and his tenure of office, see Vööbus, *History*, 134–210. Vööbus suggests his tenure of office ran from approximately 510 to 569, with the brief interlude of John of Bēt Rabban's leadership from c. 547 to 561/2 or 564 (on John, see Baumstark, *Geschichte*, 115–16 and Vööbus, *History*, 211–22).

2 See note LN 12.

3 Syr. *bar qritēh*, lit. 'son of his village'. Familial relations may have played a role in the ascent of certain figures within the Church of the East at the time. Elsewhere we are told that Job the Interpreter from Seleucia-Ctesiphon, a kinsman of Narsai, was one of two selected to replace the Catholicos Ezekiel, but the Shah supported Isho'yahb of Arzon (582–95) (*Chronicle of Siirt* 2.2.118), who himself had led the School of Nisibis prior to becoming Catholicos (cf. *Cause* 389–90).

4 Lit. 'son of martyrs'.

5 Cf. Gen 17:4.

6 Or 'love for him' (i.e. God).

because of his humility he was named a second Moses by all the community. Because the Lord knew his properties,[7] on account of this he selected him beforehand and rendered the reading of and meditation on the scriptures more dear to him than the tender shoot was to Jonah.[8]

Abraham's Learning Appropriate to What is Required in the Body

When he arrived at the measure of youth, when nature is especially full of force, impulse waxes strong,[9] all the passions of youth are enflamed as a vessel that burns with fire, the body seeks whatever belongs to it, and the soul chooses that which is opposed to it; on account of this, empowered by grace, he trampled on all those bodily things and chose these divine things, while also in this way he did not completely reject the very functions of the body, because one is not able to receive (learning) without it.[10] For although it is not possible for that divine magnificence to be known [618] except by these things proper to it, while it subtly imprints and sculpts them by deeds, nevertheless its likeness did not confer them in a participatory manner, as the folly of others (holds).[11] First, this (divine magnificence), regarding[12] everything it knows, its knowledge precedes the perfection of deeds, since unaccompanied by learning it knows everything perfectly without experience or an intermediary. But created (beings), are not only prior to their knowledge, and their coming-into-being (prior) to their essential being,[13]

7 Lit. 'the things which belonged to him'.

8 Lit. 'the tender shoot of Jonah'. The 'tender shoot' or 'young plant' (*shrurā / sherrurā*) refers to the gourd of Jonah (cf. Jon. 4:6). The same expression is used in the chapter on Theodore of Mopsuestia in a similarly scholastic context (Barhadbeshabba, *La second partie de l'histoire ecclésiastique*, 504.12). A similar expression appears at *Cause* 353.

9 Apparently following the manuscript, Nau's text places a *petaḥa* (a short *a* vowel) over the first letter of *tqp*, but this does not make sense and instead I vocalize the word as *tāqeph*.

10 The verb 'receive' (*qabbel*) can take more than one implicit direct object as it is used here, but since this verb is commonly used in pedagogical contexts for a student's 'reception' of learning from his master it seems appropriate to add this object ('learning') (see note LN 20). An alternative object may be something approximate to 'perceptions of the outside world'. The close connection between bodies and learning is apparent in a number of statements in the Neoplatonic corpus to which the East Syrians had access. Embodiment and language are both signs of our fallen state and the only means by which we can communicate truth.

11 This is a critique of 'pagan' Neoplatonists as well as Origenists who argued that human beings can directly participate in the divine attributes. The word translated here as 'in a participatory manner' is the Syriac *mshawtaphā'it*.

12 Syr. *d*, or simply 'of'.

13 The distinction between coming-into-being (*hwāyā*) and essential being (*itutā*) is addressed in note CS 67.

but also experience concerning it is prior to their knowledge. For experience is the necessity pressing it to come into being. In turn, the power to name, which is instructed by these things, is prior to the deed. In sum, that is to say, the created thing is differentiated from its creator in all of its properties.[14] If all spiritual beings are yoked by this limit of necessity, especially the soul, whose functions are heavier and more ponderous than those of (spiritual beings), it is not able to do anything individually.[15] For although its (i.e. the soul's) nature is loftier than all sensible embodiment, nevertheless since it has never seen their luminous clarity,[16] it is hence cast down from the substances akin to its form.[17] Since from the beginning of its coming-into-being it has been shut in and mixed up with the fleshly house and it has possessed with it(self) a love for it from the beginning, in the likeness of a fetus which loves those dark and narrow places in which it was formed; on account of this, even while it receives learning about something, [619] whether concerning spiritual and divine natures or in turn concerning corporeal and bodily ones, learning enters into it by the fleshy doors of the senses. Because of this there is a time when the senses cause it to stray, either by the troubled waters of their mixture,[18] by the impulse of fleshly desire, or by error and treachery, and as a camel with a bit and a dog with a leash, so they tether it to everything they want.

Because this man of God[19] experienced and knew all these things from the very beginning, he therefore thought to yoke and harness his bodily senses by means of work, vigilance both night and day, and scarce, measured-out foods, so that they might not become strong and rage against him, as also the divine Paul did: *I subject my body and enslave it, lest I who have announced (the Gospel) to others be myself rejected.*[20] He *stripped off the old human being with his manner of life and put on the new one which is renewed in the likeness of his creator,*[21] while from day to day he grew and increased in the fear of God before Mār Narsai's footstool, for a period of twenty years,

14 The use of Syr. *prish*, 'differentiated' and Syr. *dilēh*, 'property', literally 'that which belongs to it', together points to the philosophical background of such language. These are both important terms in the Syriac version of Porphyry's *Isagoge*. See note CS 11.

15 Syr. *iḥidā'it*.

16 I.e. of the spiritual beings. On this term see note LN 30.

17 Syr. *usiyas*, from Gr. *ousía*; Syr. *ādshā* is the equivalent of the Gr. *eîdos*, 'form'.

18 Syr. *muzzāgā*, which can also be translated as 'constitution'.

19 Lit. 'son of man of God', 'son of man' (Syr. *bar 'nāshā*) being a standard term for the (male) human being.

20 1 Cor 9:27.

21 Cf. Col 3:9–10; cf. Eph 4:22-4. See the conclusion of the *Cause* (note CS 558).

like a leafy tree beautiful in its fruit, [620] which is planted by a stream of water.[22]

Abraham's Ascetic Way of Life and the Awe He Inspired in Many

After this blessed one died, the glorious one succeeded him and led this assembly for twenty years. Then the brothers as well as the citizens[23] caused him trouble and made in his place as teacher Elisha of Bēt 'Arbāyē, from the village of Qozb,[24] a great as well as learned man.[25] He led the assembly for four years and he also composed many didactic and exegetical writings. He resolved the charges[26] put forward by the Magi, that is, those who are against us. Mār Abraham was again given charge to stand in the place of his master and to fulfil the office of teaching. After this holy one sat on the seat of teaching, not only because of his instruction, the illumination of his speech, and the excellence of his manner of life, but also because of the fear of God which was in him and his great humility, from all regions they gathered together to come to enjoy even just the sight of him and hear the living word of teaching from his mouth. Because in little time more than

22 Ps 1:3. Psalm 1 has a special significance here since it can be read, especially in the Peshitta version, as a programmatic statement on the East-Syrian view of learning. It is also quoted above in the beginning of the 'Life of Narsai' (p. 591). See note CS 239.

23 Syr. *bnay mdi(n)tā*, lit. 'sons of the city'.

24 Elisha 'Arbāyā bar Qozbāyē, or Elisha bar Qozbāyē, as he is usually called. In general and for his works, none of which are extant, see Baumstark, *Geschichte*, 114–15; Vööbus, *History*, 122–33. The *Ecclesiastical History* and the *Cause* disagree about his tenure of office. The former states that he led the School for four years in the middle of Abraham of Bēt Rabban's tenure of office, but the latter places Elisha's tenure directly after that of Narsai and says that it lasted seven years (see *Cause* 387). The *Chronicle of Siirt* states that Elisha left Edessa with Narsai and at the request of the patriarch Acacius (485–495/6) composed a treatise on Christianity for the Sasanian king Kavad I (488–531), which was translated into Persian (*Chronicle of Siirt* 2.1.126–27). The *Chronicle of Arbela* (70.17–19) supports the position of the *Cause*, but this text may be a forgery and Mingana, the possible forger, was aware of the *Cause* (on this issue see Appendix I). By locating Qozb in Margā, the *Chronicle* again agrees with the *Cause* (or perhaps Mingana's rendering of it), which neither locates Qozb nor gives Elisha the appellation "Arbāyā'. Vööbus suggests that his dates of tenure were from approximately 503 to 510, but this is speculative (Vööbus, *History*, 132–33).

25 On this episode, see Vööbus, *History*, 129–32, though his conclusion may be doubted. It seems more likely that the earlier and more awkward source, that is, the *Ecclesiastical History*, is more accurate.

26 The charges (Syr. *zē'ṭēmē*, from Gr. *zḗtēma*) possibly reflect an actual debate. In any case, this corresponds with his apologetic work, written for Kavad I (see note 24 above).

one thousand brothers had gathered unto him and the prior place of scribes[27] was too narrow, he took the trouble and built another house on the side of his cell, large and ample, so that it might be easier [621] for them to write in it and to complete their work. This man wholly imitated the way of life of his master, not only in fasting and prayer but also in self-denial and much abstinence,[28] while he abstained completely from eating flesh. His bed was common,[29] adorned with a blanket of animal fur and composed of a patchwork of wool. In turn, his vessels for necessities (i.e. his dishes) were passed on from those who are wise,[30] which consisted of three kinds of material, some from mud, some wood, and others gourd. His clothing and his cloak were woven of common wool. For he thought that those who are humble are among kings, according to the word of the Lord.[31] In sum, that is to say, the inhabitants of the city clung to such a love for this man that not only for the believers but also for the pagans and the Jews a secure oath was deteremined by the invocation of his name and the garments which lay upon his body were reckoned as a blessed thing by the whole community, since they experienced great powers performed by means of them, as those of the Apostles. Numerous times demons, by the mere invocation of his name, left and went away.

His Work at the School and in Teaching

[622] These are the praiseworthy (deeds) of this holy man, that is, the spiritual father, who begot many sons from the distraction of error to the truth of life. This man worked so much in his teaching that not only did he fulfil the duties[32] of the school as the order[33] demands – and (he worked so much) in

27 Syr. *bēt maktbānē*. To use a western Medieval term, this may have been the 'scriptorium' of the School. We know that manuscripts were produced there. See the colophon to British Library Add. 14471 at 108a; LXXVII in Wright, *Catalogue of Syriac Manuscripts in the British Museum*, I: 53–54. On this colophon, see also Becker, *Fear of God*, 1–4.

28 Syr. *nzirutā*, lit. 'naziriteship'. The ancient Israelite who took the nazirite vow consecrated himself to the Lord (Num. 6:1–21).

29 It is not clear how the particle *ṭāk* (from Gr. *tákha*), meaning 'perhaps', functions here.

30 The verb in this phrase is singular. However, 'vessels' is plural. Nau provides an emendation suggesting the singular 'vessel', but then translates the sentence as plural, leaving out the phrase: 'was/were passed on from those who are wise'. It is not clear if this is a reference to Abraham's actual reception of dining vessels from prior wise men or if the author is simply suggesting that such a practice of having mean utensils derives from the wise.

31 Mt 11:8. This is a paraphrase of the biblical verse.

32 Syr. *zedqē*.

33 The 'order' (Syr. *ṭaksā*, from Gr. *táxis*) may refer to the canons of the school. However,

his speech, endowed with adornment and fortified with the truth of orthodoxy, since for many years he preached[34] before the brothers – but also he wanted to produce this (teaching)[35] in his writings. Because he saw that the majority of brothers had great difficulty in finding the meaning of the scriptures from reading the volumes of the exegete,[36] since they were interwoven in Greek and dark from the loftiness of the man's speech and from the exegetes who followed after him; on account of this he wrote the greater part of them down and lucidly provided exegesis for them and, like a diligent father, adorned a table full of good things[37] and set it before them. Because he saw that they were pressed in other matters, he did not neglect even these, but rather he diligently concerned himself with them. When first he built for them a hospice[38] so that they might not stray in the city and be dispersed and mocked, as that one who said: *Who is sick and I myself am not sick?*,[39] he piled up and set therein all kinds of things and he filled it for them with all the necessities. Three times a day he would visit the sick who were in it, according to [623] the word of the Lord, which says: *I was sick and you*

---

it is possible that this could be translated here as 'his rank' or 'his station' at the School.

34 Syr. *targem* , lit. 'translate', but here means 'to produce *turgāmē*'.

35 It is not certain to what the feminine object suffix and demonstrative pronoun 'this' refers. It is most likely the 'teaching' (*mallphānutā*) mentioned earlier, but the sentence is convoluted and it could also refer to his 'speech' (*melltā*), which is also feminine.

36 'The exegete' (*mphashshqānā*) is the title commonly used for Theodore of Mopsuestia. On his influence at the School and in the sixth century in general, see Becker, *Fear of God*, 113–25 and Becker, 'The Dynamic Reception of Theodore of Mopsuestia in the Sixth Century'.

37 A similar metaphor is used in the *Cause* for Ḥenānā of Adiabene's exegetical learning (see note CS 526).

38 Syr. *'ksndwkyn* (Nau's emendation of the manuscript's *'ksdwnkyn*), from Gr. *xenodocheîon*. On this passage, see Becker, *Fear of God*, 79–81. On the *xenodocheîon* in antiquity, see for example Olivia Constable, *Housing the Stranger in the Mediterranean World: Lodging, Trade, and Travel in Late Antiquity and the Middle Ages* (Cambridge: Cambridge University Press, 2003), 35–38. It was not an uncommon institution in the region (*The Chronicle of Pseudo-Joshua the Stylite*, 42–43; see also Trombley and Watt, eds., *The Chronicle of Pseudo-Joshua the Stylite*, xlii). It was commonly associated with monasteries (*Syriac and Arabic Documents*, 123–24, Canon XXXVI of the so-called Canons of Marutā). The first of the school canons of 590 CE is: 'The host (Syr. *aksanādākrā*, from Gr. *xenodóchos*) of the *xenodocheîon* of the school shall carefully provide for the brothers that have become sick, and nothing shall be lacking in the (things) required for their nourishment and their care'. The canon then lists the restrictions that are upon him and the punishments imposed for financial infidelity (*Statutes of the School of Nisibis*, 92–93). Sick brothers are to be brought to a *xenodocheîon* according to Canon 11 of the Canons of Abrahma of Kashkar (*Statutes of the School of Nisibis*, 162).

39 2 Cor 11:29. In the preceding verse Paul refers to his concern for the larger ecclesial community.

visited me.[40] After he did these things and seemed to be satisfied for some time with the satisfaction of the brothers, he saw that they were pressed by another matter, since they did not have cells. Whatever they produced for their own sustenance they gave as a fee for their cells, and yet when they were sick many of them were worn down and constrained (to stay) with the faithful. How many times were they stripped and made naked! In turn, it was not easy for them to come and go to the church or the school, since there were some of them who had cells far away. Again, there were some for whom it was not easy to come and go because the outer doors were closed[41] by their landlords lest something be lost. How many times were they apprehended as thieves and even reviled as well for deeds of fornication! For numerous reasons on account of this after the blessed one of the Lord saw all these things and others like them, he sought a place (to build in) from Qashwi,[42] the believer and doctor of the king, and when he gave it to him, he busied himself and built eighty cells at his own expense, and he divided it into three courts. He built there baths, one for [624] the honour of the brothers, the second for the expenses of the hospice.[43] Because there was not yet a place from which the reader and the elementary instructor could be sustained, he bought a village for a thousand staters[44] and ordered that the proceeds of it go to the teachers, and if there was any surplus from that, it

40 Mt 25:36. Mt 25:31–46 commonly serves as a model for care of the poor and other forms of euergetism, e.g., Aphrahat, *Demonstrations*, XX.5 and comments in Adam H. Becker, 'Anti-Judaism and Care of the Poor in Aphrahat's *Demonstration* 20', *JECS* 10.3 (2002): 312–13.

41 Nau translates this word, *triqin* as 'closed'. Brockelmann, *Lexicon Syriacum*, 838, cites this passage alone for this word, but is uncertain about its accuracy.

42 On Qashwi's patronage, see Becker, *Fear of God*, 9–81. Vööbus, *History*, 145, cites Abū' l-Barakāt, *Miṣbāh az-zilma. Der Katalog der christlichen Schriften in arabischer Sprache*, ed. W. Riedel (Nachrichten von der königliche Gesellschaft der Wissenschaften zu Göttingen; Göttingen, 1902), 652 as another source which mentions Qashwi.

43 On the hospice, see note 38 above. On the introduction of baths to the Sasanian Empire by Balash and Kavad I, see Trombley and Watt, eds., *The Chronicle of Pseudo-Joshua the Stylite*, 19 and nn.77, 75.

44 Syr. *estērē*, from Gr. *statēr* (Mid. Pers., *ster*). The Sasanian *ster*, a multiple variant of the *dirham* (Mid. Pers. *Drahm*), the Sasanian silver unit of currency (orig. Gr. *drachmē*). (Trombley and Watt, eds., *The Chronicle of Pseudo Joshua the Stylite*, 9 n. 35, 11 n. 45; Ph. Gignoux, 'Dirham, i. In Pre-Islamic Persia', *Encyclopedia Iranica*, ed. E. Yarshater [London: Routledge & Kegan Paul, 1982–]: VII: 425–26). The same amount of money is given to a monastery by a rich layman during a locust plague in order that the monks may maintain their community (*The Histories of Rabban Hormizd the Persian and Rabban Bat-'Idta*, trans. E. A. W. Budge [2 volumes; London, 1902; repr. Piscataway, NJ: Gorgias Press, 2003], 11, line 958 (p. 153) (trans. 230); Trombley and Watt, eds., *The Chronicle of Pseudo Joshua the Stylite*, 39 n. 189). However, this source is late and therefore not necessarily reliable.

would go to the hospice of the brothers. These are the pleasing and lovely fruits of this spiritual athlete, against whom what battles arose, sometimes from the bishop of the city, at other times from the community of believers, and at still other times from pagans,[45] now is not the time for us to recount. I will set down one or two things so that the health of his soul and the aid our Lord gave him might be known.

Enemy Brothers Accuse Him

At one point evil men from among the brothers, at least in name, accused him, saying he worshipped idols and sacrificed to the luminaries, because the holy one had an icon of our Lord and a sign of the cross. When he rose at the time of the lighting of the lamps[46] he would first liturgically recite three portions[47] of the Psalter before the icon and then salute the cross. They spread news about him that the holy icon was an idol. After the matter was inquired into by the citizens and it was known that this was (merely) an accusation, they then took refuge [625] in flight and later conceived of another trick. For the holy one made at the outer door of the court of his house a barrier,[48] so that animals would not enter therein, since his door was continually open to everyone. Because he was the first to do this in Nisibis, according to the custom of the Romans, the wicked ones also spread news about him throughout the city that this was a trick that he had performed in order that everyone when entering might bow down in worship to his idol, saying that it was hidden in the walls across from the door.[49] When believers came and found that a cross was there across from the entrance of the door, Satan entered into those accusers to such a point that they said, 'The idol is

45 The Syr. *barrāyē*, lit. 'outsiders', is usually translated as 'pagans', but it could also have a less precise valence here and simply refer to people from outside Nisibis or outside the community of believers as defined by the author. See note CS 290.

46 Syr. *la-shrāgē*, lit. 'for lamps'.

47 Syr. *marmyātā*. A *marmitā* is subdivision of the Psalter. For the East Syrians there are 57 of these. See, e.g., Sebastian Brock, *The Bible in the Syriac Tradition* (Piscataway, NJ: Gorgias Press, 2006), 141 and also Thomas of Marga, *Book of the Governors* I:287 (II: 515, but ignore n. 2, which confuses the West-Syrian and East-Syrian traditions).

48 The 'court of his house' is lit. 'his court' (*dārtēh*), which could also be translated as 'his chamber'. The word 'barrier', following Nau's translation, is lit. 'daughter of a door' (*ba*(*r*)*t tar'ā*). The architectural innovation described here, which the author characterizes as a Roman custom, is unclear.

49 In the chapter on Theodore of Mopsuestia, pagans try to trick Theodore into adoring an idol by hiding it in a wall behind the church altar (Barhadbeshabba, *La second partie de l'histoire ecclésiastique*, 507–08)

hidden behind the cross'. After this was found to be false, one of them plotted to throw himself into the well of the home of the Rabban,[50] so that once he was drowned, the old man would be taken prisoner, but this (plot) also did not remain hidden. Sometimes they slandered him before the *marzbān*[51] of the city as if he were someone who had disrupted the border. Because he did not inquire into the affair, he sent his son on an embassy to the king in order to destroy the glorious one. When the divine athlete also heard this, he said: *Judge, Oh Lord, my case and fight with those who fight with me, because false witnesses have stood against me and spoken injury.*[52] After [626] many faithful were saddened due to this affair, he gave encouragement to them: *The Lord will not abandon those who fear him, but he will demand punishment of those who distress them.*[53] After the emissary went to the king and completed the will of his father – in word but not in deed – when he arrived at the Tigris, he drowned right there. He and everything with him was lost. When his father heard this, on account of the great pain he too died on the third day. All of his enemies were ashamed and hid their heads.

The Wicked Jews Attack Abraham

Afterwards, Satan incited the evil nation of the Jews, the crucifiers, against him. Although the whole city was stirred up against them, nevertheless by taking the hand of[54] the bishop of the time[55] – because they feared the city – they inclined judgment against the old man, as if he and his students[56] were the cause of the strife. Although the holy one was sick at the time and was reaching the point of death due to the intractability of the illness, everyone's eyes were nevertheless covered and not one of the faithful served as an aid to him and they exchanged the truth for falsehood. The Persian authorities sealed a decree[57] against him and against those found guilty with him.

50 Lit. 'our great one'. This was a title given to heads of monasteries as well as the head of the School of Nisibis.

51 See note SL 114.

52 Ps 27:12.

53 Ps 37:28.

54 This is possibly the same form of supplication employed in the wider region to this day. One takes the hand of another, kisses it, and then presses the kissed hand to the forehead. Such a submissive gesture makes the one entreated responsible for the one entreating.

55 This is probably Paul II (c. 554–73) (Fiey, *Nisibe*, 51–55).

56 Syr. *talmidaw(hy)*.

57 Nau suggests the emendation of *pusqānā* for *pwrsshn'* in the Ms. This is how I have translated the text, but it is possible that the emendation is not necessary and that we have the

After he was made healthy from his illness by the aid of God, he saw that his kinsmen were fleeing [627] and hiding, all the brothers were scattered, and the school was idle, and he learned the cause of this matter, then he said, 'All of them have abandoned me. *Let this not be reckoned unto them.*[58] But our Lord will arise and aid me as he always does.' What then did the father of blessings do? As soon as he heard (this) he asked God in prayer, as the old man Jacob did, and he found favour before the king and all of his administration,[59] and not only did he destroy this decree,[60] but also he gained from then onward great honours, from the king and likewise from his grandees, and his secret enemies and manifest despisers were ashamed. He re-established the school as it was before. Satan stirred up these affairs and many more than these against him.

Abraham's Sturdiness and Defence of the Doctors of the Church[61]

On the one hand, the foot of his thought did not slip from the correct confession of the true faith even in one of these affairs. On the other hand, if there was one of the brothers whose thought was weakened from the goal of orthodoxy due to one of these causes,[62] he bravely battled until he turned his thought from that distraction of error, while he himself endured all pains on his behalf, in order that he might possess a perfect human being, according to the word of the blessed Paul, and as that one who said this: *Who is it who stumbles and I am not burdened?*[63] so that because of this the Roman people had a great hatred against him [628], whether the followers

Mid. Pers. word, *pursishn*, meaning 'question', which is cognate with the standard word for 'to ask', *pursīdan*. This word can be used for questions pertaining to religion, see Henrik Samuel Nyberg, *A Manual of Pahlavi, Part II: Glossary* (Wiesbaden: Otto Harrassowitz, 1974), 163.

58 2 Tim 4:16. The postpositive particle *lam* makes explicit that this is a quotation. This line derives from (Pseudo-)Paul's description of the opposition he met in his ministry.

59 Syr. *pwlwṭy'* (voc. *pawlawṭēya'*), from Gr. *politeía*.

60 See note 57 above.

61 In view of the content of the *Ecclesiastical History* as a whole, it is appropriate that the last chapter should end with the hero defending the three most important fathers of the Church of the East, figures who play an important role in the *Ecclesiastical History* as a whole. See Narsai's defence of these three, 'Homélie de Narsès sur les Trois Docteurs Nestoriens', ed. and trans. F. Martin, *JA* 9e ser, 14 (1899): 446–92; 15 (1900): 469–525 and the discussion of this text in Kathleen McVey, 'The Memra of Narsai on the Three Nestorian Doctors as an example of forensic rhetoric', in *Symposium Syriacum III*, 87–96.

62 This word can also be translated as 'pretexts', i.e. the false accusations made against him.

63 2 Cor 11:29.

of the council or the Syrians.[64] After they suppressed every honour that the Church of Nisibis and also the holy one had at that time from the Church of Antioch for this reason, that is, that perhaps – so they said – stooping low on account of this he would abandon his confession and hold onto theirs, what then did God's chosen one do? He took care not only to guard the true faith without blemish but also to order that the name of those who openly announced it be announced in the book of life, I mean, Diodore, Theodore, and Nestorius, the vigorous athletes, these men who despised all worldly honours and possessed their confession by their own labour. After his enemies learned that he did this and that he did not want to veer off into heresy,[65] they entreated Caesar to demand (from him) an apology[66] in public speech for his confession, and that he (i.e. Abraham) produce a response to the questions springing up against him.[67] After he was asked by Caesar to ascend to him and produce a response to these (questions) and he was unable to do this, first because of his great old age and then because of the labour of his teaching, which he was maintaining, he produced in writings what was appropriate and sent them the teaching of his confession. In turn, he provided an apology for the questions which he was asked.[68] After they failed in this, [629] then they said to him, 'Remove Theodore and Nestorius from the Church and we will agree with you and the whole church will be one and of one mind'. Then he said to them, 'Is it that the names of these holy ones are loathed by you, oh wondrous ones? or their confession?' They quickly responded, 'Both of them. Their names as well as their confession.' When he heard this, the holy one was furious at them and said to them, 'Oh evil ones more evil than all! If this is true, then you are far from the whole truth. For "Theodore" means "Gift of God", "Nestorius" means "Son

64 The phrase 'followers of the council' is a rendering of Syr. *sunhādiqē* (from Gr. *sunodikós*), lit. 'synodists'. These are Chalcedonians, 'the synod' being the Council of Chalcedon of 451. The 'Syrians' are Miaphysites. This geographical designation points to the perceived dominance of Miaphysitism (later, the Syrian Orthodox or West Syrians) in Syria at the time.

65 Syr. *haraṭiqutā*, deriving from Gr. *hairetikós*.

66 Syr. *mappaq b-ruḥā*.

67 Nisibis was not under the jurisdiction of Rome and so it is peculiar that Abraham should be asked to defend his theology before Caesar, that is, Justinian. This episode and the following one seem to reflect the theological discussions that occurred in Constantinople in the 530s and 540s in the period leading up to the Fifth Ecumenical Council in 553. See, for example, Sebastian Brock, 'The Conversations with the Syrian Orthodox under Justinian (532)', *OCP* 47 (1981): 87–121 (repr. in Brock, *Studies in Syriac Christianity*, Chap. 13).

68 Again, Syr. *zē'ṭēmē*, from Gr. *zḗtēma*, see note 26 above.

of the Fast".[69] If these names are hateful to you, you are showing about yourselves that you do not love the gift of God nor are you fond of the fast of God. How could we intermingle ourselves with people who maintain this? If, in turn, their confession is loathed by you, it is clear that you do not confess the trinity nor do you believe in the primary reception (of nature) from us.[70] For these men maintain and confess thus. You are foreign to the whole truth.' After they had no response to these things, they said to him, 'We do not know what benefit there is from the remembrance of the names of these men to whom you cling in this way. But against insult and abuses you have separated yourself from the whole community.' The holy one also [630] answered them regarding these things, 'The rejection of their names is a certain denial of their confession. But if we deny their confession, we remove ourselves from the whole truth, as you yourselves do.' After these things he sent Paul the bishop[71] and others with him and they went before Caesar and apologized for the confession that they maintained and for the fathers whom they proclaimed. They then came from there with much glory.

69 Of these two etymologies, the first is accurate, while the second makes the mistake of deriving the name Nestor (with a short e) from *nēsteúein*, meaning 'to fast'. That the etymology of their names should have significance points to the tendency within Syriac Christian thought to maintain an inherent and essential connection between signifier and signified.

70 Syr. *nsibutā rēshāytā d-menan*. Syr. *nsibutā* , lit. 'taking', is the standard term for God's taking up of human nature in the incarnation, for example, in the Christological writings attributed to Michael the Intrepreter, a member of the School in the late sixth century, Abramowski and Goodman, *Nestorian Christological Texts,* 110.4 (64.2). On Michael, see Abramowski, 'Zu den Schriften des Michael Malpana/Badoqa', 1–10 and Becker, *Fear of God*, 95–96.

71 It is irregular that the head of a school should have the authority to send the bishop as an emissary. Even more odd is the fact that the bishop is being sent to the Roman Emperor, to whom he owes no allegiance. This is the same bishop Paul mentioned in note 55 above. Perhaps it is at this time that another Paul, a teacher at the School, introduced Junillus Africanus, *Quaestor Sacri Palatii* in the court of Justinian, to the exegesis of the School of Nisibis, a meeting which would later influence Cassiodorus (d. 585) and from him the Medieval Latin tradition of monastic learning. See Michael Maas, *Exegesis and Empire in the Early Byzantine Mediterranean: Junillus Africanus and the Instituta Regularia Divinae Legis* (Studies and Texts in Antiquity and Christianity 17; Tübingen, 2003) and Becker, 'The Dynamic Reception of Theodore of Mopsuestia in the Sixth Century'.

Conclusion

This blessed one maintained such a love of orthodoxy and his friends that he would endure and bear all torments on behalf of it (i.e. orthodoxy). He led the assembly for a period of sixty years, with great vigil night and day.[72] Neither completely nor quickly would he grow weary from didactic discourse,[73] but in all the school seasons he led them carefully according to their rule.[74] After he led his life with all ranks and stations according to their measure, according to the purpose of the providence of the Messiah, his life lasted a period of one hundred and twenty years.[75] His eyes did not become heavy nor did his cheeks contract nor was the polished composition of his speech spoiled. In the end he was gathered unto his fathers in peace, as a sunrise [631] that happens in its time. This is the cause[76] of the glorious deeds of the holy one. When his teaching quickly flew to the four corners (of the world) in the likeness of the rays of the sun and the whole of Persia was illuminated by his confession, he completed and fulfilled everything according to the will of God, and like unto the blessed Abraham, the first of the fathers,[77] he revealed and explained all secrets and hidden mysteries of that praiseworthy providence, and with confidence[78] and a loud voice he announced it in all the inhabited world[79] with the aid of the Messiah. To Him and to his Father and to the Holy Spirit be honour and glory for ever and ever. Amen.

The story of Mār Abraham, the presbyter and exegete of the divine scriptures, is completed.

72 The *Cause* (p. 389) also says that his tenure of office lasted sixty years.

73 Syr. *melltā d-mallphānutā*, lit. 'word' or 'speech of teaching'.

74 The Syriac word *ṭaksā* (Gr. *táxis*) can refer to the actual 'rule' of the School, that is, its canons, or it could be the 'station' or 'rank' of those Abraham was leading.

75 Gen 6:3 limits the human life span to one hundred and twenty years, though some persons, such as Sarah and Abraham, live beyond this limit.

76 This use of the word 'cause' (Syr. *'elltā*) points to the extended meaning it took on in the sixth century to refer both to a literary genre and a general interest in etiology.

77 Lit. 'head of the fathers'. For the same expression, see note SL 5 and note CS 518.

78 Syr. *galyut appē*, lit. 'revealing of the face'.

79 Syr. *'āmartā*, ellipsis for *ar'ā 'āmartā*, 'the habitable earth', a calque reflecting the Greek *oikouménē*.

BARḤADBESHABBĀ, *THE CAUSE OF THE FOUNDATION OF THE SCHOOLS*

INTRODUCTION

This fascinating, at times bizarre, text serves as an exemplar of the pedagogical understanding of Christianity that we find at the School of Nisibis and in the East-Syrian school movement in general.[1] Composed in the late sixth century, the *Cause* is written in the form of a speech addressing the incoming class at the School of Nisibis and, although it discusses a number of issues such as epistemology, psychology, cosmology, and the ineffable nature of God, it primarily recasts the history of the world as a long series of schools. The text traces out the course of cosmic history from the school God established for the angels at the time of creation up to the time of the controversial late sixth-century director of the School of Nisibis, Ḥenānā of Adiabene (d. before 612). Although the *Cause* is a key text for the reconstruction of the history and culture of the School of Nisibis, only recently have scholars begun to go beyond using the text simply as a source for the chronological history of the School.[2]

Since the text is long and sometimes obscure, I will provide a basic summary of the whole.[3] The *Cause* purports to be a speech given to the

1 The *Cause* has a confusing manuscript tradition, in part because a number of the manuscripts were perhaps lost forever during the genocide of 1915. I have therefore relegated a discussion of the manuscripts to an appendix at the end of this volume (Appendix I). For a detailed discussion of the *Cause*, see Becker, *Fear of God*, much of which is a close analysis and contextualization of the text.

2 Reinink, 'Edessa Grew Dim and Nisibis Shone Forth'; Ilaria Ramelli, 'Linee introduttive a Barhadbshabba di Halwan, *Causa della fondazione delle Scuole*. Filosofia e storia della filosofia greca e cristiana in Barhadbshabba', *'Ilu. Revista de Ciencias de las Religiones* (Madrid, Universidad Complutense) 9 (2004): 127–81, and eadem, 'Barhadbeshabba di Halwan, *Causa della fondazione delle scuole*: traduzione e note essenziali'; Theresia Hainthaler, 'Die verschiedenen Schulen, durch die Gott die Menschen lehren wollte. Bemerkungen zur ostsyrischen Schulbewegung', in Martin Tamcke, ed., *Syriaca II. Beiträge zum 3. deutschen Syrologen-Symposium in Vierzehnheiligen 2002* (Studien zur Orientalischen Kirchengeschichte 33; Hamburg, 2004), 175–92. Earlier use of the text for chronology can be found in Vööbus's *History* and T. Hermann, 'Die Schule von Nisibis vom 5. bis 7. Jahrhundert'.

3 The following summary derives from Becker, *Fear of God*, 98–100

incoming students at the School of Nisibis. The speaker regularly refers to himself in the first person and employs a rhetorical self-presentation typical of Syriac literary texts, particularly those which display the influence of a Greek rhetorical style.[4] Accordingly, the author employs a large number of Greek words.

The text begins with a discussion of the goodness, wisdom, and power of God.[5] The speaker then describes God's grace towards himself and the assembly, and refers to the future mission of the students.[6] There follows a discussion on the nature of God and on the human capacity to learn about him. God is prior in existence to the rest of creation,[7] and on account of this he would be epistemologically inaccessible to us if he had not graciously permitted himself to be known.[8] He does this through the various distinctions which exist in nature; these distinctions, when lined up side by side, form a chain of being that connects all entities, including God himself, to each other and allows us to compare them. In this way God allows himself to be spoken about by us with terms that also apply to the natural world.[9] The tools we employ to decipher the creator through his creation are the human soul and the mind within it, the workings of which the author describes in detail. The human soul is like a lamp and the mind within it is illuminated by the divine light.[10] In relation to the other aspects of the human being the mind is as a captain on a ship,[11] guiding us while aiming at perfection of both intelligence and action and at its own purification.[12] The world we live in was created in order that the rationality of the mind might be able to decipher order from the diversity of creation and from this infer God the creator.[13]

The higher beings, the angels, maintain their existence above this world.[14] Humans, who have the ability to ascend to and descend from these heights, are also given authority over creation,[15] but humanity fell because of the deceiver.[16]

4 For an excellent discussion of the development of Syriac rhetoric, see Riad, *Studies in the Syriac Preface*.

5 *Cause* 327.1–330.5

6 Ibid. 330.6–333.7

7 Ibid. 333.8–334.15.

8 Ibid. 335.1–337.6

9 Ibid. 337.7–339.14

10 Ibid. 340.1–341.7

11 Ibid. 341.8–342.11

12 Ibid. 342.12–344.7

13 Ibid. 344.8–345.6

14 Ibid. 345.7–345.14

15 Ibid. 346.1–347.9

16 Ibid. 347.10–348.3

The creation of the world in six days was a lesson for the angels to learn about the creator and serves as a model for all inferential learning about God in this world.[17] There are two types of angelic students: the lazy and the diligent. In what may be a subtle warning to the speech's audience of students who have newly arrived at the School, the text tells us how the lazy angels began to complain when God commanded them to pay honour to human beings and how on account of this they were beaten by their master and cast out of the school of heaven. In contrast, the diligent angels were given different positions within the celestial hierarchy.[18]

After describing the angelic classroom of creation, the *Cause* relates the long history of human schools, which began when God established a school for Adam in the Garden of Eden. Adam erases the law from the tablet he is given and is ejected from school.[19] The schools where Cain and Abel, Noah, and Abraham studied then follow.[20] When God makes Moses the Steward (*rabbaytā*) of the 'great school of perfect philosophy',[21] humans are no longer just pupils but begin to be instructors in their own schools.[22] Joshua receives this school from Moses; later, Solomon and the prophets have their own schools as well.[23]

The *Cause* then describes the schools of the different Greek philosophers, of the Zoroastrians, and of others who failed in their attempt to imitate the schools previously established by God.[24] After this period of decline, Jesus came and 'renewed the first school of his father'.[25] He 'made John the Baptist a Reader and Interpreter (*maqryānā w-bādoqā*) and the apostle Peter the Steward (*rabbaytā*)'.[26] The *Cause* goes on to describe the schools of Paul and the Apostles;[27] the school of Alexandria, where scripture was first interpreted;[28] the various post-Nicene schools, including that of Theodore of Mopsuestia;[29] the School of Edessa until its closure;[30] and finally the

17 Ibid. 348.4–350.5. This passage is discussed in detail in Becker, *Fear of God*, 113–54.
18 Ibid. 350.6–352.4
19 Ibid. 352.5–354.5
20 Ibid. 354.6–356.5
21 Ibid. 356.6
22 Ibid. 356.6–359.12
23 Ibid. 359.13–362.12
24 Ibid. 362.13–367.9
25 Ibid. 367.10
26 Ibid. 367.13–368.1
27 Ibid. 373.3–374.12
28 Ibid. 375.1–376.9
29 Ibid. 376.10–381.4
30 Ibid. 381.5–383.14

foundation and the different heads of the School of Nisibis.[31] The text then addresses the origins of the School of Nisibis's semester system[32] and ends with an exhortation to the students to work hard at the school[33] and an admonition to avoid contact with Satan, who would lead them astray.[34]

If we divide the *Cause* into sections based upon rhetorical transitions and changes in content, we come up with seven parts of unequal length. The following is a schematic outline of the text based upon these seven parts, divided into the subsection titles I have added to the translation below.

	Pages in the Scher Edition
1) An introductory discussion on the grace of God, who makes all things possible[35]	
Preface: goodness, wisdom, power	327–30
God's grace towards the speaker and the assembly	330–33
2) A philosophical discussion of God's nature, his angelic pupils, and the creation of man[36]	
God's priority in existence	333–34
God's epistemological inaccessibility	335–37
Distinctions and learning	337–39
Divine illumination	340–41
Mind as captain and the purification of the faculties	341–42
Perfection of intelligence and action	342–44
Reason for corporeal creation	344–45
Angelic activity above	345
The human capacity to traverse the firmament to heaven and back, and the human authority over creation	346–47
Human fall due to the deceiver	347–48
Creation as reading lesson	348–50
Lazy angels cast from heaven	350–51
Diligent angels	351–52
3) A 'scholastic' history running from Adam to the prophets[37]	
Human schools	352

31 Ibid. 384.1–393.3
32 Ibid. 393.4–394.13
33 Ibid. 395.1–396.8
34 Ibid. 396.9–397.2
35 Ibid. 327.1–333.7.
36 Ibid. 333.8–352.4.
37 Ibid. 352.5–362.12.

The school of Adam	352–54
Cain and Abel	354
Noah	355
Abraham	355–56
Moses	356–59
Joshua	359–60
Solomon	360–62
Prophets	362

4) Pagan teachers' poor attempts at the imitation of their predecessors[38]

Pagan schools	362–67

5) Renewal of the original school under Jesus and the succession of schools up to the time of Theodore of Mopsuestia[39]

Jesus the master teacher	367–73
The Apostle Paul	373–74
The post-Apostolic schools	375
The School of Alexandria and Philo of Alexandria	375–76
Arius of Alexandria and the Council of Nicaea	376
Post-Nicene schools	377
School of Diodore of Tarsus	377–78
Theodore of Mopsuestia	378–81

6) The school in Edessa, its closure and the move to Nisibis, followed by the various heads of the school at Nisibis[40]

The School in Edessa and removal to Persia	381–82
Qyorā	382–83
Narsai	383–87
Elisha bar Qozbāyē	387
Abraham and John of Bēt Rabban	387–89
Isho'yahb of Arzon	389–90
Abraham of Nisibis	390
Ḥenānā of Adiabene	390–93

7) A description of the school year, and an exhortation and admonition to the students[41]

38 Ibid. 362.13–367.9.
39 Ibid. 367.10–381.4.
40 Ibid. 381.5–393.3.
41 Ibid. 393.4–397.2.

The division of the sessions	393–94
Exhortation	394–96
Conclusion	396–97

The *Cause* can be understood as working within or at least influenced by several different literary genres or modes.[42] The text benefits from comparison with Greek protreptic, collective biography, and the chains of transmission found in philosophical, medical, Rabbinic, and patristic literature. More significantly, it seems to be a scholastic historical subgenre of the East-Syrian 'cause' genre. The 'cause' genre, or the *'elltā* in Syriac, meaning 'cause', is a scholastic genre well attested from the sixth century onwards. Most instances of this genre are aetiological discussions of East-Syrian festival days. This bears significantly on how we understand the subgenre of scholastic history, the one extant example of which is the *Cause*. It seems that the school session was treated as having the same calendrical significance as other Christian holidays and thus the existence of this subgenre points to a sacralization of the period of study at the School.

The *Cause* has a diverse intellectual pedigree and bears the traces of the various texts and ideas that could have been found at the School. Many of the theological, ethical, and exegetical interests of Theodore of Mopsuestia play themselves out in the 'cause' literature, and these and an obvious adherence to a number of Theodore's ideas can be found in the *Cause*.[43] Theodore had become the theological and exegetical authority in the Church of the East by the late sixth century and, despite a greater diversity in their thinking and exegesis than the East Syrians themselves would have cared to admit, his work remained foundational for them. The theology of the *Cause* corresponds with what we find in Theodore's works, but it also fits with a general Antiochene ethical focus on freewill and the imitation of Christ in order to restore the prelapsarian man, as opposed to the Alexandrian emphasis on Eucharistic communion.[44]

The other major influence on the *Cause* is Greek philosophical thought as mediated to Nisibis through translations of the monastic texts of Evagrius of Pontus (d. 399) and Aristotle's early logical works, as well as later Neoplatonic commentaries.[45] The Origenist literature of Evagrius of

42 On the genre of the *Cause*, see Becker, *Fear of God*, 98–112.

43 Becker, *Fear of God*, 113–25.

44 E.g., D. S. Wallace-Hadrill, *Christian Antioch: A Study of Early Christian Thought in the East* (Cambridge: Cambridge University Press, 1982), 125.

45 Becker, *Fear of God*, 126–54.

Pontus had an immense and controversial impact on East-Syrian monastic spirituality.[46] Hints of Evagrius' thought can even be found in the *Ecclesiastical History* and it is clearly attested in the *Cause*. In his systematized and further developed version of the highly Platonic spirituality of Origen of Alexandria (d. c. 251), Evagrius provided a corresponding system of kataphatic and apophatic theology. By 'kataphatic' I mean a theology that allows for affirmations about the divine nature, as opposed to an 'apophatic' one, which emphasizes the unknowability of the divine nature and, therefore, refuses to make positive assertions about it. As I argue elsewhere, we may understand the differences in epistemology between the East-Syrian schools and monasteries, the former emphasizing a kataphatic theology, the latter an apophatic one, as reflecting the hierarchy of epistemologies we find in Evagrius' oeuvre.[47] The kataphatic emphasis of the schools helps explain their heavy reliance on the Neoplatonic commentary tradition on Aristotle's logical works: the Aristotelian *Organon* is about speech, that tool which allows us to make claims about the world as well as about the characteristics of the divine.[48] As an example of the influence on the *Cause* of the Neoplatonists of the late fifth and early sixth centuries, I have included a discussion of the version of the so-called Tree of Porphyry we find in the *Cause* at the end of this volume (Appendix II).

The *Cause* relies on other sources as well. One possible source, which seems to have been interpolated into the text, is a doxographical document, which lists the views concerning the divine held by various philosophical schools as well as by Zoroastrians.[49] Such doxographical interpolations were apparently not uncommon in contemporary literature.[50] We also find the influence of other patristic literature. For example, a reference to Philo of Alexandria in the *Cause* seems to derive from Theodore's 'Against Allegorists'.[51]

46 E.g., Guillaumont, *Les 'kephalaia gnostica' d'Evagre le Pontique et l'histoire de l'origénisme chez les grecs et chez les syriens* (Paris: Éditions du Seuil, 1962). See discussion in Antoine Guillaumont, 'Les versions syriaques de l'oeuvre d'Evagre le Pontique et leur role dans la formation du vocabulaire ascétique syriaque', in *Symposium Syriacum III*, 35–41.

47 E.g, Becker, *Fear of God*, 174–78.

48 The *Organon* (lit. 'tool') is the common appellation for Aristotle's *Categories*, *De Interpretatione*, and *Prior Analytics* I.1–7.

49 *Cause* 363.7–367.2.

50 e.g., Eznik of Kołb, *On God*, trans. M. J. Blanchard and R. Darling Young (Eastern Christian Texts in Translation; Louvain: Peeters, 1998), 293–97.

51 *Cause* 375.12. Note the attempt in the manuscript tradition to turn 'Philo the Jew (*yudāyā*)' into 'Philo the Believer (*mawdyā*)'. See note CS 420 below on this passage and its possible source.

Further inquiry may uncover traces of other translations of Greek patristic material employed by the author, such as the exegetical writings of Diodore of Tarsus (e.g., the text at one point even demonstrates knowledge of West-Syrian patristic literature by citing Philoxenus of Mabbug as a source).[52] One problem in discerning the *Cause*'s sources is that what might seem to come from the Syriac version of Theodore of Mopsuestia's works may derive from some intermediary, such as Narsai, who incorporates much of Theodore's thought into his own metrical homilies (*mēmrē*).[53]

52 *Cause* 380.5.

53 Narsai, *Homilies on Creation*, 470–95.

THE CAUSE OF THE FOUNDATION OF THE SCHOOLS: TRANSLATION AND NOTES

The Cause of the Foundation of the Schools,[1] which was composed by Mār Barḥadbeshabbā of Bēt 'Arbāyē,[2] Bishop of Ḥulwān[3]

Preface: Goodness, Wisdom, Power

Preface[4]

[327] Wise architects set a firm stone in the foundation of their building so that it will fit and support the whole structure. Yet also for the wise architects of the fear of God[5] in the foundation of their building it is proper that the first stone of their speech be thanksgiving[6] to the creator.[7] The second foundation[8] after the first is his inscrutable wisdom;[9] the third then is his invincible power. Everyone who has these three (attributes)[10] is not impeded from what is properly his.[11]

1 The title, *'elltā da-syām mawtbā d-eskolē*, is better rendered as 'The Cause of the Establishment of the Session of the Schools'. I have preserved the traditional rendering to avoid confusion. See discussion of the title at Becker, *Fear of God*, 104–05.

2 Syr. *'arbāyā*, i.e. from Bēt 'Arbāyē, or Arabistān. See discussion of the author in the introduction.

3 This title appears in manuscript T and the following text up to 333.7 is found only in T. See discussion of manuscripts in Appendix I.

4 Syr. *mappaq b-ruḥā*. On this term, see Riad, *Studies in the Syriac Preface*, 179–82.

5 This expression is often translated as 'religion'. It represents the Greek *theosébeia* from which it most likely derives. Its opposite is often *deḥlat ptakrē*, lit. 'fear of idols', i.e. 'idolatry'.

6 *qubbāl ṭaybutēh*, lit. 'acceptance of his grace'. By analogy it seems the author draws an etymological connection between 'grace' (*ṭaybutā*) and 'goodness' (*ṭābutā*) in the following paragraphs.

7 This second sentence begins with the same structure as the preceding one. The reader is thus led to believe that it will conclude in the same way, but then there is a grammatical shift, which provides an elegant rhetorical touch.

8 Instead of the Syr. *shete'stā* employed above, the word for 'foundation' here is *dumsā*, 'house, building, foundation, structure', from the Latin *domus*.

9 Cf. Rom 11:33 and Eph 3:8.

10 Lit. 'is in/with these things'.

11 Lit. 'that which is his', but the Syriac *dil* often contains the philosophical sense of 'property' (*dilāytā*) since it is used to render the Greek *ídion*. However, this passage may also reflect Theodore of Mopsuestia's notion of the divine 'characteristics' (Gr. *prosónta*), e.g. F. Petit, 'L'homme créé "à l'image" de dieu. Quelques fragments grecs inédits de Théodore de Mopsueste', *LM* 100 (1987): 278f.

But regarding the nature of rational beings,[12] although it was deemed worthy of the magnitude of (God's) grace, [328] nevertheless these (attributes) are not fully grown[13] for it (i.e. that nature) nor are these things, which it promises, secure. For its goodness, because it is accidental,[14] is impeded by evil, its wisdom, because it is learned, is brought to naught by foolishness, and its power, because it is weak and temporary, is impeded by weakness. For it is necessary[15] that according to the tree also its fruit and according to the nature also the properties of the nature[16] . . . mutable also temporal things.[17] Even those things which it (i.e. the nature of rational beings) promises are diverse and mutable.[18]

But regarding the creator of times and changes,[19] not one of these weaknesses that are among us impedes him. For his goodness can be known from the fact that we ourselves did not seek from him that he bring us into being, as the testimony of scripture which says: *The world will be built on grace.*[20] And again: *The earth is full of the Lord's grace.*[21] And again: *The earth, Lord, is full of your mercy.*[22] Countless are these (passages) that tell of his graces towards us.

12 Throughout this text the Syriac *mlilē* reflects the Gr. *logikoí*, of which it at times seems to be a translation. Similarly *melltā* representing *lógos* is translated here sometimes as 'speech' and at other times as 'reason'.

13 *Syr. mshamlyātā*, 'complete, of full growth, mature'.

14 The Syriac *'āloltā* literally means 'brought in' or 'introduced', but here it has this technical meaning.

15 Syr. *ananqē*, from Gr. *anánkē*.

16 Or 'natural properties', Syr. *dilāyātēh da-kyānā*.

17 Scher supplies the emendation *wa-lphut zabnā*, 'and according to time', making the line in full: 'according to time, which is mutable, are temporal things' (note 1). Sebastian Brock suggests the simpler: *d-itaw(hy)*, rendering this: 'the nature, which is mutable and temporary'.

18 This focus on the 'diverse' (*mshaḥlphātā*) or 'changing' aspect of creation reflects the interests of Theodore of Mopsuestia, for whom the problem of humanity's changeable nature is central (Theodore of Mopsuestia, *Commentary on the Nicene Creed*, 121 [21]). This concern with diversity also fits with the Aristotelian physics popular in Neoplatonic circles.

19 Time and change are closely related concepts in Aristotelian phsyics. For example, according to the *Physics*, time is an abstraction of the rate of change (see the discussion of time at 217b29–224a17).

20 Ps 89:3.

21 Ps 33:5.

22 Ps 119:64.

Concerning the scrutiny of his inscrutable wisdom[23] his *chosen vessel*[24] Saint Paul says with wonder: *Oh the depth of wealth and the wisdom and the mind of God.*[25] [329] And again: *It is he alone who is wise.*[26] And again: *He has given wisdom to the wise and mind to those who are practised in understanding.*[27] And again: *Who is a counsellor to him?*[28]

Concerning the magnitude of his invincible power, who is it that will say that he is impeded from what is properly his? And again: *The Lord made the earth with his power.*[29] And again: *He gives power to the weary.* And again: *Who is powerful like you?*[30] And there are many other (passages) that are indicative of his invincible power.

However, regarding the nature of rational and created beings, these three things impede it from completing the good: evil, ignorance, and weakness. But regarding God, not one of these things impede (him), as we have shown from the divine scriptures. Because of this it is also right for us to observe carefully these (attributes) of God and whatsoever seems to be troublesome to us let us cast from our mind,[31] while we scrutinize these (attributes) of God, by whose grace without request[32] ... us into being and with his wisdom he has provided for our construction[33] that it be double: one of mortality,

23 The two cognate terms, *'uqqābā* and *lā met'aqbānitā* ('scrutiny' and 'inscrutable'), come from the root *'-q-b*, which is commonly used for intellectual inquiry into the nature of the divine, e.g. Ḥenānā, *On Golden Friday*, 53.6, see also 55.5; *On Rogations*, 68.5. Such activity can often have a decidedly negative valence in earlier authors such as Ephrem and Jacob of Sarug (e.g. Brock, *Luminous Eye*, 26). Such anxieties about inquiry into the divine also appear in Greek patristic literature translated in the fifth and sixth centuries, e.g., British Library Add. 14567, a sixth-century manuscript containing John Chrysostom's *On the Incomprehensibility of God*; see F. Graffin and A-M. Malingrey, 'La tradition syriaque des homélies de Jean Chrysostome sur l'incomprehensibilité de Dieu', in *Epektasis: Mélanges J. Daniélou*, ed. J. Fontaine and C. Kannengiesser (Paris: Beauschesne, 1972), 603–09.

24 Acts 9:15.

25 Rom 11:33.

26 Rom 16:27.

27 Dan 2:21. Syr. *yād'ay sukkālā*, lit. 'knowers of understanding' (cf. Payne Smith, *Compendious Syriac Dictionary*, 187). This line is also quoted at Ishai, *On the Martyrs*, 18.3–4.

28 Dan 11:34.

29 Jer 10:12.

30 Ps 89:8. This may also be translated: 'Who is like you, Powerful One?'

31 Syr. *re'yānan*. It is not always clear why one term for 'mind' is employed as opposed to another in this text.

32 There is a lacuna in manuscript T and Scher suggests the emendation 'he brought' (*ayti*) (note 1).

33 Or 'structure', Syr. *tuqqānan*. The Syr. *tuqqānā* represents Gr. *katástasis*, a term employed by Theodore of Mopsuestia to discuss the two worlds or states (*katastáseis*) of human existence

which suits those in need and pupils, and the other, belonging to the perfect, is one which suits the delight of the righteous.[34] However, by his grace he willed and by his wisdom he provided, his able power then completed and fulfilled. We receive a demonstration of these (attributes) of God from this [330] world. Just as he brought us into being, he will resurrect us by his grace and in his wisdom he will transfer us from here to there.[35] Nothing impeded that power in the first (instruction); nor also is he impeded by anything in our second instruction.[36] Because of this, it is proper to observe carefully these (attributes) of God with a sound knowledge and a firm mind,[37] and let us reckon as beneficial all the things which are done by him.

God's Grace towards the Speaker and the Assembly

But I myself, due to the weakness of my body which is tormented continually by different pains and sicknesses, would not have been able to speak with you even for one day, if that God who is acquainted with your eagerness and love for him – because of whom you left your homelands and parents, and, to put it briefly, scorned all the pleasure of this world, and loved and cherished this spiritual intercourse, which is the illuminator of souls and the place of salt for those who have lost the flavour of the taste of truth and the heavenly nourishment, and you have taken upon yourselves homelessness,[38]

(Theodore of Mopsuestia, *Commentary on the Nicene Creed*, *passim*; cf. PG 66.633c–634a). It is found in Narsai's metrical homilies (Narsai, *Homilies on Creation*, I.83–104).

34 That the former human status in the world is a training ground for the latter is a commonplace in East-Syrian literature. 'Accordingly, [because] that provider of our salvation, God our Lord, considered our lack of training and, at the same time too, the harm that would be procured for us from those reason[s] that the discourse has indicated, like a compassionate father who considers the imperfection of his children and does not put them in charge over his possessions before the time that is proper, he first arranged for us that we should live [as] in a sort of training-place in the school of this world (*b-bēt durrāshā medem b-eskolaw(hy) d-'ālmā hānā*), full of sufferings and wearisome with adversities, so that in it, at least, we might be taught as [in] a sort of gymnasium (*netyallaph a(y)k da-d-bēt agonā*), and, from the contrarieties with which it abounds, we might distinguish good from evil; and (only) then, after we had been disciplined as much as was proper and the choice of the good had been known to us, did he make ready to give us [that] world to come, which is exempt from all contradiction and in which there reigns perpetual life without end.' Cyrus of Edessa, *Six Explanations*, 122.9–21 (trans. 107); see also 9.1–27 (trans. 8) (note on line 19 *bēt nuppāqā*).

35 I.e. from this world to the next.

36 Syr. *yullphānā*. The first instruction is that which God gives by the very act of creation. For God's creation of an entity demonstrates his own existence, as can be seen below with the instruction of the angels at 348.4ff.

37 Syr. *hawnā*.

38 Syr. *aksenyā*, from Gr. *xenía*.

buffetings, poundings, deprivations, labours, and toils, vigil and wakefulness at all times towards the divine scriptures – if he in his grace had not empowered and helped me,[39] not because I was worthy, but so that you might not rest and your labour not be empty. For the divine grace is wont to do this. For it is the cause [331] of the construction[40] of the world and of our first creation.[41] For no one[42] asked God to create the created entities, except for his grace and mercy. He made known and revealed his grace especially in his words to us, in the honour that he has given us in his providence for us, in his care for us, in his forgiveness of our follies and sins. When[43] we were found to continually be wrong-doers and provokers unto anger, he in his patience lifted us and bore us with life-giving laws that from generation to generation have been established for our benefit, especially the one which was given to the Israelite people through the blessed Moses, so that they might acquire love for God and neighbour and distance themselves from the worship of idols, and confess him who alone is the true God, existing for ever.[44]

After all these things that great, glorious, and ineffable thing was also

39 The speaker's boast of suffering and God's aid helping him to endure employs a typical Pauline rhetoric. It is commonplace in the 'cause' genre for the speaker to engage in the Classical rhetorical claim of being unable to complete the task at hand and being audacious even to try (Ishai, *On the Martyrs*, 17.2–3, Ḥenānā of Adiabene, *On Golden Friday*, 55.7; Cyrus of Edessa, *Six Explanations*, 1–3 [trans. 1–3] and 101 [trans. 88]; Cf. comments in Riad, *Studies in the Syriac Preface*, 190, 197–207). Here we find a doubling of the rhetoric of suffering since the speaker attempts to win the benevolence of the audience by addressing their own suffering.

40 Syr. *'elltā d-tuqqānēh*.

41 Syr. *britan qadmāytā*. 'Accordingly, since God, more glorious than all and more exalted than all, is not only good, but also wise, it did not seem good to him that together with our first creation he should have conferred on us such dignity as he has now in our second creation made ready (and) given us.' Cyrus of Edessa, *Six Explanations*, 123.18–22 (trans. 108).

42 Scher emends the text at 331.1 by adding *'nāsh*.

43 The syntax is awkward. The phrase *hāy d-kad* connects this sentence closely to the preceding one, since the demonstrative *hāy* seems to refer to *ṭaybutā* ('grace'). Thus, God's actions described in this sentence are an example of his 'grace'.

44 Despite their strong anti-Judaism and explicit criticisms of Jewish law the East Syrians had a tradition of speaking positively about God's law. Its origins can be found in the writings of both Aphrahat, the Syriac author of the fourth century, and Theodore of Mopsuestia. See the discussion of how Aphrahat characterizes the Christian life as an observance of the law in Adam Lehto, 'Divine Law, Asceticism, and Gender in Aphrahat's Demonstrations, with a Complete Annotated Translation of the Text and Comprehensive Syriac Glossary' (PhD thesis, University of Toronto, 2003), 20–59. In his commentary on Galatians, Theodore writes about God that 'He gave us diverse laws as an aid and those modes of conduct which are according to the choice of the spirit, with the result that we do not choose the worse, but learning the good rather we run to the choice of it (i.e. the good)'. Theodore of Mopsuestia, *In epistolas B. Pauli Commentarii*, ed. Henry B. Swete (2 vols.; Cambridge, 1880–1882), I:26.23–26.

given to us: that is, the advent of Christ, through whom all the wealth of his (i.e. God's) kindness and immeasurable mercy were poured upon us. Although all these things were given to the faithful in general, nevertheless you yourselves especially enjoy them, since you study and meditate upon them and they are for you a pleasure and an excellent luxury, more than wealth of any kind.[45]

[332] Since you know from where this assembly[46] has been handed down; and how when it was in Edessa for certain reasons[47] it was uprooted[48] from there and planted in this city through the agency of the excellent and divine men, Mār Barṣaumā the bishop and Rabban Mār Narsai the presbyter;[49] and how after their deaths not only was it (i.e. the assembly) neither diminished nor did it come to an end, but God made it to abound and increase even more; and how it did not cease from the tumults and the disputes, which from time to time were awakened against it through the operation of Satan. Many advantages[50] flowed from it to the kingdom of the Persians, as the assemblies bear witness which were born out of it, which are now in many places. Therefore, for all these things we are not capable of rendering thanks to God, (that is,) for the things of which he deemed us worthy and the care which he shows for us, though we are not worthy. And we beseech from God that he guard it, establish it, and give it a foundation forever.

45 Emphasis on the pleasure derived from meditating upon God's providence reflects the larger intellectual impetus behind the 'cause' genre.

46 Syr. *knushyā*. This is a term that appears throughout this text to represent schools as communal gatherings.

47 Lit. 'causes that called' 'causes that summoned'. This is a technical idiom found in the 'cause' genre and beyond: e.g. 'In accordance with the causes which summoned us to converse with each other from time to time, ...', Thomas of Marga, *Book of Governors*, 15.3 (17); 'First then let us approach to the plan that it imposes on us and let us say, what cause called Saint Matthew, that in a book he should deliver the Gospel', Ishodad of Merv, *Commentary on the Gospels*, 2.9.16–18 (1.6); Ishai, *On the Martyrs*, 15.1.

48 The same root, '-q-r ('to uproot'), appears in a number of sources describing the closure of the school: *Chronicle of Edessa*, 8.18–19 (LXXIII); Jacob of Sarug, *Letter* 14, 59.3; Simeon of Bēt Arsham, *Letter*, 353; John of Ephesus, *Lives of the Eastern Saints*, 17: 139.9. This usage fits with the common practice of employing vegetative metaphors to discuss heresy (André de Halleux, 'La dixième lettre de Philoxène aux monastères du Beit Gaugal', 37.11, 13), but it also fits the use of 'planting' (root, *n-ṣ-b*) for the new foundation in Nisibis (*nṣibin*). See Barhadbeshabba, *La second partie de l'histoire ecclésiastique*, 606.9; *Memra on the Holy Fathers*, line 6 (*Cause* 400); John of Ephesus, *Lives of the Eastern Saints*, 17: 139.5.

49 On these two figures and their involvement in the foundation of the School of Nisibis, see the relevant passages and notes in the 'Life of Narsai', translated above.

50 Scher supplies the emendation *'udrānē saggi'ē*, 'many advantages', for a brief lacuna in T (note 1).

While it is also your concern to attend to your work, to profit and to be led by the canons that were established for you, just as those who preceded you transmitted them to you, so these good and useful things you yourselves should transmit to your successors.[51]

[333] We ourselves are grateful also to your holiness, you who continually arouse and encourage us to be neither negligent, nor slothful, nor slack in this occupation. We seek from God that he give to you a heart of wisdom, knowledge, and understanding of the things that are necessary and on account of which you have come here. After you have benefited yourselves and others here, whenever you go to your homelands, you will be seen as luminaries in the world, you will learn, and you will teach and benefit many. You will bring the erring closer to the fear of God.[52] You will bear fruit and give birth to virtuous sons through the grace and mercy of our God, to whom may there be glory forever and ever. Amen.

God's Priority in Existence[53]

Everything that exists[54] is comprehended and investigated[55] in three orders:[56]

51 The canons (Syr. *qānonē* from Gr. *kanṓn*) share a number of characteristics with this text. Their final ratification was in 602, after a new set of canons were introduced in 590 under Henānā, while the first set was established under Narsai in 496 and later ratified under Abraham of Bēt Rabban. The author's emphasis on the canons at this point in the text may reflect the need to further enforce those recently instituted under Ḥenānā.

52 The East-Syrian schools often had a missionary emphasis. See, for example, Becker, *Fear of God*, 193.

53 The other manuscripts begin at this point and Scher begins to follow C. For a close reading of 333.8 to 345.6, see Becker, *Fear of God*, 134–50 (which has a number of overlaps with the following notes).

54 Syr. *itaw(hy)* is often translated here as 'exists', especially in cases where it seems to represent a technical philosophical term.

55 Syr. *met'aqqab*. See note 23 above.

56 Syr. *ṭaksā* from Gr. *táxis*. This word comes into Syriac early and, like the Greek word, has a broad range of meanings, but generally may be translated as 'order' or 'rank'. The usage here seems to reflect the influence of Greek philosophical sources. The three perspectives one may take in looking at an entity and the upward and downward movement upon this scale corresponds to the discussion of species and genera in the *Isagoge* of Porphyry and, in particular, the use of the Tree of Porphyry later in this text (see Appendix II). We find a similar passage in Sergius of Rēsh'aynā's commentary on the *Categories* (Hugonnard-Roche, *La logique d'Aristote du grec au syriaque*, 193–94). There are also later parallels, e.g. in the preface to Ishodad of Merv's commentary on the Gospels: 'But here let us say thus briefly, that the Scriptures speak chiefly under three heads; first, when they call men just as they are, that is to say, living, rational, mortal; but secondly, above what they are, when they call us gods; and thirdly, below what they are, when they call us reptiles and worms and dust, and wolves, and foxes; but God is only names

either 'according to the order', or 'above the order', or 'below the order';[57] just as we say about a human being that he is soul and body; for this is said[58] about him 'according to the order'; or we say that he is God; and this is 'above the order' in respect to him (i.e. the human being); or we call him bull, eagle, worm, and flea, and these things are 'below the order' to him.

[334] God is spoken[59] about in two ways by creatures, either 'as he exists' or 'below the way he exists'. But 'above the way he exists' it is not possible to be spoken.[60] For if we say that he is eternally existent, infinite spirit, the cause of all,[61] this is defined[62] about him 'according to the order'. But if we say he is composed and bodily, ignorant and needful, this is composed about him 'below the order' and inexactly.[63]

---

in two ways, either as He is, as I Am THAT I Am, or as Father and Son and Spirit, or below that which He is, as fire, or as being angry or in a rage, or that He repented, or that He was a lion, etc.' (Ishodad of Merv, *Commentary on Gospels*, 2.5.10–18 [1.3–4]); or the *Book of Treasures* of Job of Edessa, the c. 800 Aristotelian and medical writer (Job of Edessa, *Encyclopædia of philosophical and natural sciences as taught in Baghdad about A.D. 817; or, Book of treasures*, ed. and trans. A. Mingana [Cambridge: W. Heffer, 1935], 23).

57 The Syriac for each of these is: *a(y)k ṭaksā*, *l-'el men ṭaksā*, and *l-taḥt men ṭaksā*.

58 Syr. *et'amrat 'law(hy)*.The focus on speaking in this and the next paragraph reflects the philosophical sense of the Greek *légesthai* ('to be spoken') and especially *katēgoreîsthai* ('to be categorized'). We find the use of the passive form of the Syriac 'to say' (*'emar*) used as as an equivalent to these Greek verbs in the early sixth-century Syriac translation of the *Isagoge*, where also the Syriac preposition *'al* reflects the Greek *katá*. Compare passages from Porphyry's *Isagoge* in its original Greek to the Syriac version: *katēgoreîsthai katá*, Greek 2.16=Syriac 4.6; Greek 2.17=Syriac 4.9; for *légesthai*, Greek 1.18=Syriac 2.10; Greek 2.17=Syriac 4.10. There are many examples of this in the *Isagoge*. See also Henri Hugonnard-Roche, 'L'Organon. Tradition syriaque et arabe', in R. Goulet, ed., *Dictionnaire des philosophes antiques* 1 (Paris, 1989), 502–28.

59 Syr. *metmallal 'law(hy)*.

60 Syr. *netmallal*.

61 This is a title for God that appears in a number of sources, including the synodal canons, e.g., Brock, 'Christology of the Church of the East', 138. Also 338.10 below. It appears in Theodore of Mopsuestia's works (*On the Nicene Creed*, 126 [25]).

62 Syr. *etthaṭmat 'law(hy)*, which is the equivalent of the Greek *horízesthai*. See Porphyry's *Isagoge* in the original Greek and the Syriac version: *horízesthai*, Greek 10.22=Syriac 24.11; Greek 11.7=Syriac 25.6; Greek 13.3=Syriac 29.10; *horismós*, Greek 1.5=Syriac 1.6 (Syriac *tḥumā*); Greek 10.20=Syriac 25.21; also see the Syriac of *De Interpretatione* 21a34 in Hoffmann, *De Hermeneuticis*, 45.9, although this is a later translation.

63 There seems to be a pun here: 'composed' (*mrakkbā*) simply means 'consisting of constituent parts', while 'is composed about him' (*etrakkbat 'law[hy]*) refers to predication. An East-Syrian example of this concern for divine simplicity can be found in Narsai, *Homilies on Creation*, II.29, where God is called 'The one without combination' (*d-lā rukkābā*). On the non-combined nature of God, see, for example, Christopher Stead, 'Divine Simplicity as a Problem of Orthodoxy', in *The Making of Orthodoxy: Essays in honour of Henry Chadwick*,

For although this term[64] 'exists'[65] agrees with both the universal and the particular,[66] nevertheless it fits and agrees exactly only with him (i.e. God), because everything that 'exists' is either an entity that has come into being or not.[67] Just as this 'coming into being'[68] is prior to 'exists', that is, 'it came into being',[69] and the former is the cause of the latter, thus in the case of he who exists, 'coming into being' is not prior to the 'exists' of the eternally existent, and that is the cause of the 'exists'. For if he were not existent and eternal, he would be an 'entity that has come into being', and if this were true, he would have a beginning and would receive his 'coming into being' from another and be equal to everything that came into being in the following two ways: in that it came into being and that it exists. But if this is defamatory to suppose in this case (i.e. in the case of God),[70] then he exists because he is an existent being and the creation exists because it came into being and began.

---

ed. R. Williams (Cambridge: Cambridge University Press, 1989), 255–69. See also *Nestorian Christological Texts*, 109.17–23(63.31–37) for a similar statement composed at about the same time at the School. See also Narsai, *Metrical Homilies*, III.650: 'Indestructible is the (Divine) Essence: because the (Divine) Essence has no structure (*rukkābā*)!'

The adjective 'composed' also resembles the Greek *súntheton*, the opposite of *haploûs*, 'simple', two terms that appear in philosophical discussions: Ammonius, *In Categorias* 35.18–36.3 (Ammonius, *On Aristotle's* Categories, 46); Philoponus, *In Categorias* 27.10–32. The second usage of the same root ('it is composed about him') derives from Aristotelian logic where any statement requires the combination of subject and predicate, e.g. *De Interpretatione* 16a12–16. For Probus's Syriac commentary on this, see Hoffmann, *De Hermeneuticis*, Syriac 69 (Latin 95); *Rakkeb* becomes even more important than the Greek *súnthesis* in the early translation of *De Interpretatione*, because it is used to render several Greek terms: Syriac 22.15=*súnthesin* (16a12) for the combination of a subject and a predicate; Syriac 22.17=the same (16a14); Syriac 24.3=*peplegménois* (16a24); Syriac 26.6=*súnthesis* (16b24); Syriac 28.10 *mrakkbā*=*súnthetos* (17a22); Syriac 26.14=*diploîs* (16b32).

64 Syr. *ba(r)t qālā*, lit. 'daught of a sound'. The sound (*qālā*) of a word is its superficial characteristic as an arbitrary signifier.

65 Syr. *itaw(hy)*.

66 The words 'universal' (Syr. *gawwā*) and 'particular' (*iḥidāyā*) reflect philosophical usage. Isagoge (Greek=Syriac): *tà kath' hékasta* 6.20=15.2 (*iḥidāyā*); *tà katà méros* 6.21–22=15.5, 17.4; *tò kath hékaston* 6.22=15.6 (*iḥidāyutā*); *toû koinoû* 7.25=17.12 (*d-gawwā*); *tò koinón* 6.23=15.7 (*gawwānāyutā*).

67 The following relies on the philosophical distinction between the two verbs meaning 'to be' in Greek, *eînai* and *gígnesthai*, represented by the Syriac *itaw(hy)* and *hwā*, rendered here as 'exists' and 'came into being', respectively. The noun *hwāyā*, based on the verb *hwā*, could be more fully translated as 'something which has come into being'.

68 Syr. *hwāyā*.

69 Syr. *hwā*.

70 Syr. *tamān*, lit. 'there'. This usage of the locative adverb seems to be modelled on that of the Greek word *ekeî*.

God's Epistemological Inaccessibility

[335] So that from this it should be certain that he is the one alone who exists from the beginning[71] before all beings,[72] even though before beings not only the (term) 'one' but also the (term) 'beginning' do not fit him.[73] For these things are established about him by analogy.[74] For he is without name and without title and he exists existentially[75] above all appellations, since he exists, and he did not come into being nor did he begin, because the appellations 'coming into being'[76] and 'beginning' were not even known until then, except by that intelligence which knows all. But he existed alone existentially, while having an essence, rich in blessings,[77] and he abided in joyous light, just as also now, being ineffable and inscrutable, yet he knew himself and he was known from himself and through himself and about himself, just as also now, although it is not possible for that manner, by which he knew himself, to be spoken or conceived of by reasoning beings. As our Lord spoke and Paul bore witness: *No one knows the Son except the Father, nor does any one know the Father except the Son.*[78] And: *No one knows that which is in a human being except the spirit of the human being*[79] *which is in him. Thus also what is in God no one knows except the spirit of God.*[80]

[336] While with these properties[81] of his he exists ineffably,[82] since thought has no place, and also time, which begins from movement, and

71 This term, *brāshit* (lit. 'in the beginning') is the first word of Gen. 1:1 and is also the name of the book of Genesis in Syriac. It derives from the original Hebrew and is not a natural Aramaic expression.

72 Again the Syr. *hwāyā*, but here the translation aims to convey the result, as opposed to the process, of coming into being.

73 Parallels to the content of the following passage can be found in earlier patristic texts, but most immediately Jacob of Sarug, *Homilies*, 3:28.10–16: God existing without name before creation; 3:6.3–8: God taking solitary pleasure in himself.

74 Syr. *peḥmā*, the root literally meaning 'equal, like, similar'. See the use of *peḥmā* in Theodore of Mopsuestia, *Fragments*, 1.15, 2.3, 2.8.

75 Syr. *itaw(hy) ityā'it.*

76 Syr. *hwāyā.*

77 See note LN 35.

78 Mt 11:27.

79 *d-barnāshā* is missing from T.

80 1 Cor 2:11.

81 Or 'these (attributes)'. See note 11 above.

82 Syr. *lā metmallānā'it.* Since speech and reason are related in Syriac (as in Greek) this adverb may also be rendered 'in a not rationalizable manner' or even 'in an uncategorizable manner'.

movement, which adheres to essence,[83] is *further from* there *than any farness* – for he is *the depth of depths*, not to be searched out or *discovered*[84] – thought does not have a path by which to go as far as that lordship, loftier than the trodden paths and ways of the mind, the swift messenger of the soul. Because the mind does not have a path by which to go there, also reason,[85] a swift horse of four feet, is lame and abstains from the course. Since, as far as thought is concerned, which is guide[86] and tutor[87] of reason, the pupils of its

83 The Syriac *ḥushshābā*, 'thought', perhaps reflects the Greek *logismós* (as opposed to, for example, *nóēsis*, which means 'intuition'). 'There is no place for thought' or 'Thought has no place' (Syr. *atrā l-ḥushshābā layt*) seems to derive from the Greek usage of *tópos* (perhaps the idiom *échein tópon*). 'Movement' (*zaw'ā*) is equivalent to the Greek *kínēsis*, which Aristotle himself suggests is not altogether different from the Greek *metabolḗ* ('change') (e.g., Hugonnard-Roche, *La logique d'Aristote du grec au syriaque*, 30: *zaw'ā = metabolḗ*). According to Aristotle, time does not exist without change or movement (*Physics* 218b21). Therefore, time can only begin with the advent of the two. Much of this can be found in *Physics* Bk. 2. Ammonius, *In Categorias* 60.24–25 (Ammonius, *On Aristotle's* Categories, 71) states: 'For time is the measure of change'. This issue was taken up in a no longer extant treatise of Sergius of Rēsh'aynā (Hugonnard-Roche, *La logique d'Aristote du grec au syriaque*, 128). The word 'essence' (*itutā*), used above, often renders the Greek *ousía*, but, since in Christological discussions the East Syrians often use *kyānā* with a meaning close to *itutā* and since *kyānā* is a word commonly used to translate the Greek *phúsis*, there is a possibility that *itutā* may derive from *phúsis* in this instance. Aristotle writes: 'For nature is the principle and cause of motion and rest for those things, and those things only, in which she inheres primarily, as distinct from incidentally' (*Physics* 192b21–23). A Syriac scholion attributed to Sergius of Rēsh'aynā reads: 'Definition of nature: the principle of movement and repose', Furlani, 'Due scoli filosofici attribuiti a Sergio di Teodosiopoli (Rêš'aynâ)', 140 (I do not have access to the manuscript, but Furlani seems to be translating *kyānā* here). The word 'adheres', Syr. *nāqeph*, is used to translate several Greek words, including *hepésthai* and *akoloúthein* (Porphyry, *Isagoge* (Greek=Syriac): 16.2=35.16, 19.13=43.2). There are several instances of this in Hoffmann, *De Hermeneuticis*, but from the later version of *De Interpretatione*: *akoloúthei* is translated thus on p. 52; see also *naqqiphutā* 48.12=*akoloúthesis* (22a14). For *hyphistánai*, see Porphyry, *Isagoge* (Greek=Syriac): 18.18–19=41.8 and *hypárchein*, ibid. 16.14–15=37.3 and 37.5; *páresti*, ibid. 22.2=47.14. The verb *nāqeph* can be variously translated in its philosophical usage as 'follows, is concomitant with, joined to, belongs to'.

84 Eccl 7:23–24. The awkwardness of the Syriac reflects problems in the original Hebrew text. This line is quoted again below at 361. Note the emphasis on God as the 'mover of all' (*mzi'ānā d-kul*) in the Syriac fragments of Theodore's commentary on Ecclesiastes (Werner Strothmann, ed., *Das syrische Fragment des Ecclesiastes-Kommentars von Theodor von Mopsuestia* [Wiesbaden: Otto Harrassowitz, 1988], 443 [p.110]). See Ramelli, *Causa della fondazione delle scuole*, 132, n. 23.

85 Syr. *melltā*, or 'the word'.

86 Syr. *huddāyā*. The 'guide of reason' is also mentioned in Ḥenānā, *On Golden Friday*, 57.3.

87 Syr. *tarrā'*. Scher wrongly suggests that this term derives from Gr. *theōría* (note 1).

eyes are blind,[88] and it would not be able to search into that powerful light, if our Lord himself had not performed his grace in us and revealed and showed us concerning his essence,[89] albeit in a manner fit only for children,[90] as Paul said: *Knowledge of God is revealed in these things*, and while showing how it is revealed, he said: *God revealed it in these things*,[91] and *to us again God has revealed by his spirit*.[92] And our Lord said: *To whomever the Son wills to reveal him*.[93] And: *I have made your name known among human beings*.[94] But if not, not even [337] this crumb of knowledge would be able to fix its gaze on that divine presence,[95] since all of his properties unspeakably transcend the thought and reason[96] of created things.

For also what we should know that we do not know, in my opinion, transcends knowledge. Therefore he who has determined that he has attained

88 This is a common motif, which ultimately derives from Plato. See, for example, Vasiliki Limberis, 'The Eyes Infected by Evil: Basil of Caesarea's Homily, On Envy', *Harvard Theological Review* 84 (1991): 163–84. For Neoplatonic examples of blinding the eye of the soul, see Simplicius, *in de Caelo* 7.74.5 (CAG 7.1; ed. J. L. Heilberg, 1894); ibid., *in Categorias* 8.8.5; the 'eye of the soul' is common: e.g. Clement, *Paed.* 2.1.2, *tò ómma tês psuchês* (ed. M. Marcovich [Leiden: Brill, 2002], 66.5).

89 Syr. *yāt*. The Syriac *yāt* is actually the archaic accusative marker used in the Peshitta of Gen 1:1. The form was not recognizable to Syriac exegetes who interpreted it as cognate with the existential particle, *it*. For example, see Ephrem's prose commentary on Gen 1:1, Ephrem the Syrian, *In Genesim et in Exodum Commentarii*, ed. and trans. R.-M. Tonneau (CSCO 152–23; Louvain: L. Durbecg, 1955), 1.1 (8/5); see also St. Ephrem the Syrian, *Selected Prose Works*, ed. Kathleen McVey, trans. Joseph P. Amar and Edward G. Mathews, Jr. (Fathers of the Church 91; Washington, DC: Catholic University of America Press, 1994), 74, n. 20. This interpretation was followed by many of the later exegetes, cf. T. Jansma, 'Investigations into the Early Syrian Fathers on Genesis: An Approach to the Exegesis of the Nestorian Church and to the Comparison of Nestorian and Jewish Exegesis', *Oudtestamentishe Studiën* 12 (1958): 101 and Antoine Guillaumont, 'Genèse 1, 1-2 selon les commentateurs Syriaques', in *IN PRINCIPIO: Interpretations des premiers verset de la Genese* (Études augustiniennes 152; Paris, 1973), 122–24.

90 Syr. *shabrā'it*. See the use of this word below (note 377). Cf. Ephrem the Syrian, *Sermones de Fide*, ed. Edmund Beck (CSCO 212–13; Louvain, Secrétariat du CSCO, 1961), 31:2 (trans. Brock, *The Luminous Eye*, 60): 'He asked for our form and put this on, and then, as a father with His children (*yalludē*), He spoke with our childish state (*shabrutan*).' See also 1 Cor 3:1–3 (though the Peshitta of this passage does not use *shabrā* for 'child').

91 Rom 1:19.

92 1 Cor 2:10. This could also be vocalized as passive: 'God is revealed'.

93 Mt 11:27.

94 Jn 17:6.

95 Syr. *shkintā*, equivalent to the Hebrew *Shekhinah*.

96 Syr. *melltā*, also 'word' or 'speech'.

knowledge even about things that are unknowable – an abortion is better than him, since it is complete stupidity. But if he knew God as unknowable, this one would be known by God as wise.

Distinctions and Learning

But because that (divine) essence is such a thing as this, let us see in what way we receive learning concerning it, and what is the difference between creatures and their creator. For although the names 'created' and 'creature' are general, they nevertheless include under themselves many genera and species.[97] Just as the name 'spirit', 'body', 'nature', or 'exists', although it is equal[98] in its external naming capacity,[99] nevertheless each one of them applies to[100] many different, dissimilar, various, and unequal things; thus also the names 'created' and 'coming into being', although equal, there are nevertheless many things under them.[101] Since[102] everything that exists is either substance or accident, each of these divisions is divided into many species, [338] these (entities) that are included under it. Therefore all substance that exists is either corporeal or incorporeal.

Body too is divided into the many distinctions that are under it: that is, then, the ensouled body and the one without soul, the one endowed with

97 Syr. *gensē*, from Gr. *génos*; Syr. *ādshē*, perhaps from the Greek *eîdos*.

98 The Aristotelian idea of the homonym lies behind this passage. Homonyms are words that share the same name but differ in definition and are thus similar only in name, but not in nature. The Syriac *shāwē b-* is used here to express the Greek prefix *homo-*. See, for example, Ammonius, *In Categorias* 6.8–10 (Ammonius, *On Aristotle's* Categories, 39). For the various renderings of the terms 'homonym' and 'synonym' in different Syriac translations of the *Categories*, see Hugonnard-Roche, *La logique d'Aristote du grec au syriaque*, 27. For example, Probus, following a Greek source, writes: 'the expression equal in name (*shawyat shmā*) (is divided) into different significations, such as the expression "dog" into "sea dog" [i.e. shark] and "land dog"', Hoffmann, *De Hermeneuticis*, 82.1–2 (Hoffmann suggests a Greek source for this example [134 note 120]). For a similar early example in Greek, see Ammonius, *In Categorias* 38.12–14 (Ammonius, *On Aristotle's* Categories, 48–49). The *Cause* thus argues in this section that the word 'exists' as it is applied to God and as it is applied to all beings is a homonym: it is the same word, but means something different in each case. This focus on homonyms can be found in other 'cause' literature (e.g., Cyrus of Edessa, *Six Explanations*, 100.8–20 [trans. 90.5–19]).

99 Syr. *ba-qrāytāh barrāytā*.

100 Lit. 'falls upon'.

101 The expressions 'created' and 'coming into being' are treated as polyonyms by the text, i.e. they have the same definition but are different names. 'But if they have their account in common but differ in name, they are called *polyonyms*, as is the case with *sword*, *scimitar*, and *sabre*', Ammonius, *In Categorias* 16.4–6 (Ammonius, *On Aristotle's* Categories, 23).

102 On the following passage, see Appendix II.

sense and the other deprived of it. Thus also the ensouled body is arranged into other distinctions: the body that is living and the one that is not, the one that moves, and the other deprived of movement; and again that one that is living and moves is divided also into other distinctions that are under it, that is, the rational and the non-rational, and again the rational into the spiritual and the psychic, and the non-rational into the living and the non-living; and again the spiritual is divided also into the limited and the unlimited, the one eternal and the other temporal, the one the cause of all things, the other is the effect that is from the cause of all things, which is God.

Because something is excellent not because it exists, but rather on account of what it is and in what manner it exists; for the former (i.e. existence) is universal, but the latter (i.e. quality) particular.[103] For a bull is better than a stone, not because it is body but because it is living and endowed with senses. A king or a priest (is better than the mass of people),[104] not because he is a human being, but by his rank and his honour. An angel [339] also is better than a human being by his immortality, and God than his creation by his essence and his eternality. For 'existing' is something in common to him and us, but this individual thing belongs to him alone. For example, the human being excels all bodies, not because he is corporeal, but because he speaks.[105] And, again, an angel (excels) all bodies, not because he is incorporeal, but because he is living and immortal. In like manner also God excels all things, not because he exists, but because of how he exists.

Although he is so high in his nature, exalted in his lordship, and distinct from everything which has come into being, nevertheless he took it upon himself to be said and spoken[106] of in the compound language[107] of creatures for the sake of our learning. For also in learning thus you find that all the lower distinctions take the appellation of the higher ones; but the higher ones are not called by the names of the lower ones. For the human being is living and ensouled of essence, but not everything that is living is a human being, such as every animal, bird, and creeping thing. And again everything which is living is ensouled, such as all plants; but not everything which is a nature

103 See note 66 above on the translation of these terms.

104 T has 'a priest than the mass of people (*w-kāhnā men quṭnā*)' and lacks 'a king'. The comparative phrase ('than the mass of people') may be an interpolation since a comparison is implicit in the passage. The absence of 'a king' from T fits with the change to the singular in the subsequent clause.

105 I.e. he is endowed with reason.

106 Syr. *net'emar w-netmallal*. See note 58 above.

107 Syr. *mamlā mrakkbā*. See note 63 above.

is ensouled, such as rocks and material[108] species, and again not everything that is a nature is a body, such as angels and souls.

Divine Illumination

[340] Nevertheless, although everything that exists is divided into all these distinctions, learning about the creator and creation is only found in these two orders,[109] I mean angels and human beings. But because these are too weak to consider that divine essence, he has established for us an invisible lamp,[110] the soul within us, and he has filled it with the oil of immortal life, and he has placed in it continuous wicks[111] with intellectual thoughts, and he has caused to be grasped in it the light of the divine mind, by which we are able to see and to distinguish, as that woman[112] who lost one of the ten *zuz*,[113] the hidden things of the creator, and to go around all of the rich treasury of his kingdom, until we ourselves also find that *zuz* upon which is stamped the glorious image[114] of him, the eternal King of Kings.[115] For (we would not be able to do this)[116] if he had not given us this light, as John says: *In it was life and the life was the light of human beings*,[117] that is, rational power, such as our Lord said: *If the light within you is darkness, how much will be your darkness*;[118] *for if the blind lead the blind, the two of them will fall into the pit*.[119] And because of this he commands us: *Walk while you have* [341]

108 Syr. *hulāyē*, an adjective deriving ultimately from Gr. *húlē*.

109 Syr. *tegmē*, from Gr. *tágma*.

110 The same Syriac word for 'lamp' appears in the Lukan parable employed below.

111 Scher notes that C adds here in the margin: 'These are things in which wicks of candles are placed, and they are made from iron and from brass; *shbr'* in Arabic is hot'. This is not true and it is not clear what Arabic word the scribe is referring to.

112 The Parable of the Lost Coin (Lk 15:8–10) received esoteric exegesis. For example, Isho'dad of Merv provides more than one interpretation, including one where 'the ten drachmae are ten Orders of Angels; the losing of one is Man, he who buried in sin as in the grave, the likeness which he received from the beginning; the Candle is the Incarnation; the Fire is the Godhead; the wick is Humanity; etc.' (Ishodad of Merv, *Commentary on Gospels*, 3.50.2–51.20 (1.180–81); Gregory of Nyssa, *On Virginity*, in Werner Jaeger et al., ed., *Opera Ascetica* (Leiden : Brill, 1952), 300.13–302.4.

113 The original Greek version uses *drachmas* as the coinage. The standard Aramaic equivalent to a *drachma* is a *zuz*.

114 Syr. *yuqnā*, from Gr. *eikṓn*.

115 This title fits the contemporary Persian context.

116 I follow Scher's insertion, since the statement would not make sense otherwise.

117 Jn 1:4.

118 Mt 6:23.

119 Lk 6:39.

the light of rationality in the divine wisdom, *lest the darkness* of error and ignorance *overtake you*.[120]

Therefore it is the lot of this rational and illuminated mind, which is the likeness of God, its maker, to dwell in two places: the one, upon the earth while clothed in a corporeal garment, going about within a fleshy enclosure; the other, in turn, up above – the portion fell to it that it might walk within the open plain of air;[121] for such as these are all the spiritual orders.[122]

Mind as Captain and the Purification of the Faculties

Now because our speech is about this mind that is within us, let us see how it is in us and what sort is its place of dwelling. For hitherto the wise men of the Greeks have been conquered (in their reasoning), since they even attribute the name of divinity to it (i.e. the mind). Now its cause and its foundation is the soul that is fettered within us, which has three cognitive faculties:[123] reason, thought, and reckoning;[124] from these are born three others, that is, desire, anger, and will;[125] the mind is above all these things,

120 Jn 12:35.

121 Syr. *ā'ar*, from Gr. *aḗr*.

122 Syr. *tegmē*, from Gr. *tágma*.

123 Syr. *ḥaylē yādo'tānē* equivalent to Gr. *dunámeis gnōstikaí, noētikaí*, or *theōrētikaí*. 'For of the cognitive faculties some are logical, others are alogical, the logical ones are the mind, thought, and opinion; the alogical ones imagination and sensation', Philoponus, *In Analytica Priora* 32.17–18 (CAG 13.2; ed. M. Wallies, 1905). Of the five cognitive faculties of the soul, the three logical ones are reason, thought, and opinion (e.g., Ammonius, *In Analytica Priora*, 24.32–33 [CAG 4.6; ed. M. Wallies, 1899]). See the editor's comment at Philoponus, *On Aristotle on the Intellect (de Anima 3.4–8)*, trans. W. Charlton (Ithaca, NY: Cornell University Press, 1991), 16.

124 Again, these are based on Greek equivalents: 'reason' (Syr. *hawnā*, Gr. *noûs*); 'thought' (Syr. *tar'itā*, Gr. *diánoia*); 'reckoning' (rendering the Syriac term) (Syr. *maḥshabtā*, Gr. *dóxa*). Similar cognitive faculties show up in the sixth-century Syriac commentary on the *Prior Analytics* attributed to Probus. A. Van Hoonacker, 'Le Traité du Philosophe Syrien Probus sur les premiers analytiques d'Aristote', *JA* ser. 9 vol. 16 (1900): 88. Probus does not divide these into logical and illogical. The text presents the five cognitive faculties as: *hawnā, tar'itā, ḥaylā meshkḥānā, fantasyā* (Gr. *phantasía*), *regshā* (Gr. *aísthēsis*) (the latter two being the non-logical parts of the soul). His term for the Greek *dóxa*, 'opinion', is *ḥaylā meshkḥānā*, in contrast to the *Cause*'s *maḥshabtā*.

125 For the three appetitive parts of the soul, see *De Anima* 414b2: 'desire' (Syr. *regtā*, Gr. *epithumía*); 'anger' (Syr. *ḥemtā*; Gr. *thumós*); 'will' (Syr. *ṣebyānā*, Gr. *boúlēsis*). See also Ammonius, *In De Interpretatione* 5.1ff (trans. Ammonius, *On Aristotle's* On Interpretation 1–8, 14); Ammonius, *In Isagogen* 11.16–18; Olympiodorus, *In Platonis Gorgiam* (ed. L. G. Westerink, Leipzig: Teubner, 1970), 12.3.12–15; David, *Prolegomena philosophiae* 79.6ff (CAG 18.2; ed. A. Busse, 1904); Alexander of Aphrodisias, *De Anima* 74.2 and 78.23 (CAG

as a wise driver and a ready captain,[126] gazing at a distance and keeping his ship laden with these treasures away from the crags of error and the thick fog[127] of ignorance.[128] While with the former intellectual portion[129] [342] he purifies[130] the learned powers of the soul,[131] not so that they then may understand one thing for something else, but so that they may grasp the truth and exactitude of things, with the other, the effectual portion, it strains clean in turn the animal powers[132] of the soul and it prepares them so that their

---

suppl. 2.1; ed. I. Bruns, 1887). The three standard forms of 'appetite' (*órexis*) are rendered by the same Syriac terms in the *Discourse on the Causes of the Universe*, the work by Alexander of Aphrodisias attributed to Sergius of Rēsh'aynā in the seventh-century manuscript, British Library Add. 14658. 99b1.16–107b.2.14; see Dana R. Miller, 'Sargis of Resh'aina: On What the Celestial Bodies Know', *Symposium Syriacum VI 1992* (OCA 247; Rome, 1994), 224.

126 Both 'driver' and 'captain' derive from the Greek (*hēníochos* and *kubernḗtēs*). The word *hēníochos* is attested in Syriac as early as Ephrem (see *Sermones de Fide*, ed. Edmund Beck [CSCO 212–13; Louvain, Secrétariat du CSCO, 1961], 3.464; 7.418). It shows up three times in the contemporary school text, Cyrus of Edessa, *Six Explanations*, 9.16; 39.22; 42.16. Brock notes instances of *hawnā* and *mad'ā* as *kubernḗtēs* at Isaac of Nineveh, *Second Part*, 17.12 nt 3 (versio). The two terms have a philosophical provenance, e.g. Aristotle, *De Anima* 413a9 questions whether the soul in the body is like a sailor in a ship. See also Anonymus, *In Categorias*, 14.32–15.3 (CAG 23.2; ed. M. Hayduck, 1883); Philoponus, *De Opificio Mundi*, 3: 584.6-22; Plotinus, *Enneads*, ed. Paul Henry and Hans-Rudolf Schwyzer (Oxford: Clarendon, 1964–1982), 4.3.21.

127 Syr. *'arpēlā*. This word is commonly used to describe the unknowability of the divine essence. See, e.g., Isaac of Nineveh, *Second Part* (versio), 5.1 n. 6 (p. 6), 5.26 n. 6 (p. 42), 10.17 n. 3 (42).

128 Ship and sailing metaphors are common. For example, Isaac of Nineveh, *Second Part*, 17.12, uses the same word for 'crag' (Syr. *shqiphā*) as the *Cause* in a similar metaphor for the dangers the intellect encounters in the world.

129 The distinction between the two parts of philosophy, the speculative (or theoretical) and the practical, is standard in the Neoplatonic commentary tradition (as well as in other philosophical literatures), e.g. Ammonius, *In Isagogen*, 6.6–7; Philoponus, *In Categorias,* 12.12ff; Olympiodorus, *Prolegomena*, 22.8–12 (CAG 12.1; ed. A. Busse, 1902). The former seeks the truth, while the latter seeks the good. These two parts of philosophy are equated with the different parts of the soul, as we find in the *Cause* where they are mapped onto its two parts. The cognitive (or intellectual) portion and the active portion of the soul, both of which contribute to the purifying process, are also clearly based on original Greek terms: 'intellectual portion' (Syr. *mnātā yadu'tānitā*, Gr. *méros theōrētikón*) and 'effectual portion' (Syr. *mnātā sā'ortā*, Gr. *méros praktikón*). Philoponus, *In de Anima* 15.520.21ff describes the parts of the soul (on Aristotle, *De Anima* 429a10).

130 See notes LN 36 and LN 39 on the language of purification.

131 The 'learned powers' (Syr. *ḥaylē yādo'ē*) may represent the Greek 'cognitive faculties' (Gr. *energeíai* or *dunámeis gnōstikaí*).

132 The 'animal powers' (Syr. *ḥaylē ḥayutānē*) represents Gr. *energeíai zōtikaí*. 'Animal' is another way of referring to the 'appetitive' faculties of the soul. In Ammonius, *In Isagogen* 11.16–8; 11.17, *zōtikaí* is a synonym for *orektikaí* (see also Ammonius, *In de Interpr*, 5.1ff).

course may not be in things that are of no benefit, but that their movements be suitable and right.[133]

For because all of the things over which the mind goes are distinct and different from one another; so that it is not drowned in their diversity and harmed by their opposition as a swimmer by the tempests of the sea, he seeks for himself, instead of a leather bottle (as a flotation device) and a light boat, a new ship of rationality by which he may go over the surface of the whole world with confidence, and he takes from it, instead of pearls and precious stones, the wisdom of the fear of God, that which is acquired by a correct knowledge.

Perfection of Intelligence and Action

For because all things doubly established in learning are divided into two kinds: intelligence and action; it is right to know that the perfection of intelligence is [343] the exact comprehension of the knowledge of all beings, the perfection of action is the excellence of good things.[134]

Therefore because there is an opposite attached to each one of these, as colour[135] is to a body, and accident is to essence, that is, to the perfection of intelligence and action;[136] on this account, rationality was sought as an intermediary that it might distinguish for us this opposition[137] from the true perfection of each one of the portions of the soul. For if the perfection of intelligence is exact knowledge of all things that exist, it is certain that its opposite is ignorance. Because of this we are in need of rationality by which we distinguish the truth from falsehood. For what is revealed to be the truth – this we grasp by healthy conviction, which is the knowledge of things. Yet whatever is borne witness to by a true demonstration to be a lie, this thing we leave out of all remembrance of truth. It is certain then that without rationality it (i.e. truth) is not distinguished correctly or known by

133 Parallels to the above passage can be found in Sergius of Rēsh'aynā's commentary on Aristotle's *Categories*, Hugonnard-Roche, *La logique d'Aristote du grec au syriaque*, 191 and comments at 203–09.

134 For this same formulation of 'knowledge' (Syr. *ida'tā*, Gr. *gnôsis*, *theōría*), 'action' (Syr. *sā'orutā*, Gr. *prâxis*) and 'perfection' (Syr. *shumlāyā*, Gr. *teleíōsis*), see Ammonius, *In Isagogen* 6.6ff and 11.18–22.

135 T has 'shadow'.

136 The analogy that colour is to body as accident is to essence derives from Aristotelian logic.

137 Opposition is common in Aristotelian physics. See, for example, the discussion of opposites in *De Generatione et Corruptione*, II.2.

those who judge these things in a human manner. For he who does not speak in the divine spirit, his teaching will be in need of lower, rational things for it to be believed by those who hear it.[138]

[344] Thus in turn also in that other portion, 'action', now if its perfection is the selection of good things, as we have shown, it is clear that evil is the opposite of the good. On account of this, we need rationality in this portion, 'action', so that it may distinguish for us the good from the evil, lest while we rush after the good we choose the evil by ignorance and we let go of the good. Since it is certain that no one willingly finds the evil and rebukes the good;[139] whatever is seen by means of this art[140] to be good, that thing is truly good; and again whatever seems evil, by necessity it certainly is evil.

Reason for Corporeal Creation

Therefore by this wonderful instrument[141] of rationality the mind paints all

138 See a similar statement in Sergius of Rēsh'aynā's commentary on the *Categories*: '[...] Without all this [i.e. Aristotle's works on logic] neither can the meaning of writings on medicine be grasped, nor can the opinions of the philosophers be known, nor indeed the true sense of the divine scriptures in which the hope of our salvation is revealed – unless a person receive divine power as a result of the exalted nature of his way of life, with the result that he has no need of human training. As far as human power is concerned, however, there can be no other course or path to all the areas of knowledge except by way of training in Logic' (trans. Sebastian Brock, *A Brief Outline of Syriac Literature* [Moran Etho 9; Kottayam: SEERI, 1997], 204). The original Syriac of this text remains in manuscript form. See also the prologue of Paul the Persian, *Introduction to Logic*, 1.1–4.25 (Syriac) / 1–5 (Latin). Compare this to Ammonius, *In Categorias* 15.4–10 (Ammonius, *On Aristotle's* Categories, 22).

139 This is a standard idea in Platonic philosophy.

140 Syr. *umānutā*, which is perhaps here equivalent to the Gr. *téchnē*.

141 Syr. *urganāwn*, from Gr. *órganon*. According to Ammonius, it is 'logic' that 'discriminates for us the true from the false and the good from the bad' (Ammonius, *In Categorias* 13.5–6 [Ammonius, *On Aristotle's* Categories, 19]). See also Simplicius, *In Categ* 14.19–22. Cf. Sergius's commentary on the *Categories*: 'Logic is the instrument that clearly distinguishes in knowledge the true from the false and in practice defines again the good from the bad', Giuseppe Furlani, 'Sul trattato di Sergio di Rêsh'aynâ circa le categorie', *Rivista di Studi filosofici e religiosi* 3 (1922): 139; see also 141. The Syriac author 'Probus' in the sixth century also follows the Neoplatonic model: 'For when art sought to adorn the soul, it saw that there are two faculties of the soul, the intellectual and the active. The intellectual is that one by which we know things; the active is that one by which we do things. While art wants to adorn that intellectual (faculty) and that active (faculty), it sent out two parts, that is, theory and practice, that through theory it might adorn the intellectual (faculty) and through practice the active (faculty). For theory teaches about the cognition of things, practice about the correcting of habits' (Hoffmann, *De Hermeneuticis*, Syriac 65.18–26, Latin 92). As stated already above, the *Organon* is also the name for the earlier part of Aristotle's logical corpus: the *Categories*,

the adorned images of exact knowledge and by it casts a glorious statue[142] of that prototype,[143] so that then the intelligence and the rationality of this mind be neither idle nor useless. Since it has no alphabet, by which it might compose names and read[144] them, receive learning about that essence, as well as make manifest the authority of his lordship, by necessity as a training exercise and a sign of his freedom, the creator established this corporeality and adorned it with powers[145] and colours,[146] and he divided it up into genera[147] and species[148] and distinguished it by figures[149] and activities,[150] and he conferred upon it individual properties.[151] [345] He brought it (i.e. corporeality) in and set it in this spacious gulf between heaven and earth. As if upon some tablet he wrote and composed all the visible bodies that it (i.e. mind) might read them and from them know that one who was the cause

---

De Interpretatione, and *Prior Analytics* I.1–7.

142 Syr. *adriyanṭē*, from Gr. *andriás*, *andriántos*. Like the Neoplatonists who follow Aristotle, the text maintains a representative view of knowledge, which means that we know things by making images in our heads about them: 'And it is not possible to think without an image' (*On Memory* 449b, 30–31); more broadly, see *De Anima* III.7

143 Syr. *tape(n)kā* (from Persian). This term is commonly used to refer to God as the original model or prototype for the human being, e.g., 'For the human being is like unto God as the image to the prototype' (Lucas Van Rompay, ed. and trans., *Le Commentaire sur Genèse-Exode 9,32 du manuscript (olim) Diyarbakir 22* [CSCO 483–84; Louvain: Peeters, 1986], 21.7–8 [see nn. 158 and 159 on pp. 28–29]). Van Rompay notes that Gr. *archétupon* shows up similarly in fragments of Theodore of Mopsuestia, the source for this metaphor. See also Cyrus of Edessa, *Six Explanations*, 97.11. At 120.20 Cyrus instead uses *rēsh tuphsā* the calque of *archétupon*. See his use of this imagery at 43.18–45.27 (trans. 37–39).

144 This word is cognate with the term *mhaggyānā*, an office at the school. It can also be translated as 'read syllable by syllable, vocalize, or meditate upon'. For a discussion of the Hebrew cognate and its oral significance, see William A. Graham, *Beyond the Written Word: Oral Aspects of Scripture in the History of Religion* (Cambridge: Cambridge University Press, 1987), 134–35.

145 Syr. *ḥaylē*, equivalent to Gr. *dunámeis* or *energeíai*.

146 Syr. *gawnē*, equivalent to Gr. *chrṓmata*.

147 Syr. *gensē*, from Gr. *génos*.

148 Syr. *ādshē*, equivalent to Gr. *eídē*.

149 Syr. *eskimē*, from Gr. *schḗmata*. The word *schema* is commonly used in Syriac. Like the Greek word from which it derives it has a diversity of meanings. In a discussion of creation it is fitting that the *Cause* uses this word to describe the different structures of the world (see also Jacob of Sarug, *Homilies*, 3:1.8; 6.15; 8.20). However, in a context where logic is being addressed this word can also mean 'logical figure', the basic configuration of argument in Aristotle's syllogistic. See for example Furlani, 'Due scoli filosofici attribuiti a Sergio di Teodosiopoli (Rêš'aynâ)', 142–45.

150 Syr. *ma'bdānwātā*, equivalent to Gr. *energeíai* or *dunámeis*.

151 Syr. *dilāyātā iḥidāyātā*, equivalent to Gr. *idiá*.

of this learning,[152] as Paul said: *They seek and search for God and from his creation they find him,*[153] and that it might take delight in desirable goods, be profited by its wonderful beauties, plait and set upon his head a crown of joys, adorned with the beauties and praises of that good Lord.[154]

Angelic Activity Above

While the dwelling place of that prior portion of the invisible ones is in the paths above and in the expanses of the firmament, as Daniel says: *The man Gabriel, whom I saw before in a vision, fluttered and flew and came from heaven,*[155] and our Lord said to the Jews: *Now you will see the heavens opened and the angels of God ascending and descending to the Son of Man,*[156] with Jacob's ladder, which also gave a hint of these things, while they have the authority to work all of the spacious plain of air, from the heights to the deep, in advantageous and refined[157] variations, as it is said: *The have the power and do his commandments and (they are) his servants*[158] *who do his will.*[159]

The Human Capacity to Traverse the Firmament to Heaven and Back, and the Human Authority over Creation

[346] But lest this lower portion be saddened and envy the honour of its higher mate, he (i.e. God) honoured it with the name 'his image and

152 For Aristotle thinking and perceiving are analogous activities (*De Anima* 427a18–21). 'To the thinking soul images serve as if they were contents of perception (and when it asserts or denies them to be good or bad it avoids or pursues them). That is why the soul never thinks without an image. The process is like that in which the air modifies the pupil in this or that way and the pupil transmits the modification to some third thing (and similarly in hearing), while the ultimate point of arrival is one, a single mean, with different manners of being' (*De Anima* 431a14–19). The source of knowledge for Aristotle is perception (as opposed to Plato, who puts the intellect first). From perception we use imagination to form an image by which to think. This is why Aristotle compares the mind to a writing-tablet (*De Anima* 430a1).

153 Acts 17:27. This is the other New Testament passage from which a notion of natural theology is often derived (along with Rom 1:19).

154 Cf. Cosmas Indicopleustes, *Christian Topography*, V.58–59.

155 Dan 9:21.

156 Jn 1:51.

157 Syr. *mṣarrphānē* can also have an active meaning of 'refining' or 'purging'.

158 Syr. *mshammshānē*. This term is also used for 'deacons' within the church, the dual usage here suggesting a further parallelism between heaven and earth.

159 Ps 103:20, 21. Cf. Cosmas Indicopleustes, *Christian Topography*, IX.3.

likeness',[160] and he placed upon it the name of his divinity:[161] *I have said, 'You are Gods and children of the Exalted all of you.'*[162] He (i.e. God) gave it (i.e. the lower portion) the power to ascend to heaven and the upper vaults[163] and, just as in a royal palace[164] and the upper chambers,[165] to go about in all the streets and ways[166] above the upper heavens.[167] Sometimes he (i.e. the lower portion) descends to take pleasure in that whole wide gulf between the firmament and heaven, while he is with himself alone[168] as if in a royal palace.[169] When he wants, he sends himself forth from there to this corporeal[170] place beneath the firmament and he flies in that fiery place and he is not scorched,[171] and he goes over the stars as if over rocks in the midst of a river, and he does not sink, and he converses with his spiritual brothers and all the orders[172] of angels with true love.[173] And because from time to time he casts the glance of his mind at the course of the sun and at

160 Gen 1:26.

161 Syr. *shmā d-alāhutēh*, or 'his divine name'.

162 Ps 82:6. See the use of this passage by Evagrius of Pontus and Bābai the Great's discussion of it in his commentary on Evagrius's *Kephalaia Gnostica* (Frankenberg, ed., *Euagrius Ponticus*, 292–94), as well as comments on this passage at Becker, *Fear of God*, 182–83.

163 Syr. *gphiphē*. This term may be a rendering of some Latin or Greek term, e.g. Lat. *arcus*. Compare this to Peshitta Job 21:33, where the same word means 'clods' (i.e. rounded). The heavens are commonly understood as 'vaulted' in the *Christian Topography* (e.g., Cosmas Indicopleustes, *Christian Topography*, II:19–22).

164 Lit. 'a palace of a kingdom'. Syr. *pālāṭin*, from Gr. *palátion*. The number of words of Greek origin in this particular passage suggests that it may ultimately rely on a Greek source.

165 Syr. *ṭriqlinē*, from Gr. *tríklinos*.

166 Syr. *plāṭawātā*, from Gr. *plateîa*.

167 On the division between heaven and earth as two worlds and much of the comogony found here, see Wanda Wolska, *La Topographie Chrétienne de Cosmas Indicopleustès, Théologie et Science au VIe siècle* (Paris: Presses Universitaires de France, 1962), 37–61, 98–105 *passim*. See examples cited at Cosmas Indicopleustes, *Christian Topography*, III.408–10.

168 Syr. *itaw(hy) bēt lēh wa-l-naphshēh*.

169 Syr. *āpadnā*. On the disputed origin of this word, see Michael Sokoloff, *A Dictionary of Jewish Babylonian Aramaic of the Talmudic and Geonic Periods* (Ramat-Gan, Israel: Bar Ilan University; Baltimore and London: The Johns Hopkins University Press, 2002), 154. For the heavens as vaulted and the solidity of the firmament, see Cosmas Indicopleustes, *Christian Topography*, III. 401–02. Cf. Cyrus of Edessa, Six *Explanations*, 140.16–141.2 (trans. 124.3–18) for a similar notion of the firmament.

170 Syr. *pagrānā*.

171 On crossing through the firmament, see also Cyrus of Edessa, *Six Explanations*, 18.12–29 (trans. 15.22–16.2), 19.13–22 (trans. 16.14–22), and esp. (trans. 124.3–18).

172 Syr. *tegmē*, from Gr. *tágma*.

173 The word translated as 'converses' (*met'nē*) can refer to sexual intimacy as well. This may explain the emphasis on 'true love', that is, non-sexual intimacy.

the changes of the moon and at the arrangement of the stars – things effected by the working of his brothers[174] – lest he be envious of them and grow sick from his corporeal service,[175] his Lord gives even to him from time to time authority over them (i.e. luminaries) [347] that by his command they may be led, as we see Joshua bar Nun, who confined one over Gibeon and that other one he fastened over the Valley of Aijalon;[176] and Isaiah commanded it (i.e. the sun) and *it turned back ten degrees* and he taught his mates that the luminaries are creatures, not creators.[177]

To put it briefly, in order to admonish him God gave him (i.e. the human being) authority[178] over everything that exists in the heights as well as in the deep, on the sea and on dry land, over the fish and over all of the creeping things, over the domestic animals and over all of the wild ones, over birds and over all quick-winged creatures, since he (i.e. God) wants him to use them, whether as his food or for his needs or for his pleasure and likewise also as his covering.

Human Fall due to the Deceiver

Because the mind did what was opposed to the first teaching that it received and it put out its eye of discernment from the understanding of rationality and it obeyed the words of its deceiver, that is, his older brother who first sinned and fell from his rank, he who is a liar and the father of falsehood, this one, who continually *acts zealously within the sons of disobedience*;[179] on account of this [348] a verdict[180] went out against him: *You are dust*

174 Cf. Cosmas Indicopleustes, *Christian Topography*, IX.3, 13–14; Narsai, *Homilies on Creation*, II.388–89; VI. 133–54. On Theodore of Mopsuestia as the source for this motif, see Gignoux's comments (Narsai, *Homilies on Creation*, 487–88).

175 Syr. *teshmeshtā pagrānāytā*. The term *teshmeshtā* is used often to refer to the liturgical service.

176 Jos 10:12. See the use of this verse at Cosmas Indicopleustes, *Christian Topography*, III.59

177 2 Kgs 20:11; Isa 38:8–9. The quoted words are closest to Isa 38:9. See the use of 2 Kgs 20:11 at Cosmas Indicopleustes, *Christian Topography*, VIII.15.

178 This is also a theme in the writings of Theodore of Mopsuestia and Narsai. See, e.g., Narsai, *Homilies on Creation*, IV:86.

179 Eph 2:2.

180 Syr. *apāphasis*. Gr. *apóphasis*. It was standard to employ this Greek word in addressing this part of the tale, e.g. Cyrus of Edessa, *Six Explanations*, 30.19, 88.25, 89.18; Narsai, *Homilies on Creation*, I.351, IV.224; Cosmas Indicopleustes, *Christian Topography*, II.88. See also the profession of faith from the Council of 585 (*Synodicon Orientale*, 135; trans. in Brock, 'The Christology of the Church of the East', 137).

and you will turn back to dust, and you will eat the grass of the field.[181] However, instruction and learning[182] he (i.e. God) did not withhold from it (i.e. the mind); rather, in many variations[183] he confers upon him learning concerning himself, lest when he neglects it[184] he perish completely and become a vessel of harm.

Creation as Reading Lesson[185]

Because the spiritual powers are prior in creation and more excellent in substance,[186] God brought forth his teaching to them, lest they fall into error and falsely suppose great things about themselves, when he wrote a scroll of imperceptible light with his finger of creative power and with (his) command, (a scroll) which he had them read with an audible voice:[187]

181 Gen 3:18–19.

182 These two terms, *mardutā* and *yullphānā*, may not be simply synonyms, but are employed to refer to profane and religious learning respectively (see 416 below). T reads: 'the instruction of learning'.

183 Syr. *shuḥlāphē*. This idea derives from Theodore of Mopsuestia, e.g. *On the Nicene Creed*, 151 (44).

184 Or 'him'.

185 Theodore of Mopsuestia's commentary on Genesis lies behind the understanding of Genesis 1 in the following passage. See discussion in Becker, *Fear of God*, 122–24. The most significant collection of Syriac fragments of Theodore's commentary on Genesis is Sachau's edition (Theodore of Mopsuestia, *Fragments*). Fragments can also be found in: Raymond M. Tonneau, 'Théodore de Mopsueste. Interprétation (du Livre) de la Genèse', *LM* 66 (1953): 45–64 and Taeka Jansma, 'Théodore de Mopsueste, Interprétation du Livre de la Genèse. Fragments de la version syriaque (B.M. Add. 17,189, fol. 17–21)', *LM* 75 (1962), 63–92. Quotations from the Greek text can be found in the *Catenae* tradition as well as in the refutation of Theodore's ideas in John Philoponus's *De Opificio Mundi*. The angels in this passage learn by analogy, an idea that also comes from Theodore's exegesis. A comparison between the creation and a reading lesson can be found earlier at Narsai, *Homilies on Creation*, II.250–54; II.352–57. On the following passage, also see A. H. Becker, 'Bringing the Heavenly Academy Down to Earth: Approaches to the Imagery of Divine Pedagogy in the East-Syrian Tradition', in *Heavenly Realms and Earthly Realities in Late Antique Religions*, ed. R. Boustan and A. Y. Reed (Cambridge: Cambridge University Press, 2004), 174–94. We find a critique of this kind of reading of Genesis 1 in Gregory of Nyssa's *Contra Eunomium*, ed. W. Jaeger (Brill: Leiden, 1960), II, 227–61 (292–302) (=Migne PG 45.2. 987–99), translation in NPNF, 2nd ser. vol. 5, 273–77.

186 Syr. *usiya'*, from Gr. *ousía*.

187 The 'command' seems to be God's jussive statement in Gen 1:3. Scher translates this line '...et à voix haute Il le lut devant eux en disant', apparently trying to avoid the oddity of the angels saying 'Let there be light'. However, God would say this before the angels say it, if 'to cause to read' (*aqri*) means to make the students repeat what the teacher says. In our own

Let there be light, and there was light,[188] and because there was an understanding mind in them, at that very moment they understood[189] that everything that comes into being comes into being from another and everyone who is in authority is commanded by someone who is in authority, and from this they knew exactly that that one who brought this excellent nature into being also created them. Therefore all of them in a group with an audible voice repaid their creator with thanks, as he (i.e. God) said to Job: *When I was creating the stars of dawn, all my angels shouted with a loud voice and praised me.*[190]

[349][191] In a similar manner we have a practice, after we have a child read the simple letters[192] and repeat them, we join them one to another and from them we put together names that he may read syllable by syllable[193] and be trained.[194] Thus also that eternal teacher did, after he had them repeat

---

classrooms we often hear the teacher say, 'repeat after me'. God is specifically analogized to a 'reader' (*maqryānā*), one of the offices in the School of Nisibis (the verb *aqri* with the preposition *'al* is similar to the Arabic usage). This passage may contain an implicit spiritualizing critique of the later reception of Jewish law since it alludes to Exod 31:18: 'he gave him the two tablets of the covenant, tablets of stone, written with the finger of God'.

188 Gen 1:3. Or 'light came into being'. The passage seems to suggest that Syriac was deemed the first language, a claim not uncommon in Late Antiquity, especially among Syriac Christians. Milka Rubin, 'The Language of Creation or the Primordial Language: A Case of Cultural Polemics in Antiquity', *Journal of Jewish Studies* 49 (1998): 322–28. See, e.g., Abraham Levene, *The Early Syrian Fathers on Genesis* (London: Taylor's Foreign Press, 1951), 86.

189 The double usage of the root *s-k-l* ('understand') may be due to the suggestive false etymology of *eskolē* ('school') from this same root. See note 413 below.

190 Job 38:7. The use of this line from Job in this context derives from Theodore's exegesis of Genesis 1 (Theodore of Mopsuestia, *Fragments*, 5). See also Cosmas Indicopleustes, *Christian Topography*, III.13.

191 See the discussion of the following passage at Becker, *Fear of God*, 130–34.

192 Syr. *ātwātā pshiṭātā*, a Syriac calque of the Greek *tà haplâ stoicheîa*, which is used to refer to the smallest and therefore indivisible components of matter in Greek physics.

193 Syr. *nehgē*. The verb rendered 'to read syllable by syllable' may also be translated as 'to vocalize' or 'to meditate'. See note 144 above.

194 Metaphors of reading and writing are common in the works of Evagrius of Pontus, especially when he addresses the lower form of contemplation, *theōría phusikḗ*. See, e.g., Evagrius' *Letter to Melania*, Frankenberg, ed., *Euagrius Ponticus*, 612, 614, 616; trans. M. Parmentier, 'Evagrius of Pontus' "Letter to Melania" I', *Bijdragen, tijdschrift voor filisofie en theologie* 46 (1985): 8, 8–9, 10, 11; repr. in Everett Ferguson, ed., *Forms of Devotion: Conversion, Worship, Spirituality, and Asceticism* (New York: Garland, 1999), 278, 278–79, 280, 281. Such metaphors show up throughout Evagrius' works: 'As those who teach letters to children trace them on tablets, thus also Christ, teaching his wisdom to rational beings, has traced it in corporeal nature' (Parmentier, 'Evagrius of Pontus' "Letter to Melania" I', 22). See

the alphabet, then he arranged it (i.e. the alphabet) with the great name of the construction of the firmament[195] and he read it in front of them that they might understand that he is the creator of all of them, and as he orders them, they complete his will, and because they are quick-witted, they receive teaching quickly. In six days he taught them a wholly accurate teaching; at one time in the gathering together of the waters and in the growth of the trees; at another in the coming into being of the creeping things; and then at another in the creation of the animals and in the division of the luminaries, with these then also in (the creation of) the birds of wing, until he made them comprehend the number ten;[196] and he taught them again something else in the creation of the human being; and from then on he handed over to them the visible creation, that like letters they might write them in their continuous variations and read syllable by syllable with them the name of the creator and organizer[197] of all. And he let them go and allowed them to be in this spacious house of the school, which is of the earth.[198] He entrusted them with a vessel much greater than this sphere which makes the luminaries to revolve,[199] in which they might continually delight themselves and not sit

---

also Evagrius of Pontus, *Kephalaia Gnostica*, 3.57 (p. 121); *Praktikos* 92 (trans. Sinkewicz, *Evagrius of Pontus*, 112). For another East-Syrian passage describing this process, see Thomas of Edessa's *On the Birth of Christ* (S. J. Carr, *Thomas Edesseni tractatus de Nativitate D. N. Christi, textum syriacum edidit, notis illustravit, latine reddidit* [Rome: R. Academiae Lynceorum, 1898], 27.15–28.5), and on this passage, see Paolo Bettiolo, 'Scuola ed Economia Divina nella Catechesi della Chiesa di Persia: Appunti su un testo di Tommaso di Edessa († ca 542)', in *Esegesi e Catechesi nei Padri (secc. IV–VII)*, ed. S. Felici (Biblioteca di Scienze Religiose 112; Rome, 1994), 152–53; see p. 154 for a discussion of similar passages in Thomas's text.

195 Syr. *shmā rabbā d-tuqqānēh da-rqi'ā*. We could translate this line more fully as 'he put the letters together with a great name which would lead to the creation of the firmament and that name is "firmament"'.

196 Ten is also important as the number of categories or predicates in Aristotelian logic. The number ten is significant in Rabbinic exegesis and also shows up in the ten *sephirot* in Jewish mysticism. It appears especially in discussions of creation (Ginzburg, *Legends of the Jews*, 5: 63, n. 1). It is also midrashically connected to the ten commandments (ibid. 3:104–06 and relevant notes). Furthermore, ten is the numerical equivalent of the letter *yod*, the first letter in God's name.

197 Syr. *mṭaksānā*, deriving from Gr. *táxis*.

198 This sentence is difficult. The 'wide' or 'spacious house' appears in Narsai's *Homilies on Creation*, I. 103, and seems to derive from Theodore's exegesis. Another rendering could be 'in this place of the school, more spacious than the earth' (*bēt rwiḥā d-bēt yullphānā d-men ar'ā*). There may be a lacuna here, since there seems to be a verb missing. See also the *Cave of Treasures*, III.15 (24–25).

199 The text is awkward. T has a lacuna at this point.

idly.[200] He endowed them with quick wings, [350] by which they might fly in this whole vehicle[201] of the open plain of air[202] and they might quickly ascend to heaven and descend to earth, just as on a ladder.[203] And he gave them freewill[204] that they might complete everything according to their desire and that they might show their good will towards their master in their service to us, as the saying of Paul: *All of the spirits are servants who are sent into service because of those who are going to inherit life.*[205]

Lazy Angels Cast from Heaven

Because one of them was negligent and did not want to read in this tablet according to the names that were written by him (i.e. God), and he forgot the meaning hidden in this book and he thought great things about himself; moreover, he envied the honour of his younger brother, as his brothers who were jealous,[206] saying:[207] 'Why is he called "this image[208] of the creator"? And why am I joined to the yoke of servitude to him and subject, spiritual to the fleshly, powerful to the weak, light to the heavy, and engaged in empty things?' At that same moment that wise master beat him with hard blows and since he did not submit to receive his punishment,[209] he took from him

200 As elsewhere, 'to sit' may have a pedagogical meaning, especially since the cognate adjective of the adverb, 'idly' (*baṭṭilā'it*), was used above for 'lazy' students.

201 This phrase is difficult. The unvocalized Syr. *mrkbt* can be either *markbat*, 'a chariot, vehicle, conveyance, ship of' or *mrakkbat*, 'composed of' (both in construct state). Instead of 'this whole vehicle of the open plain of air' we could render this phrase 'this whole (sphere) composed of the open plain of air'. Also, the passage could be relying on this ambiguity: this 'composed' thing – note the use of the same root so important elsewhere in this text (see note 63 above) – is a 'vehicle' or 'chariot', which is a common usage of this root in near contemporary Jewish 'merkavah' mysticism. Scher oddly translates this as 'les sept plaines fluides de l'air' (350).

202 Syr. *ā'ar*, from Gr. *aḗr*.

203 Cf. Jacob's ladder, Gen 28:12.

204 Syr. *mshallṭut ḥērutā*, lit. 'authority of freedom', perhaps an attempt to render Gr. *autexousía* or another technical term.

205 Heb 1:14.

206 Scher takes this as a reference to the envy Joseph's brothers felt towards him ('comme les frères de Joseph qui le jalousèrent'), but it is not clear how he came to this conclusion.

207 Cf. Narsai, *Homilies on Creation*, I.230ff; *Cave of Treasures*, III.1ff. On this theme, see Gary A. Anderson, 'The Fall of Satan in the Thought of St. Ephrem and Milton', *Hugoye* 3.1 (2000).

208 T has 'image and likeness'.

209 Beating was standard in ancient education, e.g. in *Mishnah Makkot*, 2.2, Abba Shaul exempts from paying damages the teacher who strikes his student.

his authority and threw him down [351] from his rank,[210] and he dashed him with a great force down from heaven to the earth to this place of darkness, to this dusty house, and he (i.e. Satan) continually *acts zealously within the children of disobedience*.[211]

Diligent Angels

Because the followers of Gabriel and Michael,[212] along with all of their companions, were diligent in their reading and did not neglect that blessed study; on account of this he admitted them and made them his chamberlains.[213] Before him they stand continually and enjoy revelations of him,[214] just as Daniel said: *A thousand thousands stand before him and a myriad myriads serve him*.[215] He divided them into nine orders[216] and he gave to them nine ranks.[217] Although they are all one substance,[218] nevertheless some of them he made 'Seraphs', who are interpreted as 'the sanctifying ones';[219] some of them 'Watchers',[220] who continually keep vigil before his lordship; some of them 'Cherubs',[221] who carry and solemnly bear the divine

210 The word 'rank' (*dargā*) is another school term, e.g., Narsai, *Metrical Homilies*, II.522 (p. 103).

211 Eph 2:2.

212 Lit. 'those of the house of Gabriel and Michael'.

213 Syr. *qayṭonqānē*, from Gr. *koitṓn* with the Syr. *qn'*, 'to hold, possess'.

214 Scher notes that this is in contrast to other Nestorian writers, who say that the angels only enjoy the sight of God after the final judgement (note 1).

215 Dan 7:10.

216 Syr. *tegmē*, from Gr. *tágma*.

217 The order of angels (Seraphim, Watchers, Cherubim, dominions, authorities, powers, angels, thrones, rulers) differs in various Christian texts, all of which rely on Eph 1:21 (rule, authority, power, dominion) and Col 1:16 (thrones, dominions, rulers, authorities). For example, Pseudo-Dionysius has three separate triads: Seraphim, cherubim, thrones; dominions, powers, authorities; principles, archangels, angels (with dominions and powers in reversed order at *Celestial Hierarchy*, VI.2: 201A and powers and authorities in reversed order at VIII: 237B).

218 Syr. *usiya'*, from Gr. *ousía*.

219 Scher suggests that the author falsely derives Seraph (*srāphā*) from the root *ṣ-r-p*, which means 'to clear, refine, purge' (351 n. 3). The etymology provided by the text seems to be based upon the description of the Seraphs at Isa 6.6–8.

220 Syr. *'irē*, lit. 'the woken ones'. Although this is an angelic being inherited from Second-Temple Judaism, it is not uncommon to find etymological explanations for their name (e.g., Narsai, *Homilies on Creation*, 5:503–06).

221 Scher suggests that Cherub (*krubā*) seems to be understood here mistakenly as 'cultivator' or 'ploughman' (*kārobā*) (note 4).

presence,[222] which is girt round with bands of fire. Now and then from it (i.e. the divine presence) shines forth a powerful (light)[223] underneath[224] all of them. Some of them he made 'dominions' over the nations,[225] and some of them also 'authorities',[226] who are over the kingdoms, and for some of them the name 'powers'[227] is appropriate, for they are able to accomplish his commandment, and some of them he named 'angels', which are interpreted as emissary [352] delegates.[228] Others he honours with the name 'thrones',[229] which shows the magnitude of their honour. These, as it seems, are more honoured than all of them. For others the name 'rulers'[230] is fitting, for it shows their authority over all. In brief, there is no one among them to whom he did not give some honour in reward for his learning. In this way God led this spiritual *school.*[231]

Human Schools

Let us come then to this (*school*) of ours, and let us see how he led it and in what way he dealt with it, and with what letters he composed names,[232] so it could read and be instructed.

The School of Adam

Now at the same time that he made Adam and Eve, he caused to be made

222 Syr. *shkintā*. Obviously this is cognate with the Hebrew *shekhinah*, which is used in similar descriptions of the divine hierarchy. The verb 'to solemnly bear' (*mzayyḥin*) is found elsewhere for the pomp surrounding the advent of the divine, e.g., the resurrected Christ was 'borne in a chariot (*markabtā*) like a king' (Addai Scher, ed., *Theodore bar Kōnī, Liber scholiorum* [CSCO 69; Louvain: Secrétariat du CSCO, 1960]: 170 [VIII:45]). See also note 201 above.

223 The word appears only in T.

224 Or 'in place of'.

225 Cf. Gen 32:8 (LXX), but not in the Hebrew or the Peshitta versions.

226 Syr. *shalliṭānē*.

227 Syr. *ḥaylē*.

228 The second of these two terms may be a Syriac gloss (*meshtaddrānē*) for a foreign loanword (*izgaddē*), which Payne Smith suggests is Persian (*Compendious Syriac Dictionary*, 12), but Brockelmann (*Lexicon Syriacum*, 9) posits an Akkadian origin, which is followed by Kaufman, *The Akkadian Influence on Aramaic*, 38. It may be cognate with the Neo-Babylonian *ashgandu*, which appears as a non-Akkadian family name.

229 Syr. *mawtbē*.

230 Syr. *arkaws*, the plur from the Greek *archḗ*. Eph 1:21, Col 1:16.

231 When italicized in the text, *school* is the translation of Syr. *eskolē*, from Gr. *scholḗ*.

232 See the discussion of 'composition' in note 63 above.

before them in the order of the letters the wild and domestic animals, and he whispered[233] in him (i.e. Adam) secretly so that he might read openly.[234] Adam read in this first tablet the names for all the domestic animals and for all the wild animals of the field and all the birds of the heavens. Everything Adam called them,[235] (each) living soul, that was their name. Because he repeated these unwritten letters well in the composition[236] of exact names, he (i.e. God) then introduced his *school* to the Garden of Eden and there he taught him[237] the laws and judgements. After he (i.e. God) first wrote the short psalm[238] about the tree,[239] beautiful to look at, so that he might read it and know by it the distinction between [353] good and evil, because God already knew his laxity, he warned him: *On the day that* you erase one of the letters of this tablet and *you eat from the fruit of this tree* that will grant you wisdom, *you will die*.[240] But he did not let him go only with this threat, but he promised, as a master to his student and like a father to his son, that if he should read and apply his mind to this commandment, and when asked, repeat the names that he had him read as well as show all the letters as not erased, he (i.e. God) would give him the tree of life that he might eat from it and live forever.

But because his older brother saw his honour and the tablet that was written for him, while he thought that now if he (i.e. Adam) read it as he was commanded and repeated the names that were engraved in it, not only

233 The verb *l'az* ('whisper, make indistinct or soft sounds') is used commonly for the Holy Spirit. Adam is described as naming the animals and aided in this by the power of the Holy Spirit in Rabbinic literature as well. For a number of parallels, see Ginzburg, *Legends of the Jews*, 1:61–62.

234 There is a double meaning here since the Syriac verb *qrā*, 'to read', also means 'to call out'.

235 This is the same verb as mentioned in the preceding note.

236 Syr. *rukkāb*. Again, see the discussion of 'composition' in note 63 above.

237 T has here 'and wrote for him there'.

238 The Psalter was the preliminary text of study at East-Syrian schools. For example, we are told that Mār Abā began to study it on entering the School of Nisibis (*Life of Abā*, 216.18–217.4).

239 The text seems to combine the tree of Gen 2–3 with that one described in Psalm 1. The Peshitta version of the text reads: 'Blessed is the man who does not walk in the path of the wicked or stand in the mind of sinners or sit (*iteb*) in the seat (*mawtbā*) of scoffers, but his will is in the law of the Lord and he meditates (*nethaggē*) upon his law day and night. He will be like a tree which is planted upon the stream of waters, which gives its fruit in its time and its leaves do not wither' (1:1–3). The Syriac words in brackets may take on a special nuance in an academic context.

240 Gen 2:17. The phrase 'which grants you wisdom' renders the Syriac word *mḥakmānāk*.

the name 'image and likeness' would remain for him,[241] but he would also receive perfection of nature, like the Slanderer,[242] and the arrow of death would not pierce him; on account of this he went and wrote another tablet, which was contrary to that first one, and he accused[243] God in front of them: 'Not true is this (statement) "you will die"; rather if *you eat from* that tree and transgress the commandment of your master, *you will be as Gods knowing good and evil*'.[244] To such an extent did he make that tree desirable in their eyes, like Jonah's gourd,[245] that straightaway together they broke the yoke, [354] cut the collar, and smashed the tablet on the ground and erased the letters of the commandment. When that wise instructor came and saw that the tablet was lying on the ground, that the letters were erased from it, and that they were stripped and naked,[246] straightaway he beat them like children and he expelled them from that school,[247] and he sent them to the earth from which they had been formed that they might work and eat until they would return to the earth from which they had been taken.

Cain and Abel[248]

In turn, he made that third *school*, which was with Abel and Cain. He required sacrifices and offerings as pay for his teaching, and because Cain imitated his friend the Slanderer and was jealous of the honour of his brother, on account of this he issued a murder sentence against him,[249] just as Satan

241 Here and elsewhere the text clearly maintains a theology of the image, that is, a theological perspective that emphasizes the human being's status as image of God and the Christological implications of this status. See Frederick G. McLeod, *The Image of God in the Antiochene Tradition* (Washington, DC: Catholic University of America Press, 1999), 43–85.

242 Syr. *ākel qarṣā*. This title is commonly used to refer to Satan, lit. 'eater of a gnawed or broken morsel'. It derives from an idiom meaning 'to slander' in several Aramaic dialects as well as in Akkadian. For its Akkadian origin, see Kaufman, *The Akkadian Influence on Aramaic*, 63.

243 Syr. *qaṭrgēh*, the verb *qaṭreg* deriving from Gr. *katēgoreîn*.

244 Gen 3:4–5.

245 Jon 4:6–11. See note LA 8.

246 The sense of this is unclear. In the biblical text Adam and Eve noticed their own nudity and immediately covered themselves up (Gen. 3:7). However, the text seems to suggest that it is God who noticed their nudity.

247 Syr. *bēt sephrē* is equivalent to the Hebrew *beit sepher*, the lower level house of study.

248 A less-developed version of this pedagogical reading of the Cain and Abel story can be found in Narsai's *Homilies on Creation*, IV: 306–417. On the envy of Cain, see also note LN 138.

249 Syr. *gzār dinā d-qeṭlā*. As in much of the *Cause*'s protohistory, the envy as well as the

murdered Adam, according to the Lord's saying: *That one who was from the beginning a man killer and who does not stand in truth.*[250] Because of this also he chastened this one with hard scourges of movement and unrest,[251] and he caused him to go out from before him and he said to him: *When you work the earth, it will not continue to give you its power and* because you killed your brother, you *will be avenged sevenfold.*[252] See how he honours the diligent student and what he does to the lazy one!

Noah

[355] In turn, he made a *school* full of beautiful thoughts, which bore the sign of mercy to blessed Noah for one hundred years. Since he (i.e. God) explained[253] to him daily the meaning of that glorious providence, and because he (i.e. Noah) worked beyond his power and received the teaching of the fear of God quickly and carefully, on account of this he delivered him from the punishment of the flood. He appointed him to be a substitute[254] for the world and to renew that figured work[255] which had been erased. He removed him from that accursed *school* in a ship bearing the world and he brought him to this spacious plain full of all excellent beauties, and he bore witness about this and said: *Noah was a righteous and perfect man in his generations,*[256] and he promised to him that henceforth as reward for his righteousness he would no longer curse the earth *because of the human being*, but *for all the days of the earth, sowing and reaping, summer and winter, daytime and night would not come to an end.*[257]

---

legal decision in this passage seem to reflect the social interactions of the East-Syrian school. A similar social dynamic may have existed in the Rabbinic academies. Cf. Rubenstein, *The Culture of the Babylonian Talmud*, 54–66.

250 Jn 8:44.

251 The metaphorical 'scourges' (Syr. *māragnē* from Gr. *máragna*) are the punishment of wandering which God decrees against Cain at Gen 4:12. The term *nawdā* ('wandering') derives from this biblical passage.

252 This is a conflation of Gen 4:12 and 4:15 with an exegetical addition ('because you killed your brother'). The ambiguity in the Peshitta text of 4:15 is removed by the change from the third-person singular to the second person. Scher seems to mistranslate this, 'parce que tu as tué ton frère, je te ferai payer sept pour un'. On the exegesis of this ambiguous verse, see Glenthøj, *Cain and Abel in Syriac and Greek Writers*, 202.

253 Syr. *mphashsheq*, a school term.

254 Syr. *ḥlaphtā*, i.e. 'a remnant'. It is not uncommon to find this term used for Noah, e.g. Ben Sira 44:17 and Aphrahat, *Dem.* XIII.5.

255 Syr. *ṣalmānutā*, lit. 'image-ness'.

256 Gen 6:9.

257 Gen 8:21–22; 'cold and heat' are missing from this list.

Abraham

In turn, he made another *school* in the time of the blessed Abraham. He caused Abraham to go out from his land and from the house of his family, and he brought him to the plain of Haran,[258] and there he taught him what was necessary, and afterwards he brought him to the land of Palestine. Because he tested him for a long time [356] and found him to be suitable for his tutelage,[259] he consented that he might enter his cell and repose with him.[260] In reward for his excellence he promised him that he would make his seed as great as the sands on the edge of the sea and as the stars in the sky;[261] as he said: *I know Abraham, that he commands his children and the children of his house after him to guard the ways of the Lord and to do justice and righteousness*.[262] On account of this he gave him great wealth and crowned him with a deep old age.

Moses

He then made a great *school* of perfect philosophy[263] in the time of the blessed Moses. After he made the Israelites go out from Egypt and brought them to Mount Sinai, he made Moses his steward[264] and placed upon him some of his glory and splendour, and with troops and cohorts of angels he went down to them in his love[265] to visit them and renew for them the commandments and judgements; and because it was difficult for them to receive teaching from that eternal mouth, therefore Moses was appointed as steward of the *school* to transmit to them the life-giving sounds,[266] as they themselves had requested: *You speak with us and we will listen, and let God not speak with us lest we die*.[267] Because of this Moses would speak

258 Cf. Gen 12:1ff.

259 Syr. *talmidutā*.

260 Syr. *qellāytēh*, from Gr. *kélla*. This striking metaphor for the relationship between Abraham and God seems to reflect the relations of monks and East-Syrian schoolmen.

261 Cf. Gen 22:17.

262 Gen 18:19.

263 Syr. *philāsophutā*.

264 Syr. *rab baytā* or *rabbaytā*. This is a technical term for the steward or headmaster of the School. It appears in a number of sources, including the school canons (*Statutes of the School of Nisibis*, 73–75). The term itself seems to derive from a non-religious context (Trombley and Watt, eds., *The Chronicle of Pseudo-Joshua the Stylite*, 141). The Arabic equivalent of this term is commonly used for the master of a household.

265 Or 'in his love for them'.

266 Syr. *qālē*, or 'voices'; i.e. God would speak directly with him.

267 Exod 20:19.

and God would answer him with a voice. Because he knew the harshness of their thoughts and the tyranny[268] of their heart, for [357] they too like their brothers[269] were transgressing his commandments and trampling on his teaching, he wrote the ten commandments, which he gave to them on tablets of stone so that they would not be erased, and he gave them (i.e. the commandments) to them.

When Moses and his commander[270] (i.e. Joshua) began to go down from the mountain and they heard the sound of the *school*'s clamour, then Joshua said to him: What is this *sound of battle in the camp*? And Moses responded to him*: Neither the sound of warriors nor the sound of the weak, but the sound* of sin *I hear*.[271] At that very moment *Moses became angry* and *smashed* the two tablets. After he came to the *school*, he saw a mute teacher (i.e. the golden calf) set up by them,[272] while they were making sport with him as they liked, and they exchanged truth for falsehood, Moses himself was removed from his stewardship,[273] and Joshua's honour was taken from him.[274] He was furious at this and beat that new teacher with hard straps, and he cast him down from his chair[275] and laid waste to his body *with a file*, and *he scattered its dust upon the waters*, and *he gave it as a drink* to the ashamed students, and he raised his voice in the *school* and said: *Who is on the side of the Lord? Let him come to me. Then they gathered around him, all the* prominent *brothers, the Levites*.[276] [358] As it seems, their mind had not turned toward error. He ordered them that each man should take his

268 Or 'rebellion'. This word ultimately derives from Gr. *túrannos*.

269 Scher suggests that this may be a reference to the people who lived before the flood. However, it could also be a reference to contemporary Jews (note 1).

270 Syr. *duks* from Lat. *Dux*. A title which went into Syriac via its use in Greek in the later Roman Empire (see Trombley and Watt, eds., *Chronicle of Pseudo-Joshua the Stylite*, 138), this may have been an office in some East-Syrian schools. For example, it appears in the colophon from a manuscript produced at a school in Tel Dinawar in Bēt Nuhādrā (British Library Add. 14460; Wright, *Catalogue of Syriac Manuscripts in the British Museum*, I:52–53; Hatch, *Album of Dated Syriac Manuscripts*, 211).

271 Exod 32:17–18.

272 Syr. *mawtab l-hon*, but this could also be read as *mawteb l-hon*, perhaps meaning 'giving them a lesson' (lit. 'causing them to sit'). This may be an early attestation of the tradition that the Golden Calf was animated. Cf. Qur'an 7:148–49.

273 Syr. *rabbat baytutā*.

274 The text is difficult to render with precision and may be corrupt. The reading 'they exchanged truth' comes from T.

275 Syr. *kursyēh*. This seems to be an instructor's chair or *cathedra*.

276 Exod 32:26. Certain members of the community are referred to as 'the prominent' (*qriḥē*) brothers in the school canons (*Statutes of the School of Nisibis*, 102).

sword and *go back and forth from gate to gate in the camp*, and spare not even their brothers and sons. Because they fulfilled the commandment of Moses, he said to them: You have sanctified your hands for the Lord.[277] They destroyed by the sword anyone in whom there seemed to be some signs of love for the calf after the drinking of water.

The mind of Moses was pacified. Then he prayed to their master again in order to entreat him to be reconciled to his students and not consider their foolishness, because they were children. After God had also accepted Moses' entreaty, he ordered him to make for himself tablets like those earlier ones and to write upon them those ten sayings[278] and to go down and read them. For the purpose of according honour to Moses, and as a sign that his entreaty was accepted,[279] he poured on his face a powerful light and an excellent glory, and he entrusted the *school* to him and made him teacher in his stead. He (i.e. God) recused himself from teaching those mad people, and after he went down and had them read those ten sayings and they agreed to repeat them and observe everything that was commanded, Moses himself too, that novice teacher from the race of mortals, wrote them new commandments, many [359] and more subtle than those (ten sayings), as he said: *I gave them commandments which are not pleasing, and judgements by which they would not live*;[280] the human being who does them lives by them.[281]

He led that *school* for a period of forty years in the desert of Horeb. Anyone who had to ask a matter[282] from the Lord would come to Moses. He would sit diligently from morning until evening so as to resolve their questions and inquiries.[283] Anyone who disputed his teaching, he would have them beaten with the hard scourges[284] of a sword. Some he would bring

277 Paraphrase of Exod 32:27–29. 'You have sanctified your hands for the Lord' is an accurate gloss for the Peshitta Hebraism, *mlaw idaykon*, which in turn represents the Hebrew, *mil'ū yedkhem* (Exod 32:29).

278 Syr. *petgāmin*, or 'words, phrases, verses'.

279 This is an exegetical explanation of Exod 34:29–35, where the actual reason for the light from Moses' face is not described.

280 Ezek 20:25.

281 Cf. Lev 18:5. Scher also has trouble identifying this line.

282 Syr. *melltā*, lit. 'word'. This resembles the Rabbinic usage of the term.

283 This clearly derives from an institutional context. Teachers and judges 'sit' (*yāteb*) and resolve (*neshrē*) 'questions and inquiries' (*shu'ālayhon w-zēṭēmayhon*, the latter deriving from Gr. *zḗtēma*). The question-and-answer genre was employed in the East-Syrian schools. See Bas Ter Haar Romeny, 'Question-and-Answer Collections in Syriac Literature', in *Erotapokriseis: Early Christian Question-and-Answer Literature in Context*, Proceedings of the Utrecht Colloquium, 13–14 October 2003, ed. Annelie Volgers and Claudio Zamagni (Louvain: Peeters, 2004), 145–63.

284 Syr. *esqṭē*, from Gr. *skûtos*.

to pass that they be swallowed by the earth, others (he punished) with the burning of fire, and others he would stamp excommunication upon them, as he did upon Aaron and Mariam. [285] He restricted her so that she would sit outside the camp for seven days and then confess her folly. Because he showed this care for the *school*, at the time of his death, God ordered that he not be buried by them, but he and his holy angels served him and buried him on the mountain.[286]

Joshua

At the time of his death, he handed over the *school*, as he was instructed by the Lord's providence, to Joshua bar Nun, his commander, that he might be the teacher for it and do within it [360] whatever was proper.[287] Joshua also, after he made them enter the land of promise and laid waste to the errant nations before them, divided the inheritance for them justly and departed to his Lord. Scripture bears witness about these things: *At that time there was no king in Israel and everyone would do whatever was pleasing in his own eyes*[288] until the time when Samuel was selected as a prophet and David as king, and he (i.e. David) taught them in accordance with the former teaching.

Solomon[289]

In turn, the wise Solomon made a *school*. He taught those within his household as well as outsiders,[290] as it is said: *All of the kings of the earth came to*

285 Syr. *qataresis*, from Gr. *kathaíresis*. The phrase *qataresis d-ḥermā ṭāba' (h)wā* ('he would stamp excommunication') seems to reflect some technical usage. The passage refers to Moses' dispute with Aaron and Mariam at Numbers 12.

286 This exegetical apology for Moses' misdeeds treats as an honour what is understood as a punishment in the standard reading of the text. For Moses' burial by angels, see, e.g., Isho' bar Nun, *Questions on the Pentateuch*, 43.

287 Another example of a pedagogical interpretation of the relationship between Joshua and Moses can be found in Thomas of Marga's *Book of Governors* where Mār Māran'ammēh and Babai of Gebiltā are compared to Joshua and Moses (Thomas of Marga, *Book of Governors* 174, trans. 347).

288 Judg 21:25.

289 The works cited in the following passage are appropriately those ones pseudepigraphically attributed to Solomon in antiquity.

290 'Outsiders' (Syr. *barrāyē*), a calque of Gr. *hoi éxō*, is a term used for non-Christian books and thinkers, and therefore can be translated simply as 'pagans'. See note 310 below, and note LA 45.

hear the wisdom of Solomon.[291] For because when he reigned[292] he sought nothing other than the wisdom to hear judgement; on account of this God also made him great and wealthy with it (i.e. wisdom) more than anyone else, as he said: *Behold I have given you wisdom, since there was no man like you among the kings before you, nor after you will there be one like you for all time.*[293] Scripture bears witness about him and says: *He was wiser than everyone*, and he spoke about the powers and activities of every body, [294] *from the cedars of Lebanon to the plant*[295] *which clings to the wall, and he spoke about* [361] *the domestic animals, about the birds, about the creeping things and about the fish.*[296] Sometimes he would call his student 'son' and say to him: *Listen, my son, and receive my instruction and the years of your life will be many.*[297] And again he would say: *for everything a time, a time for everything under the sun.*[298] Sometimes he taught about God and would say to his pupil: *Watch your foot whenever you go into the house of God, and go near to hear, sacrifices are better than gifts of fools.*[299]

Because there were many at that time who thought that they comprehended and understood God,[300] as well as his power, his wisdom, and his activity, he (i.e. Solomon) alone said: Not one of these things is comprehended by the thoughts of creatures and fleshly things. *I said that I have learned wisdom. And it is far from me more than that which was farness, and depth of depths,*[301] that is, who will discover the divine nature? *And who is the man who will enter after the king in judgement, and then with the one who made him?*[302] *The heavens are high and the earth is deep and the heart*

291 1 Kgs 4:34.

292 Syr. *qām b-malkutā*, lit. 'stood in kingship'. The idiom, *qām b-* (lit. 'stood in' or 'arose as') can mean 'to be occupied with', 'to undertake', but is also sometimes used to render Gr. *proestánai*, 'to be set over, govern, direct'.

293 1 Kgs 3:12.

294 The language of this inserted phrase derives from philosophical and theological usage.

295 The Hebrew (1 Kgs 4:33) has 'hyssop', but it is not clear to what plant the Syriac (*lwp'*) refers; cf. Löw, *Aramäische Pflanzennamen*, no. 176. The word derives from a root which means 'join' or 'add'.

296 1 Kgs 4:31, 33.

297 Prov 4:10.

298 Eccl 3:3.

299 Eccl 4:17. The Hebrew of this verse can be read variously and the Peshitta rendering is awkward.

300 The two verbs, *adrek(w)* and *qām(w) 'al*, literally mean 'tread upon' and 'stand over', thus further conveying the hubris of such action.

301 Eccl 7:23. See the discussion of this difficult verse in note 84 above.

302 Eccl 2:12.

of the king and God is not investigated.[303]

In short, in the time of his old age he convened and brought together to himself the whole, entire people, and he taught about the weakness of this (present) way of life, and he showed that it would indeed pass away and be dissolved [362] along with the desire for it and that all of its construction is vanity.[304] And counselling what is more advantageous, he says: *Fear the Lord and guard his commandments, because the Lord brings into judgement all deeds, according to all that is hidden and revealed, whether it be good or bad.*[305]

Prophets

In turn, the rest of the prophets also made a *school*, as we learn from the story of the blessed Elisha the prophet. He, according to the tradition that he received from his master Elijah, proceeded in this same path. For a long time he taught in it what was necessary and needed,[306] as the scripture teaches: *The sons of the prophets said to Elisha: 'This place here in which we sit is too narrow for us. But let us go to the Jordan and let us cut from there, each man one beam, and let us make for ourselves a shelter. You too should come with us.' And he said to them: 'go* and do it; I am also coming with you'.[307] (This) demonstrated that the sons of the prophets built a *school* there in the desert. On this account they went out into the desert: so that they might collect their thoughts (away) from the clamour of the world and be able to receive teaching from their master.[308]

303 Prov 25:3. The Peshitta lacks 'and God'. Scher takes T's reading, 'divine king', instead of 'king and God'.

304 The text inserts Syr. *tuqqānēh* ('its construction') into Eccl 1:2. See note 33 above.

305 Eccl 12:13–14, but part of the passage is missing. Scher mistakenly attributes this to Proverbs.

306 T reads here: 'Again the blessed prophet Elisha made a *school* and great assembly, according to the tradition he received from his master Elijah over a long period of time and he taught in it what was just and needed'.

307 2 Kgs 6:1–3, but with some phrases missing. Again, as mentioned above, 'to sit' may have a scholastic sense.

308 The Peshitta itself contributes to this transformation of the prophets into a series of teachers and students. In 1 Kings Elijah's 'servant' (Hebr. *na'ar*, lit. 'young boy'; LXX *paidárion*) is translated as his 'student' (Syr. *talmidā*). This change is repeated in references to Elisha's 'servant' Gehazi (1 Kgs 18:43; 19:3; 2 Kgs 4:12, 25, 38; 5:20). Gehazi is also characterized as a student of Elisha in Rabbinic exegesis (e.g., b. Sanhedrin 107b).

Pagan Schools[309]

Lest there be a great burden in our speech, we shall abstain from (speaking about) the many assemblies [363] that the rest of the prophets made, and we come to those of the profane[310] and of the philosophers,[311] those who also sought to imitate these assemblies which we have considered. Because the foot of their teaching was not set on the truth of faith[312] and they did not grasp the *beginning of wisdom*, that it is the *fear of God*;[313] on account of this they fell from the truth completely. Because they compare things with themselves,[314] they do not understand, but *while thinking themselves to be wise, they were fools* since *they feared and served creation more than their creator.*[315]

For Plato first made[316] an assembly in Athens.[317] More than a thousand men were gathered before him, so they say. Even Aristotle was there before him. One day, while he was interpreting, after he looked and did not see Aristotle, he spoke thus: 'The friend of wisdom[318] is not here. Where is the seeker of the beautiful? I have a thousand and not one, but one is more than a thousand.'[319]

309 The author seems to rely on a doxographical document in in 363.7–367.2.

310 Syr. *barrāyē*, lit. 'outsiders'. This term is commonly used for non-Christian books or ideas. See note 290 above.

311 Syr. *philāsophē*. Elsewhere in the *Cause* 'philosophy' is treated as something worthy of aspiring to, but here 'philosophers' are treated negatively.

312 There is a pun in this line since the word for 'truth' literally means 'solidity' or 'firmness' (*shrārā*).

313 Prov 1:7. The word rendered as 'beginning' is literally 'head' (*rēshā*).

314 Scher (as well as Ramelli, *Causa della fondazione delle scuole*, 145 n. 91) finds this line obscure. Syr. *henon b-hon*, translated here as 'with themselves', may be a rendering of Gr. *en heautoîs*.

315 Rom 1:22, 25. Romans 1 is an important passage for the natural theology promoted in the text. See note 153 above.

316 Following T. C has an awkward plural at this point (*'bad*[*w*]).

317 It is likely that the material on Plato at the Academy does not derive from the tradition of anecdotes on him, but rather from the biographical tradition of Aristotle. This also occurs in the Arabic sources, although there is also a distinct biographical tradition of Plato in Arabic. See, for example, comments at Alice Swift Riginos, *Platonica: The Anecdotes concerning the Life and Writings of Plato* (Leiden: Brill, 1976), 216.

318 Syr. *rāḥmā d-ḥekmtā* is a calque of Gr. *philósophos*.

319 This anecdote derives from the biographical tradition concerning Aristotle. See Baumstark, *Aristoteles bei den Syrern*, b-g and 1–130 and Anton-Hermann Chroust, 'A Brief Summary of the Syriac and Arabic Vitae Aristotelis', *Acta Orientalia* (Hauriae) 29 (1965–66): 23–47. See also Diether R. Reinsch, 'Das Griechische Original der Vita Syriaca I des Aristoteles', *Rheinisches Museum* 125 [1982]: 106–12) and Ingemar Düring, *Aristotle in the Ancient*

Although he (i.e. Plato) taught correctly about God and spoke about his only-begotten[320] son as the word[321] begotten from him according to nature[322] and about the holy spirit as the hypostatic[323] power that proceeds [364] from him,[324] nevertheless when he was asked by his fellow citizens[325] whether or not it is right to honour idols, he passed on the tradition[326] to them that it is requisite that they be held in honour, and he said: 'It is necessary to sacrifice a white cock to Asclepius'.[327] Although he knew God, he did not praise and confess him as God, *but he was lacking in his thoughts and darkened*[328] in misunderstanding.

Also about the soul he passes on the tradition[329] that it migrates from body to body. Sometimes it abides in creeping things, at other times in wild animals, sometimes in domestic animals, at other times in birds, and afterwards in human beings, and then it is raised up to the likeness of angels and it passes through all the orders[330] of angels. Then it is strained and made pure and returns to its place above.[331] Regarding women he commanded that they be (held) in common, as the Manichees say.[332]

Biographical Tradition (Göteborg: Elanders, 1957), 184–87, 469–70, but note the comments on Düring's work in Dimitri Gutas, 'The Spurious and the Authentic in the Arabic Lives of Aristotle', in *Pseudo-Aristotle in the Middle Ages: The Theology and Other Texts*, ed. J. Karyae, W. F. Ryan, and C. B. Schmitt (Warburg Institute Surveys and Texts 11; London, 1986), 15–36 (repr. in *Greek Philosophers in the Arabic Tradition* [Aldershot: Ashgate, 2000], Chap. 6).

320 Syr. *iḥidāyā*, equivalent to Gr. *monogenḗs*.

321 Syr. *melltā*, equivalent to Gr. *logos*.

322 Syr. *kyānā'it*.

323 Syr. *qnomāyā*.

324 Other contemporary texts from the same cultural milieu also maintained that Plato supported the idea of the trinity. Sebastian Brock, 'A Syriac Collection of Prophecies of the Pagan Philosophers', *OLP* 14 (1983): 203–46 (repr. in *Studies in Syriac Christianity*, Chap. 8).

325 Lit. 'sons of his city'.

326 Syr. *ashlem*, lit. 'handed over', 'transmitted'.

327 This saying attributed to Socrates on his death (Plato, *Phaedo* 118A) seems to have become a commonplace. For example, Tacitus mentions it in his description of Seneca's suicide, which is clearly modelled on that of Socrates (*Annals*, 15.60–64).

328 Rom 1:21. Again, Romans 1 is being employed to promote natural theology and to condemn those who have been led astray. See note 315 above.

329 Syr. *mashlem*.

330 Syr. *tegmē*, from Gr. *tágma*.

331 This description of metempsychosis derives ultimately from Book X of Plato's *Republic*, but through various intermediaries. The language of purification is similar to what we find above (see notes 129 and 130).

332 It was a commonplace to refer to the sharing of wives within Plato's utopian community as described in the *Republic*. The reference to Manichees (*mannināyē*) is inaccurate and the author (or a scribe) may be confusing Manichaeism with Mazdakism, a tendency within

After he died, Aristotle received the assembly.[333] He turned and rejected the teaching and former tradition of his master and established his very own. With the other foul things he devised, he also said this: 'Providence and divine care[334] are only to the point of the moon, and from there to here he (i.e. God) entrusted his providence to the authorities'.[335]

There was an assembly and teaching also in Babel of the Chaldaeans, those who for a long time have spoken falsely of the seven (planets) and the twelve signs of the zodiac.[336]

[365] There was also (an assembly) among the Indians and in Egypt, those (peoples) whose perversity it is difficult for us to repeat.[337]

Epicurus and Democritus too made an assembly in Alexandria.[338] They

---

Zoroastrianism that flourished in the sixth century. Patricia Crone, 'Kavad's Heresy and Mazdak's Revolt', *Iran* 29 (1991): 21–42; Zeev Rubin, 'Mass Movements in Late Antiquity – Appearances and Realities', in *Leaders and Masses in the Roman World*, ed. I. Malkin and Z. W. Rubinsohn (Leiden: Brill, 1995), esp. 179–87; Ehsan Yarshater, 'Mazdakism', in *The Cambridge History of Iran*, vol. 3, pt. 2, ed. Ehsan Yarshater (Cambridge: Cambridge University Press, 1983), 991–1024.

333 We find similar terms in the Syriac translation of an abbreviated life of Aristotle: 'When Plato died, Speusippus, because he was his nephew, received (*qabbel (h)wā*) the residence of Plato, and he sent for Aristotle that he might stand at the head (*nqum b-rēsh*) of the residence of Plato'(Baumstark, *Aristoteles bei den Syrern*, g lines 1–3). The use of *qabbel* here and its Hebrew cognate in Mishnah Avot (1:1, 1:3, 1:4, 1:6, 1:8, 1:10, 1:12, 2:8) reflects the various words based on the Greek root √*dech-*, 'to receive,' used in succession lists: *diadéchomai* ('to receive in turn'), *diádochos* ('successor'), and *diadochḗ* ('succession'); see note SL 15. On the idiom *qām b-*, see note 292 above.

334 On this term (Syr. *bṭilutā*), see Riad, *Studies in the Syriac Preface*, 85–86.

335 This is a common doxographical tradition. This simplification of Aristotle's cosmology has possibly been influenced by the Pseudo-Aristotelian *De Mundo*, which was translated into Syriac in the sixth century (Paul de Lagarde, *Analecta Syriaca* [Leipzig, 1858]: 134–58). See, e.g., A. P. Bos, 'Clement of Alexandria on Aristotle's (Cosmo-)Theology (Clem. Protrept. 5.66.4)', *Classical Quarterly* 43 (1993): 177–88, esp. 180–82. The addition of 'authorities' (*shalliṭānē*, Gr. *árchontes*) to this scheme is a later Neoplatonic extrapolation of the distinction between the sub- and supra-lunar worlds.

336 Syr. *malwāshē*. It is a commonplace to introduce the Chaldeans in any discussion of astrology in Classical sources. Syriac responses to astrological fatalism are attested as early as the early third century in Bardaiṣan of Edessa, *'The Book of the Laws of the Countries' or 'Dialogue on Fate'*, ed. and trans. Han J. W. Drijvers (Assen: Van Gorcum, 1965; repr. Piscataway, NJ: Gorgias, 2006). See F. Stanley Jones, 'The Astrological Trajectory in Ancient Syriac-Speaking Christianity', in L. Cirillo and A.van Tongerloo, eds., *Atti del terzo congresso internazionale di studi 'Manicheismo e oriente cristiano antico'* (Manichaean Studies 3; Louvain, 1997), 183–200, esp. 188–94.

337 The extreme criticism of and silence regarding these two ethnic groups may be in response to their well-known zoolatry.

338 Neither Democritus (d. c. 370 BCE) nor Epicurus (d. 270) had any connection to

said that this world is eternal and exists on its own, while saying that there were fine bodies, which do not fall under the senses because of the excellence of their fineness. They name these things without body 'grains'.[339] They say that these are inanimate,[340] without reason, without beginning, without birth, and without end in their multitude.

There was also an assembly of those who are called 'natural philosophers'.[341] These, too, established the beginning upon inanimate elements.[342] They deny there is a God or (divine) forethought, but (they say) that the powerful plunders and the weak is plundered, along with the rest of the things (they say).

Thus also Pythagoras, although he made an assembly and taught about the one God, who is the maker of all and also its guide, he nevertheless corrupted in other (matters).[343]

Zoroaster,[344] the Persian Magus, also made an assembly of a *school*, in the time of Bashtasp [366] the king.[345] He gathered many assemblies unto himself and they received his error, since his teaching suited their blindness. He taught them (that there are) four gods in one cohort – Ashoqar, Frashoqar, Zaroqar, and Zurwān[346] – but he did not demonstrate their work and service. Afterwards he affirmed two other gods – one he called Hormizd, the other

---

Alexandria. As atomists it is not uncommon for the two to be mentioned together, cf. Hermann Diels, *Doxographi graeci* (Berlin: G. Reimer, 1879), 285–86, 316, 330.

339 Syr. *perdē*, i.e. atoms.

340 Syr. *d-lā naphshā*, lit. 'without soul', but in a philosophical context *naphshā* refers to the 'vegetative' soul.

341 Syr. *phusiqāyē*, from Gr. *phusikoí*.

342 Syr. *esṭukhsē*, from Gr. *stoicheîa*.

343 For another positive Christian perspective on Pythagoras (d. c. 500 BCE), see Sebastian Brock, 'A Syriac Collection of Prophecies of the Pagan Philosophers', *OLP* 14 (1983): 203–46 (repr. in *Studies in Syriac Christianity*, Chap. 10).

344 Syr. *Zardusht*.

345 Vishtāspa, or Gushtāsp, known as 'Hystaspes' in the Greek sources, was the semi-mythical king who endorsed Zoroaster's teachings.

346 Syr. *'shwqr prshwqr zrwqr zrwn*. C has *bdkshy*, which is missing from T. The former are the three hypostases of Zurwān, e.g., R.C. Zaehner, *Zurvan: A Zoroastrian Dilemma* (Oxford: Clarendon, 1955), 219–25. At 439–40 Zaehner reproduces the translation of this passage from Joseph Bidez and Franz Cumont, *Les mages hellénisés, Zoroastre, Ostanès et Hystaspe d'après la tradition grecque* (Paris: Les Belles lettres, 1938), vol. 2, 100. Despite earlier scholarly claims, it seems that Zervanism was merely a tendency within Zoroastrianism: see Shaul Shaked, 'The Myth of Zurvan: Cosmogony and Eschatology', in *Messiah and Christos*, ed. Ithamar Gruenwald et al. (Tübingen: Mohr Siebeck, 1992), 219–40 (repr. in Shaul Shaked, *From Zoroastrian Iran to Islam: Studies in Religious History and Intercultural Contacts* [Aldershot: Ashgate, 1995], Chap. 4).

Ahriman[347] – and he said that the two of them were born from Zurwān and that the one is completely good, Ahriman perfectly evil. These (two) created this whole world: the good one, the good things, the evil one, the evil things. After that, he spoke of twenty-four others, who in their whole cohort are thirty, just as the number (of days) of the months.[348] He said it is not right to slaughter animals because Hormizd is in them. Whatever is to be offered as sacrifice, they ought to first break its neck with rods until it is dead, and thus it (i.e. the neck) should be cut so that it is unaware while suffering. He said that it is necessary for a son to take his mother in marriage, [367] his daughter, or his sister, and the rest of the things (he said). He does not allow the dead to be buried, but rather (he teaches) that they should be exposed so that they may be torn to pieces by birds.

The errant ones made these assemblies. Although they[349] established them on this pretext of being a benefit to themselves and others, they nevertheless were found from the result of their deeds to be as error, destruction, and ignorant darkness, because all of them together broke the yoke and cut the bands of that eternal Lordship, as David said: *The truth has perished from the earth.*[350] Jeremiah said: *Lord, your eyes are upon faith*,[351] that is, upon the truth of your essence,[352] because *while thinking in themselves that they were wise, they were fools.*[353] In another place he says: *they were ashamed of the thing in which they put their trust.*[354]

Jesus the Master Teacher

On account of this, the circumstances demanded that the illuminated mind, the great teacher, the eternal radiance, the living Word of God, should come. He renewed the first *school* of his father, which the errant ones had

347 Syr. *hwrmyzd 'hrm*. In Zervanism the forces of good and evil are born as twins. Hormizd and Ahriman are later renderings of the Avestan Ahura Mazda and Angra Mainyu respectively.

348 On the Zoroastrian sacred calendar, see, e.g., Mary Boyce, *Zoroastrians: Their Religious Beliefs and Practices* (London: Routledge & Kegan Paul, 1979), 70–74.

349 According to T.

350 Scher suggests this is Ps 12:2, but it more likely derives from Mic 7:2: 'The pious one (*ḥasyā*) has perished from the earth'.

351 Jer 5:3.

352 This is the unknowable divine essence (*itutā*). Cf. *Cause* 335–7.

353 Rom 1:22. The section began above at 353 with a quotation from Romans 1.

354 Cf. Jer 48:13.

corrupted.[355] He cried out and said to them: *Come to me all of you who are weary and bearers of heavy burdens and I will give you rest.*[356] He made John the Baptist a reader and instructor[357] and [368] the apostle Peter the steward of the *school*,[358] as he said: *The Torah and the prophets prophesied until John.*[359] *Henceforth the kingdom of heaven is proclaimed and everyone will throng to enter it.*[360] Because of the great care that John showed for this *school* – sometimes rebuking, at other times teaching, and then sometimes reproving the evil and the lazy in the wilderness at the bank of the Jordan; on account of this, he was furnished with the baptism of repentance for the remission of sins. Our Lord bore witness to this: *Among those born of women no one arose* like him.[361] After he (i.e. John) revealed and showed that spring of wisdoms and that true teacher in the sight of all the crowds, (saying) 'This is the one who *takes up the sin of the world*',[362] then all the crowds began to throng around him (i.e. Jesus) and listen to his teaching. The glory of John began to decrease and his assembly to grow small, while that of our Lord became great and was added to day by day,[363] as he (i.e. John) said: *It is fitting that he grow and I be diminished.*[364]

After our Lord arose as[365] the head of this *school* and many crowds gathered unto him, then he selected from them prominent brothers,[366] that is, followers of Peter and John.[367] He had them go up a high mountain, as his father did on Mount Sinai. There he taught them [369] necessary things

355 Christ's capacity to renew creation is a common feature of Theodore of Mopsuestia's thought (*On the Nicene Creed*, 144 [39]: 'He renewed also all the creatures and brought them to a new and higher creation [*tuqqānā*]', or 181 [68]) and is found in the 'cause' literature, e.g., Cyrus of Edessa, *Six Explanations*, 89.7–21 (trans. 77.11–24).

356 Mt 11:29.

357 These are both offices at the East-Syrian school. The former is an instructor in reading and perhaps preliminary interpretation, while the latter is less clearly defined in the sources (Becker, *Fear of God*, 87–89).

358 Syr. *rabbaytā d-eskolē*.

359 Mt 11:13. The order of 'the Torah' (*urāytā*) and 'the Prophets' has been reversed.

360 Lk 16:16.

361 Mt 11:11.

362 Jn 1:29.

363 This is the first of several instances where the author correlates the decline of one school and the ascent of another. It is a rhetorically effective way to link the two and subject the former to the latter. See also *Cause* 376 and 386.

364 Jn 3:30.

365 See note 292 above.

366 See note 276 above.

367 Syr. *d-bēt*, or 'those who were with'.

about his father and about him, and about the manner and about the goal[368] of his teaching. He was interpreting[369] all of the difficulties of the Law and he illuminated before them all the allegories and figures[370] of the Old (Testament), as he said: *I have not come to loosen the Law, but to fulfil it.*[371]

Just as painters depict the likeness, not with glittering colours appropriate to the exact original, but with coal or with dark lines, and once it has taken its nature and a form that fits the true image,[372] then they adorn the image with bright pigments possessing glittering colours like the original, so in like manner that great teacher of the world did.[373]

What do I mean by this? For, behold, even workers of brass, when they want to cast a likeness of a human being, they depict all the limbs on the ground first, and afterwards they depict (it) in wax and balance the parts of the body, and then they melt gold or brass and pour it over the wax.[374] When the wax is consumed, at that moment the solid[375] and permanent likeness of brass is cast, the wise not considering the destruction of the former likeness as a loss. [370] Rather, this is seen as the wisdom of the craftsman, who through the destruction of those former things sets up a true[376] likeness that remains and does not come apart.

Thus also that master teacher first used this order according to the childishness of the students.[377] Because that likeness of true learning was about to be melted and effaced, he sent his beloved son and he was melted and poured[378]

368 Syr. *nishā*. See note 14 above in the introduction to the *Ecclesiastical History* of Barḥadbeshabbā.

369 Syr. *mphashsheq*.

370 Syr. *pelā'tā*, 'parables, allegories, proverbs', and *ṭelānyātā*, lit. 'shadows, shade'.

371 Mt 5:17. The author's understanding of the Sermon on the Mount as an exegesis of the Old Testament corresponds to the original tenor of the Matthean text.

372 Syr. *yuqnā*, from Gr *eikṓn*.

373 Following T. C has 'worlds'.

374 Syr. *qē'rutā*, from Gr. *kērós*.

375 Syr. *sharrirā* can mean both 'solid' and 'true'. This passage plays on this double meaning.

376 See the previous note.

377 Syr. *ṭaksā*, from Gr. *táxis*. This is related to the usage above (see note 56). God humbles himself ontologically to speak to our 'childishness' (*shabrutā*). See also the use of a cognate term above at 336 (note 90).

378 This passage is difficult and may be corrupt. In *etpshar* (or: *etpashshar*) *w-naskēh* ('he was melted and poured') the same subject is employed first with a middle/passive verb and then awkwardly with an active verb. The conjunction is found only in T. The verb *etpshar* (or: *etpashshar*) may also have a double meaning since it is also used for interpretation, though usually only of dreams ('he was interpreted').

his teaching upon that former likeness.[379] He revealed and spoke to us about that true likeness of the trinity, the future way of life, the annulment of the things of old, and the destruction of the weak things. He fastened in our mind the exact truth,[380] as it is said: When he went down from the mountain and many crowds gathered unto him, *he opened his mouth and taught them and said, 'Blessed are the poor in spirit, for theirs is the kingdom of heaven'*,[381] and the rest. Sometimes, it was said, he boarded a *boat* and began to speak his teaching *in allegories* to the crowds.[382] In turn, at other times in the temple and in the synagogues he would do this, as he said to the Jews*: I was with you everyday while I was teaching in the temple and you did not seize me*.[383] To such an extent did his students multiply that from this the head priests and the Pharisees were filled with envy towards him as they themselves even said: *Have you not* [371] *seen that the whole world follows him? If we let him do thus, everyone will believe in him*.[384] Just as the likeness of brass was the fulfilment of the likeness in wax, not an annulment, since although the wax was dissolved, nevertheless its likenesses exist, so also the Messiah is not a dissolver of the Law and the likeness which he made in it,[385] but their fulfilment and completion, as he said.[386]

When he was thirty years old,[387] he produced his teaching and he renewed the former *school*.[388] He established strong definitions of philosophy;[389] he

379 Behind this passage we can see Theodore of Mopsuestia's notion of Christ as the perfect image of God, e.g., Frederick G. McLeod, *The Roles of Christ's Humanity in Salvation: Insights into Theodore of Mopsuestia* (Washington, DC: Catholic University Press, 2005), 124–43.

380 Lit. 'exactness of truth'. The term 'exactness' or 'precision' (*ḥattitutā*) shows up a number of times in this text and seems to be a virtue advocated in both teaching and interpretation. Cf. Theodore of Mopsuestia, *On the Nicene Creed*, 160 (51), 174 (63).

381 Mt 5:2–3; Lk 6:17 seems to be implied by the descent from the mountain. It is not clear because the Sermon on the Mount was explicitly referenced just above.

382 Mt 13:2–3. The beginning of this sentence is unclear.

383 Mk 14:49.

384 Jn 12:19; 11:48.

385 Or 'with it'.

386 Compare this to the citation of Mt 5:17 above.

387 Lit. 'after the time of thirty years'; cf. Lk 3:23.

388 This is ambiguous since the adjective *qadmāytā* can also mean 'first'. How it is translated depends on whether it refers to the 'first' school of the angels at the time of creation, the 'first' school of Adam, or simply the schools 'prior' to the decline into pagan schools.

389 Syr. *tḥumē ḥayltānē d-philāsophutā*. The term *tḥumā* represents Gr. *hóros* or *hórismos*, the philosophical 'definition'. A 'Book of Definitions' is falsely attributed to Michael the Interpreter (*bādoqā*), a member of the School of Nisibis in the sixth century. Cf. Abramowski, 'Zu den Schriften des Michael Malpana/Badoqa', in *After Bardaisan*, 1–10.

resurrected wisdom, which had died; he gave life to the fear of God, which had ceased; he showed the truth, which had been lost; in brief, all the species of teaching he forged and fastened in the ears of the faithful, as the separate parts of a statue.[390] He rebuked evil, put a stop to error, and condemned falsehood. After he wrote them a testament in the upper room at the time of his passion,[391] he led his *school* and went out to the Kidron valley.[392] There he taught them great, wonderful, and exact things all night long.[393] Because at that time their senses were too weak to receive the complete teaching, [372] he said to them: *I have much to say to you, but you are not able to bear it now. But once the spirit of truth has come, it* will teach *you the whole truth.*[394]

After he arose on the third (day), as he said (he would), for a period of forty days he went about with them in the world and taught them many things. At the time of his ascent into heaven, he chose from them twelve prominent brothers[395] and ordered them (to do) what was necessary and needed. He said to them: Go out and *make students of all the nations. Baptize them in the name of the Father, the Son and the Holy Spirit, and teach them to guard everything that I have ordered you. Behold I myself am with you for all days until the end of the world.*[396]

Simon, the steward of the *school*,[397] he made head of all of them and he ordered him to pastor and lead the men, women, and children.[398] After he (i.e. Jesus) ascended to heaven, they also did as they were ordered. They went out and preached in every place, as Mark testifies: *Our Lord was helping them and confirming their words with the signs they were performing*,[399] after they

390 Syr. *adriyanṭē*, from Gr. *andriás*, *andriántos*. This word may be singular or plural. It is ambiguous since the Syriac plural marker is sometimes simply used to mark the *eta* (*ē*) of Greek words. In this case it would be a hypercorrection since the original Greek word does not have an *eta*.

391 This is a reference to Jesus instituting the Lord's supper and announcing the new covenant (or testament) (Mt 26:28; Mk 14:24; Lk 22:20; Syr. *diyatēqē*, from Gr. *diathḗkē*) at the Last Supper (Mt 26:20–30; Mk 14:12–25; Lk 22:7–23), which took place in an upper room (Syr. *'elēytā*, Gr. *anágaion*) (Mk 14:15; Lk 22:12)

392 Jn 18:1.

393 On the focus on exactitude, see note 380 above.

394 Jn 16:12–13. The original text has 'will guide' where this text inserts 'will teach'.

395 See note 276 above.

396 Mt 28:19–20. This reading is from T.

397 Syr. *rabbaytā d-eskolē*.

398 Scher notes: 'Jean, xxi, 15. La version dite Pschitta porte: Pais mes agneaux, mes moutons et mes brebis; les commentateurs chaldéans les expliquent par hommes, enfants et femmes' (note 3). cf. Ishodad of Merv, *Commentary on Gospels*, 3.225.5–7 (1.287).

399 Mk 16:20.

had first made a *school* in that upper room, where[400] our Lord transmitted to them Passover (as a tradition),[401] until they received the Holy Spirit.[402] Afterwards they came [373] to Antioch. There they made students of and baptized many, as Luke says: *Then the students were called Christians in Antioch.*[403]

The Apostle Paul

After a short time, our Lord chose the diligent student and careful teacher, Paul the Master,[404] to teach all the gentiles.[405] This one, who went beyond both those before him and after him, brought brothers together in many places and made a *school*, first in Damascus, afterwards in Arabia,[406] then in Achaea and in Corinth, for two and a half years.[407] Then after fourteen (years) he went up to Jerusalem and saw the Apostles and returned to his work.[408] With much labour and fatigue he was fighting in his work – as he said: *Who is sick and I myself am not sick? Who is scandalized and I myself do not burn?*[409] – even against all the different heresies[410] and doctrines until he changed them to the manner of his teaching. After he came from Corinth to Ephesus and found there twelve people who were students of Christianity, he spoke with them openly for three months, as Luke makes known in the Acts of the Apostles, and he was instructing them about the kingdom of God.[411] Because some people reviled his teaching, Paul then distanced himself from them. [374] He chose true *students from among them and everyday he would speak with them in the school of the man whose name*

400 The text may be corrupt here since the particle *d* is only occasionally used in this locative sense without the antecedent being picked up again in the relative clause.

401 Syr. *ashlem* is rendered more fully here in order to bring out its scholastic sense. Syr. *peṣḥā*, like Greek term and its Romance cognates, means both Passover and Easter.

402 Cyrus of Edessa, *Six Explanations*, 144–51 (trans. 127–33) expounds on the idea that Jesus had to stay with them until the Spirit came.

403 Acts 11:26.

404 Or 'Paul the Great', 'the Great Paul'.

405 Lit. 'nations'.

406 Following T, since C has 'Thrace'.

407 As Scher points out, there is a discrepancy with Acts 18:11, which states that this was only for a year and a half (note 2).

408 This refers to the so-called Council of Jerusalem (Gal 2:1–14; Acts 15).

409 2 Cor 11:29.

410 Syr. *heresis*, from Gr. *haíresis*.

411 Acts 19:7–8. This passage may be referring to Paul's famous *parrhesia* (2 Cor 3:12, 7:4; Phil 1:20; Philem 8; Acts 28:31; also in the pseudo-Pauline texts).

was Tyrannus. This was for two years until all who lived in Asia received *the Word of God.*[412]

For until this point we did not have the noun '*school*', which is interpreted as 'place for learning understanding'.[413]

After Paul completed his teaching in every place, he was crowned with Peter in Rome due to Nero's evil. The whole group[414] of the twelve departed to our Lord. Then the evil foxes began to peek out from their dens and were seeking to enter and ravage the pleasant vineyard and to pull down that former tradition which our Lord transmitted to his apostles. The side of Satan began to grow strong; the *school* of the members of the household (of the Lord) began to be brought low. When the master teacher saw that his side had been brought low and that the side of his adversary had grown strong, he then selected and established in his *school* skilful[415] teachers to manage it according to his will.

The Post-Apostolic Schools

[375] Now that with God's help we have arrived at this point, it is right for us to show how a *school* began to exist after that glorious band of Apostles, and at what time the scriptures began to be interpreted, by whom and where, and then gradually we will be brought to this (*school*) of ours.

The School of Alexandria and Philo of Alexandria

For a great abundance of instruction was in Alexandria, as we said earlier.[416]

412 Acts 19:9–10. The original text has 'heard' where this text inserts the more scholastic 'received'.

413 Syr. *bēt yullphānā d-sukkālā*. The term *bēt yullphānā* is commonly translated as 'school', but this would confuse the sense of the passage, which offers a false etymological link based on a supposed shared root, *s-k-l*, between Syr. *eskolē* (Gr. *scholḗ*) and the wholly unrelated word *sukkālā* ('understanding'). An interest in etymology is not uncommon in the 'cause' genre, e.g., Ḥenānā, *On Rogations*, 69.14–71.16, esp. 71.13; *On Golden Friday*, 62.1.

414 Syr. *shi'tā*. This term shows up below and in the school canons for what seems to be a certain liturgical practice at the School (*Statutes of the School of Nisibis*, 79).

415 Syr. *mhirē*. This Ancient Near Eastern term originally used of scribes found its way into Syriac, e.g., Jacob of Sarug, *Homélies contre Juifs*, 1.1–2; cf. Ezra 7:6 and Ps 45:2. See also the *Mēmrā on the Holy Fathers* below, lines 9 and 10.

416 The word rendered 'instruction' in this paragraph, Syr. *mardutā*, originally referred to a 'beating' (cf. *al-adab* in Arabic). It seems to represent Greek *paideía*, since it refers to learning that is not necessarily Christian (cf. *Life of Abā*, 219.7). This passage may correspond with the only other previous reference to Alexandria up to this point in the text, that is, the reference

Because of its renown and antiquity, they would come there from everywhere to receive philosophical learning. Because reading is a habit in humans,[417] someone who had received Christian teachings happened to have[418] a zeal for instruction, so that he even established a school of the divine letters[419] in this city, lest only the instruction of those (i.e. pagan philosophers) be considered. Along with the readings of scripture he wanted to add interpretation to them, as an ornament, that is, of the scriptures. On account of this he introduced something illusory into the holy books. The leader of this *school* and exegete, Philo the Jew,[420] invented it. After he was occupied in this craft, he began to interpret (the holy books) allegorically,[421] while he put a stop to the historical method completely.[422] Those wise men did not understand that they should not teach only empty things alone [376], but rather (they should teach) the teaching of the truth that ornaments the divine books. *They loved human praise more than the praise of God.*[423] For this reason many would come to Alexandria. That *school* of philosophers almost ceased and this new one became strong.[424]

---

to Epicurus and Democritus at 365. However, it is possible that the text is reflecting its source (e.g. 'as we said earlier'), since it is not clear why it states that Philo put a stop to the historical method, the beginning of which was never mentioned.

417 Instead of *qeryānā*, Scher supports the variant reading, *meryānā* (from the verb *marri*, 'to contend, strive emulate, imitate'; cf. *mmaryānā*, 'one who imitates'), found in T, although this word is not attested and the verb is only found in the *pa"el* form (note 1).

418 Lit. 'was found with'.

419 Syr. *bēt yullphānā d-sephrē alāhāyē*. It is perhaps relevant that *sephrē*, a term used also for other forms of literature, is used here instead of *ktābē*, the term used more often to refer to scripture.

420 Philo of Alexandria (c. 20 BCE–c. 50 BCE), the hellenized Jewish philosopher whose works had a major influence on Christian exegesis. C has *mawdyā* ('the one who confesses [or: acknowledges]') instead of *yudāyā*, 'Jew'. It was common in the early Church and the Middle Ages to transform the influential Alexandrian thinker into a Christian. Theodore of Mopsuestia's *Treatise against the Allegorists*, in *Fragments syriaques du Commentaire des Psaumes (Psaume 118 et Psaumes 138-148)*, ed. L. Van Rompay (CSCO 435–36; Louvain: Peeters, 1982), 11.15–13.24 (14.27–16.5): Origen of Alexandria went astray due to his learning the allegorical method from the Philo the Jew. This text may be a source for the above passage.

421 Syr. *peletānā'it*. See notes 370 and 382 above, where 'allegory' (*pele'tā*) is used in a positive sense.

422 Syr. *tash'itā*, lit. 'story, history'. This is the standard Syriac term for the so-called historical method. In general, see Frances M. Young, *Biblical Exegesis and the Formation of Christian Culture* (Cambridge: Cambridge University Press, 1997), esp. 169–76.

423 Jn 12:43.

424 See note 363 above. Note the use of *'elltā* ('reason', 'cause') here and elsewhere in this section in particular. It may suggest that an aetiological interest in the origins of exegesis and the difficult relationship between Antioch and Alexandria guides this passage.

Arius of Alexandria and the Council of Nicaea

After Philo died, the wicked Arius, who promised much instruction in the divine books, was then present in Alexandria. When he was invited to undertake this interpretation, because profane[425] instruction had been received by him, he promised also to interpret the scriptures. On account of this he proceeded to the new invention of a corrupted faith. Out of his great pride he said that the Son is a created being.

For this reason an ecumenical council[426] gathered in the city of Nicaea concerning him.[427] That council anathematized him and was active there under the authority of Eustathius,[428] bishop of Antioch, for three months.[429] It disputed all the heresies that had sprung up from the time of the Apostles until then. There was disputation of all the heresies for forty days and the replies of the fathers against them for fifteen days, aside from the canons and the reasons for them, which were for three days.[430]

Post-Nicene Schools

[377] After everyone went home, the blessed Eustathius made a *school* in his city, Antioch, and Jacob[431] in Nisibis – since this holy man was also at that council – and Alexander[432] in Alexandria, and others in other places, but we do not intend to demonstrate all of these. Jacob made Mār Ephrem exegete,

425 See note 310 above.

426 Syr. *sunhādāws*, from Gr *súnodos*; Syr. *tēbelāyā*, from *tēbel*, corresponds to the Greek *oikoumenikós*, from Gr. *oikouménē*.

427 The First Council of Nicaea in 325 CE.

428 Eustathius of Antioch, who after serving as bishop of Beroea became bishop of Antioch in the early 320s, only to be deposed after 330. He played an active role at Nicaea. His strident anti-Origenism may explain the favour he is shown here. There is no evidence that he founded any school.

429 Scher suggests 'months' as an emendation for 'years' (note 2).

430 On the reception of the Council of Nicaea in the Church of the East, see Arthur Vööbus, ed. and trans., *The Canons ascribed to Marutha of Maipherqat and related sources* (CSCO 439–40; Louvain: Peeters, 1982). I follow Scher's emendation to the text (note 3). Instead of 'days', the manuscripts for some reason read 'prophets'.

431 Jacob of Nisibis (d. 338) was the Nisibene bishop to attend the Council of Nicaea. He became a representative figure of Nicene orthodoxy in the Syriac churches.

432 Alexander of Alexandria was bishop of the city until his death in 326. He attended the Council of Nicaea and worked actively against Arius whom he had condemned at a local council in 318.

Alexander Athanasius.[433] Eustathius was cast into exile[434] and entrusted the assembly to Flavian.[435] This holy man made Diodore his friend and partner.[436] The two of them maintained the assembly of Antioch with the whole teaching of orthodoxy,[437] since they did not fear the threats of Valens the King,[438] nor the evil of the Arians, the errant ones, but they continued to complete their labour sometimes outside the city, at other times within it.

School of Diodore of Tarsus

After Flavian became bishop, the blessed Diodore went out to a monastery. Then Diodore maintained a *school* in that monastery for a long time. Many gathered unto him from all regions, including the blessed Basil,[439] John,[440] Evagrius,[441] [378] and the Master Theodore,[442] and they were with him and

433 Athanasius of Alexandria (d. 373), the well-known bishop of Alexandria of the fourth century, attended the Council of Nicaea as a deacon of his predecessor, bishop Alexander. His works began to be translated into Syriac by the late fourth century. See, e.g., R. W. Thomson, *Athanasiana Syriaca* I–IV (CSCO 257–58, 272–73, 324–25, 386–87; Louvain, 1965–77).

434 Syr. *eksāwriya'*, from Gr. *exoría.*

435 Flavian, bishop of Antioch (381–404), had to deal with the continuing schism caused by the deposition of Eustathius.

436 On Diodore of Tarsus, see note SL 28.

437 Syr. *ārtādāwksiya'*, from Gr. *orthodoxía.*

438 The emperor Valens (364–78) was an Arian.

439 Basil of Caesarea (330–79) was an important Greek patristic author translated into Syriac from the fifth century onwards and this is probably why the author wants to associate him with Diodore. See, e.g., D. G. K. Taylor, ed. and trans., *The Syriac Versions of the De Spiritu Sancto by Basil of Caesarea*, CSCO 576–77 (Louvain: Peeters, 1999); Robert W. Thomson, 'The Syriac and Armenian Versions of the Hexaemeron of Basil of Caesarea' (Studia Patristica 27; ed. E. A. Livingstone: Louvain; Peeters, 1993), 113–17, and R. W. Thomson, ed., *The Syriac Version of the Hexaemeron by Basil of Caesarea* (CSCO 550; Louvain, Peeters, 1995). For a general discussion, see David G. K. Taylor, 'St. Basil the Great and the Syrian Christian Tradition', *The Harp* 4.1–3 (1991): 49–58. In the *Life of Ephrem* the eponymous hero in fact travels to Caesarea where he meets Basil. For their meeting, see *Life of Ephrem* 643.11–649.10 (in *Acta martyrum et sanctorum syriace*, vol. 3).

440 John Chrysostom (c. 347–407). Despite his Antiochene tendency, his works were a major source of exegesis and theology of all the post-Chalcedonian churches. His influence on East-Syrian exegesis begins to appear around the time of the composition of the *Cause*. See Molenberg, 'Silence of the Sources', 153–54.

441 Evagrius of Pontus (d. 399). He certainly was not a student of Diodore, but his popularity in the Church of the East would have been an impetus for creating this fictional link between the two, thus legitimizing Evagrius' works.

442 Or 'Theodore the Great', i.e. Theodore of Mopsuestia.

they learned from him the interpretation of scripture and their traditions.[443] For he was a man perfect in these two things – in the teaching of philosophy and in the explanation of scripture – more than all the rest.

Theodore of Mopsuestia[444]

After this holy man (i.e. Diodore) was sought for the work of the bishopric of Tarsus and each one of his students migrated elsewhere, then the blessed Theodore remained in that monastery and for a long time he alone took on the work of teaching. Not only was he teaching with the true word of teaching,[445] but also with writings, at the request of the fathers. With the strength of grace he produced an interpretation of all the scriptures and a disputation against all heresies.[446] For until the time when grace brought this man into being and to the abode of human beings, all the parts of teaching, the interpretations, and the traditions of the divine books – in the likeness of different species, from which is made the image of the King of Kings – were dispersed and cast everywhere in confusion and without order among all the earlier writers and fathers of the catholic church.

After this human being had distinguished the good from the evil and was trained in all the writings and traditions of those of former times, then like a skilful doctor, he collected into one whole[447] all the [379] traditions and chapters which were dispersed, and he compounded[448] them skilfully and intelligently, and from them he prepared (as a drug) one complete remedy

443 On this passage, see Reinink, 'Edessa Grew Dim and Nisibis Shone Forth', 85–86.

444 The Council of Bēt Lāpāṭ of 486 affirmed Theodore's position within the Church of the East: 'Nobody among us should have doubt concerning this holy man because of the evil rumors which the heretics have spread about him. For he was reputed during his lifetime to be illustrious and eminent among the teachers of the true faith, and after his death all the books of his commentaries and his homilies [were] approved and clear to those who understand the wise meaning of the divine Scriptures, and who honor the orthodox faith. For his books and his commentaries preserve the unblemished faith, as the meaning which befits the divine teaching in the New Testament. [His works] destroy and reject all of the teachings which strive against the guidance given the prophets and against the good tidings coming from the apostles. If anyone therefore dares, secretly or openly, to traduce or to revile this teacher of truth and his holy writings, let him be accursed by the Truth [itself]' (*Synodicon Orientale*, 211; trans. Gero, *Barṣauma*, 45).

445 This refers to his actual teaching and may be rendered alternatively as 'his true didactic discourse' (*melltā sharrirtā d-mallphānutā*).

446 For Theodore's numerous works known in Syriac, see 'Abdisho''s *Catalogue*, Chap. XIX (*Bibliotheca Orientalis* III.1.30–35).

447 Syr. *shalmutā*, 'harmony, agreement, whole'.

448 The use of the verb *rakkeb*, 'compose, compound', recalls its use above (see note 63).

of a teaching, perfect in beauties; this (remedy) which uproots and puts an end to the sickly diseases from the minds of those who eagerly approach its teaching,[449] since although there are diseases and pains in our body, nevertheless among all the pains there is no pain worse and more bitter to human souls than the disease of ignorance. Just as those who make a statue[450] forge each and every one of the parts of the image separately, and afterward compound them one after another, as the order of workmanship demands, (to make) a complete statue,[451] thus also the blessed Theodore composed, ordered, fitted, and placed each and every one of the parts of this teaching in the order that truth demands, and forged from them in all his writings one perfect and wonderful image of that essence, rich in blessings.[452] What was said of Solomon was fulfilled in him: *He was wiser than everyone* before and after him.[453] He managed in this practice for a period of fifty years. After he was led to the bishopric of Mopsuestia, he would prostrate himself regularly at the grave of the blessed Thecla and from her he would seek help so as to receive the power to interpret the scriptures.[454]

[380] When he departed for his Lord, because the blessed Nestorius[455] was chosen for the patriarchate[456] of Constantinople, he entrusted the work of teaching in Mopsuestia to Theodoulos,[457] his student, the length of whose life, so they say, was until the time of Mār Narsai and Barṣaumā, the bishop. These blessed ones went and saw him there and were blessed by him.[458]

449 T has 'writings'. Instead of the 'remedy', this whole clause may also have 'Theodore' as its subject.

450 See note 390 above.

451 T has 'and they make a statue'.

452 See note LN 35.

453 1 Kgs 4:31.

454 On the cult of St Thecla at Seleucia, see Stephen J. Davis, *The Cult of St. Thecla: a Tradition of Women's Piety in Late Antiquity* (Oxford: Oxford University Press, 2001), 36–80, and Catherine Burris and Lucas Van Rompay, 'Thecla in Syriac Christianity: Preliminary Observations', *Hugoye* 5:2 (2002). Barhadbeshabba, *La second partie de l'histoire ecclésiastique*, 515.6–9 says that Theodore was buried next to Thecla's remains.

455 On Nestorius, see note SL 41.

456 Syr. *paṭriyarkutā*, derives from Gr. *patriárchēs*.

457 Theodule, d. 492. 'Abdisho''s *Catalogue*, Chap. XXI (*Bibliotheca Orientalis* III.1.37).

458 We have no evidence of Narsai and Barṣaumā visiting Mopsuestia. Such a visit would have occurred during their stay in Edessa, although this is doubtful. Rather, the text may be simply making more explicit the links between Theodore of Mopsuestia and these important founding figures of the East-Syrian school movement. This story is repeated by a later source (*Chronicle of Siirt* 2.1.114).

Even that Aksenāyā,[459] the evildoer, bore witness about this, saying about him that he was alive until his own time.

Although these (affairs) were managed in this way, nevertheless, Rabbula,[460] bishop of Edessa, although from the beginning he demonstrated an appearance of friendship towards the illustrious exegete and would meditate upon his compositions, nevertheless because, when he went up to Constantinople to the assembly of the fathers,[461] was accused of using blows against his clergy,[462] and made the (following) apology: 'Our Lord also struck (people) when he entered the temple', then the exegete stood and rebuked him, 'Our Lord did not do this, but to the rational he spoke with speech,[463] "Remove these from here", and he overturned the tables, but the bulls and the sheep he expelled with lashes',[464] he (i.e. Rabbula) buried this hatred [381] in his heart, and after his (i.e. Theodore's) death he had his writings burned in Edessa, apart from these two (commentaries), which were not burned, one on *John the Evangelist* and the other on *Ecclesiastes*.[465] These were not burned, so they say, because they were not yet translated from Greek into Syriac. These things will suffice about him.

459 Syr. *Aksnāyā*, from Gr. *Xénos*. This refers to Philoxenus of Mabbug (Halleux, *Philoxène de Mabbog*, 14 and n. 16). This reference suggests that Philoxenus' works were read at Nisibis, despite his being an archenemy of Dyophysitism.

460 Rabbula of Edessa (412–435). On him, see note LN 73. Ibas's *Letter to Mari* states that Rabbula became an adversary of Theodore because he publicly opposed him (trans. Doran, *Stewards of the Poor*, 171–73 and Price and Gaddis, *The Acts of the Council of Chalcedon*, 2:297). See Michael Gaddis, *There is No Crime for Those who have Christ: Religious Violence in the Christian Roman Empire* (Berkeley: University of California, 2005), 259–60. Also, see the late version of events in Michael the Syrian, *Chronicle*, ed. J.-B. Chabot (Bruxelles: Culture et Civilisation, 1963), II: 424 (French trans. IV: 436).

461 It is not clear what council this would be. The author seems to be expanding on the *Letter to Mari*.

462 Syr. *qliriqē*, from Gr. *klērikós*.

463 The sense here relies on the double meaning of Syr. *melltā*, since humans are *mlilē*, 'endowed with speech' and 'rational'.

464 The use of Syr. *phrāgelē*, from Gr. *phragéllion* (Jn 2:15), suggests that this passage relies on the more detailed of the descriptions of the so-called cleansing of the temple from Jn 2:13–16 (cf. Mk 11:15–17; Mt 21:12–13; Lk 19:45–46).

465 Again, the author may be expanding on the *Letter to Mari*. For the former of these two commentaries, see Theodore of Mopsuestia, *Commentarius in Evangelium Iohannis Apostoli*, ed. J.-M. Vosté (CSCO 115–16; Paris: Respublica, 1940); Theodore of Mopsuestia, *Commentary on the Gospel of John*, ed. and trans. George Kalantzis (Strathfield, NSW: St Pauls Publications, 2004).

The School in Edessa and Removal to Persia

But let us show then how this divine assembly was transferred to the land of the Persians, and by what cause and by what means. The blessed Mār Ephrem then, whom we mentioned a little earlier, after Nisibis was handed over to the Persians, moved to Edessa and lived there the rest of his life.[466] He made a great assembly of the *school* there.

Not even after his passing did this study cease, but through the diligent students that were his they made the assembly of the *school* greater by many additions, and day by day it progressed due to the brothers who would come thither from all quarters. When Mār Narsai, Barṣaumā,[467] who became the bishop in Nisibis, and Ma'nā, [382] bishop of Rewardashir,[468] heard the news of this assembly, because they were lovers of wisdom, at once they went thither with the rest.

Qyorā

The head and exegete of that *school* was an enlightened man whose name was Qyorā, who was completely a person of God.[469] To such an extent was this man swallowed up by love for the business (of the *school*), that he embraced the complete practice of interpretation,[470] of reading instruction,[471] and of vocalization,[472] as well as church homily.[473] Although he was fasting and abstinent, nevertheless he would strenuously complete all this labour. However, in this one thing he was anxious: up to then the interpretations of the Exegete were not translated into the Syriac tongue, but rather he would interpret extemporaneously from the traditions of Mār Ephrem. These, as they say, were transmitted from Addai the Apostle,[474] who was in early times

466 Lit. 'all the time of his life'. This more literal rendering may be correct, since it is possible that any information on Ephrem comes through the Edessene tradition, where little is known of his life in Nisibis. In the Vita tradition, for example, his life in Nisibis is given short shrift. The city of Nisibis was part of the capitulation the new emperor Jovian made to the Persians after Julian the Apostate's defeat in 363 CE.

467 See note LN 65.

468 Syr. *wrdshyr*. On Ma'nā, see note SL 66.

469 See the comparison of this text with a similar passage in the *Ecclesiastical History* in Appendix III (cf. Vööbus, *History*, 10–11, 14, 61, 64).

470 Syr. *mphashshqānutā*.

471 Syr. *maqryānutā*.

472 Syr. *mhaggyānutā*, or 'basic literacy', or 'spelling'.

473 Syr. *āmorutā d-'ēdtā*.

474 By the fifth century, Addai was commonly understood to be the apostle who founded

the founder[475] of that assembly of Edessa, because he and his student went to Edessa and planted there this good seed. For also what we call the tradition of the *school*, we do not mean the interpretation of the Exegete, but rather these other things that were transmitted from mouth to ear of old.[476] Then [383] afterwards the blessed Mār Narsai mixed them into his homilies[477] and the rest of his writings.

After the interpretation of Theodore went into Syriac, then also it was transmitted to the assembly of Edessa, then that man took his rest with the whole assembly of brethren. After these holy ones were in that assembly at the feet of the blessed one for a long time, they received from him the interpretation of the divine books and their traditions. They read and were instructed also in the books of the Exegete.

Narsai

After that man, the exegete of the *school*, took his rest, then the whole brotherhood asked Mār Narsai to stand at the head of the assembly[478] and to fulfil its needs, because among all of them there was no one there like him. When Mār Narsai refused, he said to them: 'I myself am not able to bear the whole labour of the *school* as our master did. For he was rich in two things: in bodily health and in spiritual grace with old age. But if you make (someone else) reader and elementary instructor, perhaps I will be able to interpret.' After they did everything that he asked, then that blessed man led

---

the Christian community in Edessa, e.g. *Doctrine of Addai*, ed. and trans. G. Phillips (London: Trübner, 1876); repr. with new translation, G. Howard (Texts and Translations 16; Ann Arbor: Scholars Press, 1981). See Ramelli, *Causa della fondazione delle scuole*, 157 n. 165.

475 Syr. *nāṣobā*, lit. 'planter'. There is a play on words here with the name of the city Nisibis (*nṣibin*). The vegetative metaphor continues further on in this passage.

476 There seems to have been a specific 'tradition' of the School, which was occasionally passed on separately, even in later periods (e.g., Isho' bar Nun, *Questions on the Pentateuch*, 36). See Lucas Van Rompay, 'Quelques remarques sur la tradition syriaque de l'oeuvre exégètique de Theodore de Mopsueste', in *Symposium Syriacum IV 1984*, ed. H. J. W. Drijvers et al. (OCA 229; Rome, 1987), 33–43. Also, Gerrit J. Reinink, 'The Lamb on the Tree: Syriac Exegesis and anti-Islamic Apologetics', in *The Sacrifice of Isaac: The Aqedah (Genesis 22) and its Interpretations*, ed. E. Noort and E. Tigchelaar (Leiden: Brill, 2002) (repr. in Reinink, *Syriac Christianity under Late Sasanian and Early Islamic Rule*, Chap. 15), 115–17, 122–23.

477 Syr. *mēmrē*, here probably 'metrical homilies'. For a list of incipits of Narsai's published metrical homilies, see Sebastian P. Brock, 'The Published Verse Homilies of Isaac of Antioch, Jacob of Serugh, and Narsai: Index of Incipits', *Journal of Semitic Studies* 32.2 (1987): 279–313.

478 See notes 292 and 333 above.

the assembly for a period of twenty years, while daily leading the choir and giving interpretation.[479]

[384] Then Barṣaumā came to Nisibis and was chosen to be bishop. Maʻnā[480] went to Persia and received there the yoke of priesthood.

When the business of the assembly was proceeding in order, then Satan troubled and mixed them up, as is his habit. When Mār Narsai migrated from there, he came to Nisibis and settled in the Monastery of the Persians.[481] For his thought was to go down to Persia. Barṣaumā, after he heard this, sent his archdeacon[482] and he ordered that he enter the city with great honour. After he entered and the two of them greeted one another and attended to one another for a few days, Barṣaumā entreated him, if he desired, to settle[483] there and to make an assembly of the *school* in that city, while (Barṣaumā) would help him with all the necessities. As it was difficult in the eyes of Mār Narsai, then Barṣaumā said to him: 'Do not think that your removal from Edessa and the scattering of the assembly were accidental,[484] oh my brother, but rather [385] that it was the providence of God. If it is (the case) that you should liken this to that which occurred in Jerusalem after the ascension of our Lord, you would not be mistaken. For also the band of Apostles was there and the gift of the spirit and the signs which were done and the different powers. Because they were not worthy, their *house was forsaken desolate*,[485] according to the saviour's word.[486] The Apostles then *went out to the ways* of the Gentiles *and to the narrow paths*[487] of paganism, and

479 Syr. *emar si'tā w-pushshāqā*, lit. 'he spoke choir and interpretation'. See note 29 in the introduction to this volume.

480 On Ma'nā, see note SL 66.

481 Since Nisibis was within the Persian Empire, the name of this monastery suggests that it had an ethnic component. Having a Persian name, Narsai himself was perhaps ethnically a Persian and therefore went to a Persian monastery. On ethnic monasteries and schools in the region, see Becker, *Fear of God*, 64–68.

482 Syr. *arkidyaqāwn*, from Gr. *archidiákonos*.

483 This is probably the correct translation, but there is the possibility that this word, which literally means 'to sit', should be rendered as 'study' or 'teach', following scholastic usage (cf. Syr. *mawtbā* and the Hebrew cognate, *yeshivah*). See notes 200 and 307 above.

484 Syr. *shḥimā*, lit. 'black, blackened', then 'common, rough, simple, ordinary, lay, secular'.

485 Mt 23:38.

486 The 'they' here is an elliptical reference to the Jews. The destruction of the Temple and its prediction by Jesus (as depicted in the Gospels) are common tropes in the early Christian anti-Jewish tradition.

487 Lk 14:23. Syr. *bēt syāgē*, lit. 'places of walls, hedges, enclosures', represents Gr. *phragmoí*.

gathered everyone whom they found, good and evil.[488] They made students, baptized and taught, and in a short time the gospel of our Lord flew through all the world. It seems to me that the scattering of this (i.e. your) assembly is similar.[489] If you listen to me and settle[490] here, everywhere there will be a great benefit from you. For there is no city in the Persian realm able to receive you like this one. It is a great city, set in the borderlands, and from all regions they (i.e. people) are gathered unto it. When they hear that there is an assembly here, especially that you yourself are its leader, many will throng here, especially because now heresy has begun openly to gaze out from its surroundings in Mesopotamia. You will be as a shield to us and a strenuous labourer. Perhaps between you and me [386] we will be able to expel evil from our midst. For it is said: *Two good men are better than one, in that there is a better reward in their labuor. If one becomes strong, two of them will stand against him.*'[491]

After he (i.e. Barṣaumā) put his (i.e. Narsai's) mind to rest with (words) such as these, then he (i.e. Narsai) consented to do this. At once he commanded and did all the things that were necessary and useful for the *school*. In a short time they increased to such an extent – not only Persian and Syrian brothers who were near by, but also a majority of that assembly of Edessa came to it – so that as a result glory ascended to God. From this cause[492] also assemblies increased in the Persian realm. Edessa grew dark and Nisibis grew light. The Roman realm was filled with error, and the Persian realm with knowledge of the fear of God.[493] He led this assembly for forty-five years.[494] He also composed up to three hundred homilies, and more including his other writings.

[387] Barṣaumā composed many commentaries[495] along with other teachings. The two of them, according to the will of God, were led away and migrated to their Lord. For it is not our intention to speak about their way of life, but the manner of their teaching.

488 Mt 22:10.

489 The syntax is not exactly clear.

490 Lit. 'sit'. See note 483 above.

491 Eccl 4:9.

492 This is the same word (Syr. *'elltā*) from which the 'cause' genre receives its name. We can see here the aetiological interest of the genre as a whole.

493 See note 363 above concerning the trope of reversal.

494 See note LN 180.

495 Syr. *turgāmē*.

Elisha bar Qozbāyē

Mār Elisha from the village of Qozb,[496] a great man, trained in all the subjects of the ecclesiastical and profane books, received the work of interpretation. (It was) for seven years. He also composed many writings: a refutation of the charges of Magianism,[497] a disputation against heretics, commentaries[498] on all the books of the Old (Testament) according to the Syriac tongue.

Abraham and John of Bēt Rabban

After this blessed man was gathered unto his fathers in peace and in deep old age, then Mār Abraham[499] received his labour – servant,[500] kin, and [388] cellmate of Mār Narsai.[501] This man, so they say, they would formerly call Narsai, and after his father brought him to this blessed man, he changed his name and called him Abraham.

Furthermore, they say of John of Bēt Rabban[502] that his former name was Abraham. After he came to them, they called him John, so that he would not be called by the name of his master, and John, so that he would not be called by the name of his partner.[503] Because the two of them drank from the spring of wisdoms,[504] on account of this, these men were able to lead this assembly in all (matters) of the fear of God.

For John also laboured a great labour in this assembly. If it is right to speak the truth – all the beautiful arrangements[505] that are in it come from

496 Syr. *bar Qozbāyē*. On Elisha, see note LA 24.

497 Syr. *shrāyā d-zēṭēmē* (Gr. *zḗtēma*) *da-mgushutā*. The 'charges' would have been against Christianity. See also note 283 above.

498 Syr. *mashlmānwātā*, the same word is translated as 'traditions' above.

499 Abraham of Bēt Rabban, d. 569.

500 Syr. *ṭalyēh*, lit. 'his young man'.

501 The term for cellmate, Syr. *bar qellāytā*, may be a mistake for *bar qritēh*, lit. 'son of his village', which we find in the *Life of Abraham of Beth Rabban*, 616 above (see the synoptic comparison of these two passages in Appendix III). This possible mistake appears also in *Chronicle of Siirt* 2.1.114. See 356 above where sharing a cell is used as way of describing Abraham's relationship with God.

502 John of Bēt Rabban. Not much is known of him. Numerous works are attributed to him by 'Abdisho', *Catalogue*, Chap. LVI (*Bibliotheca Orientalis* III.1.72). See also Vööbus, *History*, 211–22; Baumstark, *Geschichte*, 115–16.

503 The redundancy of this sentence is obscure. Syr. *ḥabrā* means 'friend, partner, companion' and its Hebrew and Babylonian Jewish Aramaic equivalents are commonly used in Rabbinic literature for study partners.

504 See above at 368 where this term is used for John the Baptist.

505 Syr. *ṭukkāsē*, deriving from Gr. *taxis*.

this holy man. He also composed interpretations of and commentaries[506] on the books, a disputation against the Jews, and a refutation of Eutyches.[507] Indeed three homilies[508] were composed as well by him, one when Khusrau conquered Najran,[509] because he was there at the court[510] at that time on account of a suit for the *school*, one of prayer,[511] and the other on the plague, along with the other writings.

[389] After he went to rest due to the great plague,[512] all of the burden remained on Mār Abraham. With great fasting, continual prayer, strenuous vigils, and constant labours night and day, he led the assembly for a period of sixty years, while interpreting, leading the choir,[513] and resolving questions.[514] He also composed commentaries[515] on the Prophets, Ben Sirach, Joshua bar Nun, and Judges.[516] What labours he laboured because of the *school*, what buildings he built, and what benefits he benefited it with,[517] the matter does not need our speech, since deeds are more apparent and brilliant than the rays of the sun and all the land of the Persians was illuminated with his teaching. Like Abraham, the first of the fathers,[518] he was also father of many

506 Syr. *mashlmānwātā.*

507 On Eutyches, see note SL 44.

508 Syr. *mēmrē.*

509 Khusrau I Anushirvan ('The Immortal Soul') reigned 531–79. On him, see Arthur Christensen, *L'Iran sous les Sassanides* (Osnabrück: Otto Zeller, 1971), 363–440. The Sasanians expanded in the sixth century into South Arabia, e.g., Winter and Dignas, *Rom und das Perserreich*, 131–33.

510 Lit. 'at the gate'. It was common in the ancient and medieval Near East to use terms meaning 'door' or 'gate' to refer to the king's court (e.g. Arabic and Ottoman *Bāb*), which would here be Seleucia-Ctesiphon. However, on the mobility of the 'Porte', see Florence Jullien, 'Parcours à travers l'*Histoire d'Īšō'sabran*, martyr sous Kosrau II', in *Contributions à l'histoire et la géographie historique de l'Empire Sassanide*, ed. Rika Gyselen (Bures-sur-Yvette: Group pour l'Étude de la Civilisation du Moyen-Orient, 2004), 179–80.

511 Syr. *bā'utā*. This often refers to intercessory prayer.

512 This was no doubt related to the 'Justinianic' plague of the sixth century. In general, see Lawrence I. Conrad, 'Epidemic disease in central Syria in the late sixth century: some new insights from the verse of Hassan ibn Thabit', *Byzantine and Modern Greek Studies* 18 (1994): 12–58. See Vööbus, *History*, 220 for using this to date his death. Ramelli, *Causa della fondazione delle scuole*, 162 n. 180, suggests that this is the plague that occurred under the Catholicoi Joseph and Ezekiel (552–80).

513 See *Cause* 383 and note 29 in the introduction to this volume.

514 Syr. *shārē shu'ālē*. See note 283 above.

515 Syr. *mshalmānwātā.*

516 On his works, see 'Abdisho''s *Catalogue*, Chap. LV (*Bibliotheca Orientalis* III.1.71).

517 On Abraham's building projects and work at the school, see the 'Life' above.

518 Lit. 'head of the fathers'. For the same expression, see note SL 5 and note LA 77.

nations, begot spiritual sons without limit, and took up a beautiful name in the two kingdoms of the Romans and the Persians.

Isho'yahb of Arzon

After this holy, blessed father was also gathered unto the storehouse of heavenly life, as the bringing in of a heap of grain in its time,[519] Mār Isho'yahb the Arzonite received his practice and worked [390] in it vigorously for two years. Then he became weary from it and went and became bishop in Arzon. Afterwards he was chosen for the patriarchal duty.[520]

Abraham of Nisibis

Mār Abraham the Nisibene received the chair of interpretation – a great man, learned in all things, zealous, diligent, and a teacher of the fear of God, hardworking as well as careful. After he worked with this spiritual talent and drew with this same yoke for one year, he also departed to his spiritual fathers.

Ḥenānā of Adiabene

Mār Ḥenānā the Adiabenene[521] received his rank, this man who was adorned with all (virtues),[522] with humility, and with instruction in all the rest of the matters that the labour of interpretation requires. If someone should say that he was chosen for this from the beginning, he would not be wrong. This is certain from the manifest result of his deeds, since he was tested and proven in many things. Although this man's whole quiver sufficed against the flock of Satan, the Slanderer incited against him much quarreling, great strife, clamour, controversies and schisms without end, but that hidden providence did not allow [391] one of the arrows of the evil one to pierce him. Rather, while placing his foot on the rock of faith and setting his shoulder to spiritual

519 Abraham died in 569 CE.

520 Lit. 'the work of the patriarchate' (*'bādā d-paṭriyarkutā*). Isho'yahb I became Catholicos of the Church of the East in 582. See Baumstark, *Geschichte*, 126.

521 Ḥenānā of Adiabene, the controversial head of the School of Nisibis from 571 to c. 612. Two extant instances of the 'cause' genre are attributed to him: *On Golden Friday* and *On Rogations* in Scher, ed., *Traités*, 53–82). On the events during his tenure of office which may have led to the decline of the School, see Becker, *Fear of God*, 198–202.

522 See note LN 74.

labour, he worked in the spiritual arena,[523] continually without cessation and without negligence, according to the divine will, while being occupied with and meditating upon the reading of the scriptures and their interpretation,[524] day and night, reading and offering everything to this practice, as the blessed Paul did. Because of his great love for the matter, the trustworthiness of his word, and the great treasure house of his soul, it did not suffice for him to only transmit interpretation in word, but also he wanted to depict for us in writings his thought and opinion concerning all the verses and chapters in the scriptures, Old (Testament) as well as New (Testament), depicted according to Theodore the Exegete. Many homilies and disputations were also produced by him.[525]

[392] All of us pray that God will add to his life, like the blessed Hezekiah, because like a great royal treasure, his soul is rich with all the sciences of the scriptures, and like a king's table which is adorned with all sorts of foods,[526] thus he is continually a spiritual table set up before us, filled with dainties of the scriptures and embroidered with various sorts of teaching of the holy lection and salted with the elegant speech of the philosophers. Everyone who is nourished by this man is not in need of other food, but, as *every scribe who is made a student to the kingdom of heaven*, it is said about him that *he brings out from his treasures new and old things*[527] and nourishes the souls that are hungry, so also sometimes from the Old (Testament), and at other times from the New (Testament), but sometimes from the writings of his predecessors, he feeds us with his writings.[528]

He is tranquil, compassionate, and long-suffering, and he does not seek his own honour as all others do. Behold, his writings travel[529] everywhere. Even where he is distant, through his writings he is close by and teaches.

523 Syr. *esṭadyāwn*, from Gr. *stádion*. Agonistic metaphors had long been a cliché in early Christian literary culture.

524 Syr. *pushshāqayhon*. This may also be translated more concretely as 'their commentaries'.

525 Syr. *mēmrē wa-drāshē*. There was a shift to writing in prose through the sixth century due to the influence of Greek exegetical literature. Therefore, the *mēmrē* attributed to Ḥenānā may be prose works, in contrast to those of Narsai, for example.

526 A similar metaphor is used in the 'Life of Abraham of Bēt Rabban' for his reformation of the exegesis of the School (see note LA 37). The preceding clause seems to refer to Isa 38:5.

527 Mt 13:52.

528 The text published by Mingana ends here. It then continues with material unattested elsewhere. See the 'Mingana Fragment' and Appendix I.

529 Syr. *rādyān*. This may also mean 'instruct' or 'chastise'.

Report of him and his glory are spread in all the distant *schools* as in the ones nearby through the mouth of all his students. Because of this man we ask and seek from God that when [393] it is pleasing to that universal providence and it causes him to migrate from us to itself, it will choose one for us from his sons and students, though he be inferior by comparison to him, one who is trained in his ways and his habits and retains his traditions,[530] and honours his memory continually as a son would his father.

The Division of the Sessions

This is the cause of the assemblies told in brief. The (school) session was arranged and set[531] in the two seasons of summer and winter, not in an ordinary way,[532] but because the human being is double, (composed) of soul and body. These things are not able to exist[533] one without its companion. Therefore the fathers arranged things so that, just as we care for this psychic nourishment,[534] thus they distinguished for us times that are also convenient for us for the labour of bodily nourishment. For also our Lord when he taught the Apostles the aim[535] of spiritual prayer, because it (i.e. the soul) is not able to exist without this bodily (nourishment), he said to them: *Give us today our daily bread.*[536] He also showed that this too is by necessity required. Thus also Paul taught: *We did not bring anything*[537] *into the world and it is certain that we are not even able to bring anything out of it. Because of this, food and covering are sufficient for us.*[538] Thus also the fathers did, that is, in the two times [394] that they arranged for us there are the two labours: before the summer session is the harvest, and then the session of the Apostles.[539] Before the winter session is the labour of the figs and olives,

530 Syr. *mashlmānwātēh*. This may also refer to his actual writings ('commentaries').

531 Syr. *mawtbā*. The idiom here seems to reflect a technical usage and it serves as evidence that the school calendar was understood as part of the holy calendar since 'holidays' too are 'set'; see Ishai, *On the Martyrs*, 48.8.

532 Syr. *law shḥimā'it*. This could also be rendered as 'not without forethought'. On the meaning of *shḥimā*, see note 484 above.

533 Lit. 'stand'.

534 Or 'of the soul'.

535 Syr. *nishā*, equivalent to Gr. *skopós*. See note 14 in the introduction to Barḥadbeshabbā's *Ecclesiastical History* above.

536 Mt 6:11; lit. 'give us today the bread of our need'.

537 Scher emends the text, changing *lam* to *lā* (note 2).

538 1 Tim 6:7.

539 The canons of Narsai suggest that there was originally only one school session (*mawtbā*) (*Statutes of the School of Nisibis* 77–78, 110). On this passage, see Becker, *Fear of*

and then the winter session. They taught us to occupy ourselves diligently in the two of them. However, we should know which labour was for the sake of which. For this spiritual one is not for the sake of the bodily, but rather the bodily for the sake of the spiritual. Thus also one of the wise men says: All human beings seek to live so that they may eat, but I myself eat so that I may live.[540]

Exhortation[541]

Therefore the divine assembly is a likeness of the four faces in that it gazes upon and sees all regions, assuredly as the chariot of Ezekiel,[542] likewise also it is seen by all (regions). Because of this, it is fitting for those who lead their lives[543] within it to walk[544] in a manner becoming to this business and to listen to the word of our Lord who said: *Seek first of all after the kingdom of God and his justice, and all these things will be given in addition unto you*.[545] Our own commerce is spiritual and our labour is in heaven. *From there we await the one who gives us life, our Lord* [395] *Jesus the Messiah*; according to the word of the blessed Paul, *he will change the body of our lowly state and make it a likeness of his glory*.[546]

For not as those who beat the air do we run, nor again do we labour for something uncertain,[547] but rather for the great hope of spiritual knowledge. Because of this, before everything let us acquire love for the business (of the school) as well as for each other. Let us reward the masters with due honour, so that they too will conduct themselves[548] with us in joy and good will, according to our weakness. For if those who occupy themselves with worldly games before earthly kings, although they are honoured with

---

God, 105–06. On the Rabbinic *metivta*, see, e.g., David M. Goodblatt, *Rabbinic Instruction in Sasanian Babylonia* (Leiden: Brill, 1975), 76–92.

540 This saying was attributed to Socrates in a number of ancient sources, e.g. Diogenes Laertius, *Lives of the Philosophers*, ed. H. S. Long (Oxford: Clarendon, 1964), 2.34

541 It is standard practice in the 'cause' genre to end by exhorting the audience to virtuous conduct. In those instances of the genre where the portions of the text are formally divided into separate chapters this exhortation entails a distinct chapter.

542 Ezek 1:1–28.

543 Syr. *metdabbrin*, etpa. 'conduct oneself, act, or live'.

544 'To walk' is a common metaphor taken from the Hebrew Bible for leading one's life.

545 Lk 12:31. The words 'and his justice' are a biblical variant.

546 Phil 3:20.

547 1 Cor 9:26.

548 Syr. *netdabbrun*. See note 556 below on the noun cognate with this verb.

a worldly honour, hold themselves away from anything that hinders the labour of their craft, as the blessed Paul said: *How much more is it right for us to hold our mind away from anything that is against our craft!* [549] For not only before *outsiders* does the Apostle command us *to walk* with right behaviour[550] and to be in order, (saying): *buy your opportunity*[551] *and let your word be all the time seasoned with grace as with salt.*[552] For, if those who are chosen by earthly kings for a certain deed, even if they are raging and licentious, from then onward desist from these former (ways) [396] and become peaceful and pleasant, how much more is it right for us to do this! If it is the case that whenever someone is invited to enter the royal house, before he takes food, on that day he guards himself carefully, lest they see in him disorder and reject him and expel him from there, how much more is it right for us – we who have been invited to the heavenly wedding feast – to adorn ourselves with deeds suitable for that wedding feast, so that our Lord may not say to us: *My friend, how have you entered here when you do not have wedding garments?* If only this alone were the shame! But he says: *Bind his hands and feet and remove him to the outer darkness.* If only it were temporary! But he says: *There there will be crying and gnashing of teeth.*[553]

Conclusion

So then lest we be struck by this scourge,[554] let us labour diligently, according to the aim[555] of our learning, while we adjust our way of life[556] to our didactic

549 The source of this quotation is unclear.

550 The biblical text has *ḥekmtā* ('wisdom') instead of *eskēmā*.

551 Syr. *qē'rsā*, from Gr. *kairós*.

552 Col 4:5–6. Scher suggests there is an omission here (note 3). The switch from indirect to direct speech is awkward.

553 Mt 22:12–13; Mt 22:11ff is incorporated in a similar manner into the final exhortation at Cyrus of Edessa, *Six Explanations*, 135.1–136.7 (trans. 119.22–120.28) and 158.21–159.13 (140.2–22). Tamcke, *Der Katholikos-Patriarch Sabrīšō I. (596–604) und das Mönchtum*, 31–32 for Ḥenānā's reading of this text; cf. Ishodad of Merv, *Commentary on the Gospels*, 2.145.12–15 (1.86).

554 Syr. *esqṭā*, from Gr. *skûtos*.

555 Syr. *nishā*, equivalent to Gr. *skopós*. See note 14 in the introduction to Barḥadbeshabbā's *Ecclesiastical History* above.

556 The expression 'way of life' here and in the following line is the Syriac *dubbārē*. The chapter title of several of the concluding exhortations of the 'cause' genre is 'an exhortation to virtuous conduct' (*martyānutā d-'al dubbārē shappirē*) (e.g. Cyrus of Edessa, *Six Explanations*, 3.28 [trans. 3.24]). The following expression, 'our didactic reading', is literally 'the reading of our learning' (*qeryānēh d-yullphānon*)

reading, as our Lord said: *Thus let your light give light before people*, that is, your way of life, *so that they may see your good deeds and glorify your father who is in heaven*,[557] and remove the evil one from your midst. Do not mix yourselves with him, so that he may be ashamed. Crucify yourselves to the world. Strip off the old [397] man with all of his ways. Put on the new man who through knowledge is renewed in the likeness of his creator,[558] to Whom and to his Father and to the Holy Spirit be glory and honour forever and ever.

Completed is the *Cause of the Foundation of the Schools*.[559] Glory to God and to the sinner Thomas forgiveness of sins. Truly and amen.[560]

557 Mt 5:16.

558 Cf. Eph 4:22–24; Col 3:9–10. Cf. Theodore of Mopsuestia, *Commentary on the Nicene Creed*, 118 (19).

559 See note 1 above on the translation of the title.

560 M has 'Completed is the *Cause of Foundation of the Schools*. Glory to God and to the sinner Sabrisho' forgiveness. Amen.'

THE MINGANA FRAGMENT: TRANSLATION AND NOTES

See the discussion of this brief passage and its authenticity in Appendix I.

VI. And in these two years (during) which the assembly of Nisibis ceased on account of Khusrau the King,[1] many students went to Seleucia-Ctesiphon[2] where Mār Abā had been recently teaching, whom the king was fond of, …[3] so that he might prepare a path[4] for war with the Romans.[5] When the students assembled again, some of those who had gone to Seleucia-Ctesiphon returned, some did not, because they were also reading the writings of the Exegete[6] there, as (in) our assembly of Nisibis. Those ones did not return who were there to help them with the interpretation and meditation, such as Ishai and Rāmisho',[7] and Wardashir,[8] Karka d-Ledan,[9] Kashkar,[10] and Shoshan[11] were then illuminated, and these two assemblies began to proceed in the path of learning and secure ways, while guiding the spiritual ship of the church between storms without fear.

VII. But when the fathers sought to select another head in the place of Joseph,[12]

1 Khusrau I (531–579). See note CS 509.

2 Lit. 'the cities'. Cf. Arab. *al-madā'in*.

3 Mār Abā was Catholicos c. 540–552. There is a lacuna in the text, but the syntax is clear otherwise.

4 Lit. 'tread his path'.

5 The text is describing events which occurred during the second Sasanian-Roman war of the sixth century (640–662). Winter and Dignas, *Rom und das Perserreich*, 57–65, 124–29.

6 I.e., Theodore of Mopsuestia.

7 These were two important figures at the School of Seleucia in the sixth century. The former composed the extant 'cause' text, *On the Martyrs*, 15–52. Both appear at *Chronicle of Siirt*, 2.1.158. On the two of them, see also Vööbus, *History*, 175–76 and Baumstark, *Geschichte*, 123.

8 See notes SL 54 and SL 66.

9 See note SL 71.

10 See note LN 132.

11 Susa, a city in Khuzistan.

12 The controversial Catholicos (551–566/7) who was deposed. See *Bibliotheca Orientalis* III.1.432–35; Barhebraeus, *Chronicon Ecclesiasticum* II, ed. J. B. Abbeloos and T. J. Lamy

Khusrau the King, after he had returned from the Roman Empire,[13] was not pleased with this, because he had previously been his doctor. However, when he saw that they were seeking this in common,[14] he was somewhat frightened and asked, though with great severity, the fathers to choose another in his place. Afterwards the king changed his mind and returned to his previous (opinion) because of the cunning wiles of Joseph. He showed by his manner of speech that if they should expel him, he would again obstruct the assembly of Nisibis. He did this because Joseph hated our divine assembly. He declared to the king that the readers and elementary instructors were seeking to rebel against him. Or, perhaps (the king changed his mind) because God, praise be to his grace, took pleasure in this, because the teaching of Mār Ḥenānā was not much loved within the assembly, and this (was the case) also among his students[15] while he was still teaching, and this (was so) due to the thicket of commotion that Satan had planted also in this assembly of ours, as is his habit. His exegetical teachings[16] ceased to go on their path.

VIII. Then Paul,[17] bishop of the city, went to the gate of the King with a number of presbyters and deacons.[18] The gate of mercies was opened for him and his entreaty was received before the King of Kings. He made manifest the cunning wiles of Joseph against the King of Kings and against the Church of God. The king then gave permission that the assembly be opened and that another head be appointed.[19] They selected Ishai the teacher, and Paul and the rest were not happy with him until they selected Ḥazqi'ēl, a friend of the king and a student of Mār Abā.[20] He had come with the king to Nisibis during this upheaval of the kingdom, which occurred in our days against the Romans.[21] May the Lord give to all of them power and strength to lead their flock with tranquility and relief, and may they delight the lambs that are deposited with them with the teaching of life.

(Louvain-Paris, 1874), 95–97; *Chronicle of Siirt*, 2.1.176–81; Wright, *History*, 121; Baumstark, *Geschichte*, 124; Labourt, *Le Christianisme dans l'Empire Perse*, 192–97.

13 Syr. *bēt rhomāyē*.

14 Syr. *knishā'it*, or 'as an assembly' (cf. Syr. *knushyā*).

15 Syr. *b-talmidutēh*.

16 Syr. *durrāshē da-mphashshqānutā*.

17 Paul, bishop of Nisibis, student of Mār Abā, played an important role in the deposition of the catholicos Joseph (Fiey, *Nisibe*, 51–55).

18 On the 'gate' of the king, see note CS 510.

19 On the School of Seleucia, see Becker, *Fear of God*, 157–59.

20 See also *Chronicle of Siirt* 2.1.192.

21 This war ended in 562.

PORTION OF THE *MĒMRĀ ON THE HOLY FATHERS*: TRANSLATION AND NOTES

Addai Scher appended to his edition of the *Cause* part of a *mēmrā*, that is, a metrical homily, which he found in the library of the Chaldean episcopate of Diyarbakir in a seventeenth-century manuscript containing homilies of Narsai.[1] The *mēmrā* was composed by Rabban Surin,[2] a head of the School of Nisibis in the seventh century, but a marginal note explains that some of the lines in the text were written by his student, Jacob the Great. Unfortunately Scher only reproduced those lines of the text which he deemed of historical importance. The manuscript he used has probably been destroyed, but at least one copy of the text is extant in Berlin.[3]

Mēmrā on the Holy Fathers, Mār Narsai, Mār Abraham, Mār John, which was produced by Rabban Surin, their student and spiritual son

In this path our blessed teachers went, Master Narsai, Mār Abraham, and Mār John ... From Edessa[4] they began the labours of teaching and they completed the course of their way of life in the city of Nisibis.[5] ... After the time that Edessa[6] went a-whoring and was an adulteress with the calf,

1 *Cause* 399–402; see Addai Scher, 'Notice sur les Manuscrits Syriaques et Arabes conservés à l'archevèché Chaldéen de Diarbékir', *JA* 10 (1907): 361–62, Ms 70. The manuscript is dated 1328 of the Greeks, i.e. 1639 CE, and produced in the Monastery of Michael of Tar'el in Adiabene.

2 Baumstark, *Geschichte*, 196–97.

3 Baumstark (ibid.) suggests that there is another copy of this text in a liturgical collection of Narsai's works. However, his citation for this is Eduard Sachau, *Verzeichniss der syrischen Handschriften der Königlichen Bibliothek zu Berlin* (Berlin: A. Asher, 1899), 57 (Sachau 174–76) (pp. 190–97), #10, which is identical with Narsai's homily on Diodore, Theodore, and Nestorius: 'Homélie de Narsès sur les Trois Docteurs Nestoriens', ed. and trans. F. Martin, JA 9e ser. 14 (1899): 446–92; 15 (1900): 469–525. Perhaps the Surin text has been interpolated into the homily, but Baumstark does not state this and someone would have to check the actual manuscript in Berlin. Completed in 1881, it may ultimately be related to Diyarbakir 70.

4 The Greek name of the city is transliterated here in the Syriac, *'ds'* (Gr. Edessa).

5 Syr. *Ṣobā*. This is the later Syriac name for Nisibis.

6 Syr. *Urhāy*.

which the demon of Egypt[7] moulded and sent, and which was set up there, the assembly with its teachers migrated and came to Nisibis, and it became great and large and cast down sinews, also roots. Wondrous Narsai and Mār Barṣaumā planted, also they consolidated. Little by little it became great and it was abundant with leaves and fruit. … Thirty years and a little more the glorious one lived and he did not slacken nor become silent from the battle with the errant ones. … Mār Michael, the student of truth, a skilled scribe,[8] – speech is too small to repeat the tale of his story. … Mār Elisha who is named bar Qozbāyē,[9] he became a student to the teaching of the skilled scribes. The athlete of truth (girded)[10] himself against sin, and he demonstrated the truth of his faith and rebuked ungodliness. Mār Isho'yahb, who was from Arzon, succeeded him. He worked, was successful, and was selected Catholicos. Mār Abraham bar Qardāḥē[11] inherited his seat and he cast the mould of his words according to those before him. There were afterwards from generation to generation other teachers until at one time Rabban Surin arose. In this path the just lover of the just went, and he began and finished by the power of the aid which is from grace. Fifty years he worked in this spiritual field and he did not yield to the difficult times that battled against him. Inasmuch as he was loved a love of his lord was upon him (greater) than anything. In the likeness of the just he endured the scorn of the foolish, and he did not weary from the fight against the demons. Demons and men battled with the just and modest one, and the demons were shamed and the just one was victorious by the power of the spirit. He became a student to the mastership[12] of the words of truth. He composed a homily[13] of the glory of the righteous ones with the speech of his mouth. This homily was written by him about the holy ones, the followers of Mār Narsai, Mār Abraham, and Mār John. He imitated them in their faith and their way of life, and like a son and an heir he inherited the seat of their teaching. He produced exegeses and composed homilies as well as commentaries,[14] and he deposited a treasure of teaching for his heirs.

7 I.e. Cyril of Alexandria (d. 444). Cyril is commonly referred to as simply 'the Egyptian'.

8 A common expression, e.g. Jacob of Sarug, *Homélies contre Juifs*, 1.1.

9 The text is *br qrbn'* (*bar qurbānē*), but I follow Scher's suggested emendation (the alteration from *zayin* to *resh* and *yod* to *nun* are both understandable mistakes to make in the Syriac script).

10 The text is unreadable here. Scher suggests *ḥayyeṣ*.

11 Lit. 'son of the smiths (of small articles)'. This seems to be Abraham of Bēt Rabban.

12 Syr. *rabbanutā*.

13 Syr. *mēmrā*.

14 Syr. *turgāmē*.

APPENDIX I
ON THE MANUSCRIPT TRADITION OF THE *CAUSE OF THE FOUNDATION OF THE SCHOOLS*

The manuscript tradition of the *Cause* is confused due to both the imprecision of previous scholars and the tumultuous modern political history of the region from which the manuscripts derive. The *Patrologia Orientalis* edition of the *Cause* was produced in 1907 by Mār Addai Scher (1867–1915), Archbishop of the Chaldean Catholic Church in Siirt, a city south-west of Lake Van in south-eastern Turkey. Aside from his pastoral duties, Scher was an active scholar who published numerous works on Syriac literature and history as well as part of the edition and French translation of the Arabic *Chronicle of Siirt*, or the *Nestorian History* (*Histoire Nestorienne*) as it is also called. Scher was murdered in 1915 amidst the catastrophic upheaval that took place in what is now south-eastern Turkey during and after World War I.[1]

In his edition of the text of the *Cause* Scher used three manuscripts:

C Ms 109 Episcopal Library of Siirt; dated 1609.

T Ms 82 Episcopal Library of Siirt; many blanks for those words and phrases not understood; 16th century.[2]

M Ms from the Church of Mār Guryā in the diocese of Siirt; incomplete at the beginning and the end; more recent; closer to C in content.

Scher also relied upon a fourth text, a selection of the *Cause* provided by Alphonse Mingana in the introduction to his edition of the works of Narsai.[3] Scher refers to this text as A. C serves as the base text, while

1 For Scher's life and bibliography, see J.M. Fiey, 'L'apport de Mgr Addaï Scher (+1915) à l'hagiographie orientale', *AB* 83 (1965): 121–42 and Rudolf Macuch, *Geschichte der spat- und neusyrischen Literatur* (Berlin: Walter de Gruyter, 1976), 402–05. For an example of how the ancient martyrological genre is still alive and kicking, see A. S. Assad, 'Addai Shir 1867–1915', *The Harp* VIII/IX (1995–96): 209–20. For the context of his death, see David Gaunt, *Massacres, Resistance, Protectors: Muslim–Christian Relations in Eastern Anatolia During World War I* (Piscataway, NJ: Gorgias, 2006), 250–56.

2 For both C and T, see Addai Scher, *Catalogue des manuscrits Syriaques et Arabes conservés dans la bibliothèque épiscopale de Sèert* (Kurdistan) (Mosul, 1905).

3 Narsai, *Homiliae et Carmina*, 32-39 ('Integra Narratio').

Scher's translation often relies on readings from T presented in the critical apparatus. Scher's text is based solely on T for the introductory portion (pp. 327.1–333.7), since this part of the *Cause* is not extant in C. M is rarely cited and only towards the end of the text. Scher's citation practice and apparatus are occasionally inconsistent.

Along with C, T, M, and A, Scher mentions a fifth manuscript, which comes from the Chaldean monastery of Notre-Dame des Sémences (Our Lady of the Seeds), not far from the Monastery of Rabban Hormizd (2 km from Alqosh and 40 km from Mosul in northern Iraq). He does not include this manuscript in his list of abbreviations and thus does not seem to have used it. We know he saw the manuscript in 1902 when he visited the monastery, after which he produced the catalogue for its library. The manuscript is incomplete at the end and dated to approximately the 15th century, according to Scher, who labelled it Ms 52 Notre-Dame des Sémences in his 1906 catalogue.[4] It was later labelled Alqosh 65 in Vosté's catalogue of 1929.[5] The difference in labels comes from the fact that the books of the Chaldean monastery of Rabban Hormizd near Alqosh were moved to the library of Notre-Dame des Sémences in 1869.[6]

C and T were probably destroyed in the same events that led to Scher's death.[7] The whereabouts of M are unknown but it may also be lost forever. The preface to a Turkish translation of the *Chronicle of Siirt* contains an account of the intentional burning of the library at Siirt in 1915.[8] The Notre-Dame des Sémences collection was moved to Baghdad at a certain point and its exact present condition is unclear (=Chaldean Monastery Baghdad 181).[9] As of July 2003 – that is, after the mass looting of cultural and civic institutions permitted by the American forces occupying Iraq – the collections in Baghdad were intact.

4 Addai Scher, 'Notice sur les Manuscrits Syriaques conservés dans la bibliothèque du Couvent de Chaldéens de Notre Dame-des-Sémences', *JA* 10 ser 7 (1906): 499.

5 Jacques Marie Vosté, 'Catalogue de la Bibliothèque Syro-Chaldéenne du Couvent de Notre-Dame des Semences', *Angelicum* (Rome) 6 (1929): 27. Vööbus refers to it by this name.

6 Alain Desreumaux, *Répertoire des bibliothèques et des catalogues de manuscrits syriaques* (Paris: CNRS, 1991), 84–85.

7 Ibid. 230–31.

8 Adday Şer, *Siirt Vakayinamesi: Doğu Süryani Nasturi Kilisesi Tarihi* (trans. Celal Kabadayı; Istanbul: Yaba, 2002), 8–9.

9 P. Haddad and J. Isaac, *Syriac and Arabic Manuscripts in the Library of the Chaldean Monastery Baghdad, Part I, Syriac Manuscripts* (Baghdad: Iraqi Academy, 1988) [Contents in Arabic], 89.

With regard to the stated authorship of the *Cause*, the authorial attributions in the manuscripts themselves are difficult to confirm. Scher's belief that the two Barḥadbeshabbās were the same person may be reflected in his edition of the *Cause*.[10] The author's name provided in the title of the work in the PO edition is 'Mār Barḥadbeshabbā 'Arbāyā, Bishop of Ḥalwan'. This appears in the two copies from Scher's own hand (Ms 394 Bibliothèque Nationale de France and Ms Vat. Syr. 507) and probably also in Sharfeh Patr. 80, which was probably made from the Vatican copy. However, the catalogue entry for Notre-Dame 52/Alqosh 65 has only 'Barḥadbeshabbā 'Arbāyā', and Mingana 547, probably a copy of this manuscript, has 'Mār Barḥadbeshabbā 'Arbāyā'. The manuscripts are all late and since most of them are now missing, it is unclear whether a solution to the question of the author's name will be found through the authorial attributions in individual manuscripts. There is the slim chance that new manuscripts of the *Cause* will one day come to light. The text was composed in the late sixth century. It is possible that it was copied at some point in the centuries between its composition and the present manuscript attestation, and that all copies have not yet been found. However, this is doubtful.

There are also other modern copies of the *Cause*. According to Vööbus, Alqosh 155 (= Chald. Mon. 486) is a copy of Siirt 82.[11] (This manuscript is presumably with Ms 52 Notre-Dame des Sémences in Baghdad, if it still exists, but it is not clear if it actually contains or contained a copy of the *Cause*.) As mentioned above, two modern copies were produced by Scher himself. Syriac Ms 394 Bibliothèque Nationale de France is among François Nau's papers in Paris and seems to have been sent to Nau by Scher.[12] There is also now a copy in the Vatican library (Ms Vat. Syr. 507).[13] Vosté states that this was sent by Scher to Father J. Tfinkdji, vicar of the Chaldean Patriarch of Beirut, and that in September 1926 it was deposited in the Vatican library by Vosté himself as a martyr's relic.[14] Both of these manuscripts are

10 For an early formulation of this opinion, see Scher, 'Étude supplémentaire sur les écrivains syriens orientaux', 15.

11 Vööbus, *History*, 177 n. 171.

12 Françoise Briquel-Chatonnet, *Manuscrits syriaques: de la Bibliothèque nationale de France (nos 356–435 entrés depuis 1911), de la Bibliothèque Méjanes d'Aix-en-Provence, de la Bibliothèque municipale de Lyon et de la Bibliothèque nationale et universitaire de Strasbourg* (Paris: Bibliothèque national de France, 1997), 112–13.

13 Arnold Van Lantschoot, *Inventaire des manuscrits syriaques des fonds Vatican (490–631): Barberini oriental et Neofiti* (Studi e testi 243; Vatican, 1965), 39.

14 Vosté, 'Catalogue', 27 n. 1; see also Desreumaux, *Répertoire*, 112–13. (See notes 5 and 6 above).

annotated, the former most likely being the source for the PO edition itself. Another manuscript, Sharfeh Patr. 80, which is mentioned by Vööbus, was probably made from the copy that would eventually be sent to the Vatican.[15] Further inquiry could be made concerning the manuscripts of the *Cause*, but access to those in Baghdad is needed first. Scher's notes in the Paris manuscript may also prove helpful.

There is one final manuscript, Ms Ming. Syr. 547, which is a modern copy and points to a possible problem with Mingana's scholarly precision, or perhaps even his truthfulness.[16] In his edition of the metrical homilies of Narsai Mingana does not specify from which manuscript he draws his excerpts of the *Cause* (A, according to Scher). In the catalogue entry for Mingana 547 he states that it is this manuscript which he used. However, there are two problems with this. First, Mingana's catalogue says that the *Cause* of Barḥadbeshabbā is in folio pages 69b–83a. However, neither Mingana 547 itself nor the published microfiche of it contain the last two pages (82b–83a). They simply stop mid-sentence at the end of 82a (PO Edition 377.5) and thus within the *Cause* well before any of the material covered in the extract printed in Mingana's edition of Narsai's works, which begins at *Cause* 381.5 and goes through 392.9 (not including the material unattested elsewhere). Mingana mentions in the catalogue entry that a page is missing from the manuscript and there is evidence that a single page has been torn out of the actual manuscript.[17] Thus, according to Mingana's statement in the catalogue, all of the material in the Narsai edition would have to fit on two manuscript pages. This is impossible.

Furthermore, the contents and order of Mingana 547 are the same as the manuscript mentioned by Scher in his introduction to the *Cause*, but which he did not seem to have used in his edition, that is, Ms 52 Notre-Dame des Sémences (later Alqosh 65 and then Baghdad Chald. Mon. 181) (perhaps 15th century), mentioned above. Mingana 547 is dated to c. 1880 and thus must be a copy of Notre-Dame des Sémences 52/Alqosh 65. However, this *Vorlage* of Mingana 547 lacks approximately two pages of material which Mingana published and which cannot be found in any other manuscript (i.e.

15 Behnam Sony, *Fihris al-makhtūtāt al-batriyarkīya fī Dair al-Sharfa - Lubnān* ('Le catalogue des manuscrits du Patriacat au Couvent de Charfet – Liban') (Beirut, 1993), Ms 797 (p. 307), 'sabab ta'sīs al-madāris' on fol. 15–23.

16 Alphonse Mingana, *Catalogue of the Mingana Collection of Manuscripts* (Cambridge, 1948–1963), col. 1015–16.

17 I thank Philippa Bassett, archivist at the University of Birmingham, for examining the manuscript for me.

the 'Mingana Fragment').[18] It is unlikely that this material fell out of both Mingana 547 and its *Vorlage*. In any case, if this material was actually part of the manuscript then it would have to be an interpolation.

Scher does not mention the interpolated material being in Notre-Dame des Sémences 52/Alqosh 65, the manuscript upon which Mingana 547 is based. He certainly handled the manuscript and of course later edited the text of the *Cause*. Furthermore, although he did not use Notre-Dame des Sémences 52/Alqosh 65 in his edition, he did use the printed text of Mingana from the Narsai edition, apparently because he thought it had come from another manuscript tradition. In the introduction to his edition to the *Cause*, he does not seem to be been aware that Mingana 547 is simply a copy of a manuscript to which he already had access.

With regard to the 'Mingana Fragment', Scher recognizes the oddity of the passage, which is clearly out of place in the *Cause*. He opines that it is not part of the original composition, but that it has been added by a later copyist as a supplement to the original text, inserted into 'le manuscrit de M. Mingana'.[19] J. B. Chabot translates this passage into French, but questions it.[20] J.-M. Fiey, who was the first to raise a firm challenge to the very authenticity of Mingana's *Chronicle of Arbela*, refers to this fragment as 'un texte d'origine douteuse'.[21] But Vööbus, who suggests that the *Cause* has been 'supplemented', accepts this material as historically authentic and employs it as the main source for a temporary closure of the School of Nisibis.[22]

These problems suggest that we should be suspicious of the text Mingana published, especially since the content of the 'interpolation' is strange in itself. The material added is not from after the time of Ḥenānā or the author (c. 590s), but refers to mid-sixth-century events, and yet seems to confuse things by setting Ḥenānā in this mid-sixth-century context. Perhaps Mingana conflated two manuscripts by accident, or even intentionally. Or, even worse, there remains the possibility that this interpolation is in fact a forgery.

As anyone who works within Syriac Studies knows, Alphonse Mingana (1878–1937) was a scholar whose method was occasionally questionable,

18 Narsai, *Homiliae et Carmina*, 38–39 (sections VII–VIII).

19 *Cause* 324.

20 J. B. Chabot, 'Narsai le Docteur et les origins de l'école de Nisibe', *JA* 10e série, vol. 6 (July-August 1905): 170–73. Cf. Samir, *Alphonse Mingana*, 9.

21 J.-M. Fiey, 'Topographie Chrétienne de Mahozé', *OS* 12 (1967): 407 (repr. idem, *Communautés syriaques en Iran et Irak des origins à 1552*, Chap. 9).

22 Vööbus, *History*, 155–60, or see ibid. 176 for his further use of the text.

possibly even disingenuous and deceptive. The famous example of this is his 'discovery' of the so-called *Chronicle of Arbela*, the authenticity of which has been impugned by scholars of no mean reputation.[23] Furthermore, problems with Mingana's work continue to be discussed. For example, in his study of the *Acts of Mār Qardāgh* Joel Walker supports the need for scholarly suspicion in using Mingana's editions,[24] while Chip Coakley has found instances of Mingana's theft of manuscripts from Rendel Harris's collection.[25]

Mingana's edition of Narsai's metrical homilies remains the only published version of much of Narsai's work. It lacks critical scholarly tools and it is clear that Mingana catholicized the text at certain points.[26] If the interpolation to the *Cause* was an invention or, at least, a disingenuous insertion, we should consider whether Mingana could have had certain goals in publishing such material. Why would he publish this questionable fragment?

Mingana understood the publication of this material to be a challenge to Labourt's rendering of the history of the School of Nisibis as presented in his synthetic history of Christianity in the Sasanian Empire: 'From this narrative of Barḥadbeshabbā it is clear what sort of corrections should be brought to bear upon the work of J. Labourt: *Le Christianisme dans l'empire Perse, sous la dynastie Sassanide* (1904)'.[27] It is not clear what points in Labourt's reconstruction would be challenged by this new material.[28]

23 The text of the *Chronicle* can be found at: A. Mingana, ed. and trans., *Sources Syriaques I* (Leipzig: Harrassowitz, 1907) 1–168 and P. Kawerau, ed. and trans., *Die Chronik von Arbela* (CSCO 467–68; Louvain: Peeters, 1985). See criticisms in Julius Assfalg, 'Zur Textüberlieferung der Chronik von Arbela. Beobachtungen zu Ms. or. fol. 3126', *OC* 50 (1966): 19–36 and J.-M. Fiey, 'Auteur et date de la Chronique d'Arbèles', *OS* 12 (1967): 265–302. Sebastian Brock supports the authenticity of at least some of the work, 'Syriac Historical Writing', 23–25. There is discussion in Samir, *Alphonse Mingana*, 12–14. Edward G. Mathews, Jr's review of Ilaria Ramelli's 2002 translation and commentary of the *Chronicle* provides a good introduction to the problem and the scholars who have weighed in on this issue, *Il Chronicon di Arbela: Presentazione, traduzione e note essenziali* (Madrid: Universidad Complutense Madrid, 2002) at http://ccat.sas.upenn.edu/bmcr/2003/2003-11-01.html.

24 Walker, *The Legend of Mar Qardagh*, 287–90.

25 J. F. Coakley, 'A Catalogue of the Manuscripts in the John Rylands Library', *Bulletin of the John Rylands Library* 75 (1993): 109–13.

26 'It was not a critical edition. It was intended to be a reading book for Chaldean priests, not a book for scholars. For that reason, the homilies were slightly expurgated to suppress some Nestorian affirmations' (Samir, *Alphonse Mingana*, 8).

27 'Ex hâc narratione Barhadhbchabbae liquet quales correctiones afferendae sint operi D. J. Labourt: Le Christianisme dans l'empire Perse, sous la dynastie Sassanide (1904)' (Narsai, *Homiliae et Carmina*, 40, misquoted in Samir, *Alphonse Mingana*, 11).

28 The bulk of Labourt's discussion appears at *Christianisme dans l'empire Perse*, 288–301, but the narrative portion is primarily pp. 288–93.

However, Labourt does question at one point the historicity of Mār Abā's founding of the School of Seleucia, which is alluded to at the beginning of the 'Mingana Fragment'.[29] Mingana's criticisms of J. B. Chabot's work on the School and its sources would suggest that he was perhaps including this material in part as a way to attack Chabot. However, I have not found any precise correspondence between his criticisms of Chabot and the interpolated material.[30]

29 Ibid. 169–70 n. 3. However, on 291 he seems to accept this tradition.

30 Mingana, *Réponse à M. l'abbé J.-B. Chabot, à propos de la chronique de Barhadbshabba.*

APPENDIX II
THE TREE OF PORPHYRY IN THE *CAUSE OF THE FOUNDATION OF THE SCHOOLS*

Despite a silence in the sources concerning formal philosophical study at the School of Nisibis, it is clear from the works produced there that members of the School had some acquaintance with the early echelons of the Greek philosophical curriculum of Late Antiquity, specifically Aristotle's logical works and their commentary tradition. The plethora of philosophical material we find in the *Cause of the Foundation of the Schools* provides an excellent example of this. Much of the dependence on Greek philosophical sources is highlighted in the notes of the translation above and I have discussed this material in detail elsewhere.[1] However, here I would like to look at one instance of the text's use of Aristotelian logic and the later Neoplatonic commentary tradition. The passage from the *Cause* under consideration relies on a Christianized version of the so-called Tree of Porphyry from Porphyry's third-century *Isagoge*.

The *Isagoge* of Porphyry of Tyre was a key text in the late antique and Medieval curriculum of learning, among Greek- and Latin-speaking Christians and eventually among Jews, Christians, and Muslims working within Islamic sciences and philosophy. It is in fact the most influential work in logic and one of the most influential books in philosophy in general. Written as an introduction to Aristotle's *Categories*, it defines and describes the relationship between the five different ways in which a subject can relate to a predicate, or the 'predicables', as they are called.[2] According to Porphyry, the five predicables are Genus, Species, Difference, Property, and Accident.[3]

1 Becker, *Fear of God*, 126–54.

2 For an edition with a long, useful introduction to the text, a French translation, and the Latin version of Boethius, see Porphyry, *Isagoge*, trans. A. de Libera and A.-P. Segonds, intro. and notes A. de Libera (Paris: Vrin, 1998). Also now there is the extensive commentary on the *Isagoge* by Jonathan Barnes, Porphyry, *Introduction* (Oxford: Clarendon, 2003). For a critical text, see the CAG edition. There is no one definitive study on the *Isagoge*'s wide influence in Greek, Latin, Syriac, Arabic, etc.

3 Porphyry actually confuses Aristotle's system by treating genus and species as different predicables.

The *Isagoge* was the first text in the Neoplatonic school curriculum and several commentaries on it from the later Neoplatonists are extant.

The most famous portion of the *Isagoge* is the so-called Tree of Porphyry. The Tree is part of a passage in which Porphyry attempts to demonstrate by example the relationship between genus and species. The original Tree of Porphyry is as follows:

> Substance then is also a genus; under it is body; and again under body animate body, and under this is animal; thus again also under it is rational animal, after which is set man; under man are Socrates, Plato and the rest of men. Of all these substance is the genus of genera,[4] and it is a genus only, while man is the species of species,[5] and it is a species only. Body is a species of substance and a genus of animate body. But then also animate body is a species of substance and a genus of animal, etc.[6]

This passage may be schematized in the following manner:

> Substance → Body → Animate (or Ensouled) → Animal (or Living) → Rational Animal → Man

In the above line each entity is a genus of what is on its right and a species of what is on its left. Thus, substance is not a species nor is man a genus. There is no broader genus to which substance may belong, while the species man is made up of particular men, such as Socrates and Plato.

The first translation of the *Isagoge* into Syriac was completed around the turn of the sixth century and was part of a steady stream of Greek philosophical works to be translated and taken up within Syriac-speaking intellectual centres, first by West Syrians, and later East Syrians, in Sasanian Mesopotamia and beyond.[7] The first translation of the *Isagoge* into Syriac is attributed to the famous West-Syrian translator, Sergius of Rēsh'aynā (d. c. 536 CE).[8] The close connections between early Edessene Christianity, as

4 Translation of Greek: *tò genikṓtaton*, 'the most generic'.

5 Translation of Greek: *tò eidikṓtaton*, 'the most specific'.

6 Porphyry, *Isagoge*, 4.21ff ; trans. from Porphyry the Phoenician, *Isagoge*, trans. E. W. Warren (Toronto: Pontifical Institute of Mediaeval Studies, 1975), 35–36; Syriac version 9.26–10.8 (Brock, 'The earliest Syriac translation of Porphyry's Eisagoge').

7 Hugonnard-Roche, *La logique d'Aristote du grec au syriaque*; Sebastian P. Brock, 'From Antagonism to Assimilation: Syriac Attitudes to Greek Learning', in *East of Byzantium: Syrian and Armenia in the formative period*, ed. N. G. Garsoïan, T. F. Mathews, and R. W. Thomson (Washington, DC: Dumbarton Oaks Center for Byzantine Studies, 1984), 19–34 (repr. in Brock, *Syriac Perspectives on Late Antiquity* [London: Ashgate, 1984]).

8 Brock, 'The earliest Syriac translation of Porphyry's Eisagoge'. This attribution is questioned in Henri Hugonnard-Roche, 'Les traductions syriaques de l'Isagoge de Porphyre et la constitution du corpus syriaque de logique', *Revue d'Histoire des Textes* 24 (1994): 293–312.

well as Syriac Christianity in general, and Antioch, which have been clearly traced out by modern scholars (and were acknowledged even in antiquity), have been used to explain the first influx of philosophical literature into Edessa and from there further transmission eastward.[9] However, as the sixth century progressed, the circuits of transmission became more complex and texts went through various routes.[10] Furthermore, the heavy dependence on the later Neoplatonic transmission of this material suggests that Antioch was of less importance than direct connections to Alexandria.

The Tree of Porphyry apparently served as a useful teaching device and was at times transmitted separately from the *Isagoge* as whole. It is an easy didactic tool, one that could remain in the student's memory and later be reworked and used as one chose. Its popularity in Syriac can be seen not only in the translation of the *Isagoge*, but also the version of the Tree found in Paul the Persian's sixth-century *Introduction to Logic* (see below) and in the separate version we find in the seventh-century manuscript, British Library Add 14658.[11]

> The division of universal substance (Gr. *ousía*): Substance is divided into body and non-body. Body is divided into ensouled and not ensouled. Ensouled body is divided into animal, living-plant, and plant. By body then are known wood, dry stuff, and stones. Animal then is divided into rational and non-rational. Rational then is divided into human and god. Human is divided into Socrates and Plato. Non-rational animal is divided into cow, horse, and the rest of the four footed (animals), and creeping (things), the bird, flying (things) and whatever lives in the water. [12]

A schematization of this passage is as follows:

> Substance → Body → Animate (or Ensouled) → Animal (or Living) → Rational → Human → Socrates

9 See, for example, a number of the articles in H. J. W. Drijvers, *East of Antioch: Studies in Early Syriac Christianity* (London: Ashgate, 1984).

10 Becker, *Fear of God*, 127–30; Walker, *The Legend of Mar Qardagh*, 180–90.

11 Wright, *Catalogue of Syriac Manuscripts in the British Museum*, III: 1154–1160 (Ms DCCCCLXXXVII).

12 *pullāg usiya' d-gawwā (the text is rubricated up to this point): usiya' metpalgā l-gushmā w-lā gushmā, gushmā metpleg la-mnaphphshā w-lā mnaphphshā, gushmā mnaphphshā metpleg l-hayyutā wa-l-ḥayyut nṣebtā wa-l-nṣebtā. b-gushmā dēn lā mnaphphshā metyad'in qaysē (w-) yabbishē w-kēphē. ḥayyutā dēn [lā] metpleg la-mlilā wa-l-lā mlilā, mlilā dēn metpleg l-bar 'nāshā w-l-alāhā. bar 'nāshā metpleg l-soqratis wa-l-plāṭon. ḥayyutā lā mliltā metpalgā l-tawrā wa-l-susyā wa-l-sharkā d-arb'at reglē w-raḥshā wa-l-ṭayrā wa-l-praḥtā w-l-aylēn da-b-mayyā mdayyrin.* The text is in a column of twenty-three lines in the manuscript.

This version of the Tree shows clear connections to the later Neoplatonic versions, such as the tripartite division of the 'animate' that we also find in the commentaries attributed to Elias and David.[13] There is no obvious evidence of Christian interpolation.[14]

The *Cause* contains an idiosyncratic version of the Tree and provides its earliest Syriac attestation in East-Syrian literature. The variations of the *Cause*'s version of the Tree from the original reveal something of the later Neoplatonic and Christian tradition on which the *Cause* depends. In fact, what might be considered the misuse of the Tree within the *Cause* demonstrates how the early reception of this material was not a simple taking up of Greek texts and ideas, but rather a negotiated appropriation, which could lead to a peculiar use of the transmitted material.

The Tree as it appears in the *Cause* is as follows:

> Since everything that exists is either substance[15] or accident,[16] each of these divisions is divided into many species, these (entities) which are included under it. Therefore all substance that exists is either corporeal or incorporeal. Body too is divided into many differences that are under it. That is, then, the ensouled body and the one without soul, the one endowed with sense and the other deprived of it. Thus also the ensouled body is arranged into other distinctions: the body that is living and the one that is not, the one that moves, and the other deprived of movement; and again that one that is living and moves is divided also into other distinctions that are under it, that is, the rational and the non-rational, and again the rational into the spiritual and the psychic, and the non-rational into the living and the non-living;[17] and again the spiritual is divided also into the limited and the unlimited, the one eternal[18] and the other temporal, the one the cause of all things, the other is the effect[19] that is from the cause of all things, which is God.[20]

13 It also shares with the works of Elias and David a division of the different animal species. See note 29 below.

14 This fits with the disputed suggestion that the manuscript in which it is found belonged to the Syriac-speaking, pagan philosophical community of Harran (Becker, *Fear of God*, 129). However, other texts in this manuscript are certainly Christian.

15 Syr. *usiya'*, from Gr. *ousía*.

16 Syr. *gedshā*, the Syriac equivalent of Gr. *sumbebēkós*.

17 Non-rational is a species of living. To say that there are living things that are non-rational is redundant. However, the passage goes a step further and states that non-rational has non-living under it as well. This is said perhaps to avoid the suggestion that the rational/non-rational dichotomy applies only to living things and not to God and the angels.

18 Syr. *ityā*, or 'existent'.

19 Such a phrase may derive from the East-Syrian theological tradition. See Brock, 'The Christology of the Church of the East', 138.

20 *Cause* 337.13–338.10.

The word 'under' used in this passage means 'subject to, subordinate to'. The idea that there would be existents in a genus above substance seems to derive from a loose usage of the word 'exists'. The Syriac *itaw(hy)* can mean both 'to be' or 'to exist', but also 'to exist eternally or truly' in the philosophical sense of the Greek word *eînai*. Whereas elsewhere in the *Cause* (e.g. 334.7–334.15) the philosophical sense is employed, for example, when the author states that only God can truly 'exist', here the more common sense of the word is being used. To 'exist' in this case refers also to things that come into and go out of being, commonly expressed by the Greek verb *gígnesthai*. The dichotomy we find in the passage between accident and substance is basic to Aristotelian philosophy. All of Aristotle's categories, except substance, are accidentals. There cannot be further division under accident in the Tree because there can be no science of accidentals.[21]

Some of the further distinctions drawn by the *Cause*'s Tree derive from the philosophical tradition. For example, distinctions the *Cause* makes under the category of the spiritual, differentiating between limited and unlimited and cause and effect, can be traced to philosophical sources. The further distinctions created by introducing the properties of 'movement' and 'sensation' clearly derive from Aristotle and the commentary tradition on his works. In book I of *De Anima* Aristotle summarizes his predecessors' views on the nature of the soul as generally falling into two categories, the soul as principle of movement (*kínēsis*) and as principle of sensation (*aísthēsis*). In book II he begins his own definition. 'Making then a beginning of our inquiry we say that ensouled is distinguished from soul-less by living.'[22] 'Living' he previously defined as having 'self-nourishment, increase, and decay'.[23] 'Soul' has various faculties. The most common is the nutritive, which even plants share.[24] This is the faculty of growth and self-maintenance. 'Living' belongs to all living things but it is specifically the 'animal' that has sensation (*aísthēsis*).[25] Movement (*kínēsis*) is also one of the faculties of 'soul', though it is not necessarily a faculty of every ensouled entity.[26] Thus, 'ensouled' in the Tree of Porphyry is what we would commonly call 'living', but does not necessarily entail 'movement' or 'sensation' (e.g. it is

21 Jonathan Barnes, *Aristotle* (Oxford: Oxford University Press, 1982), 57.
22 *De Anima* 413a20–22.
23 Ibid. 412a14–15.
24 Ibid. 413b7–8.
25 Ibid. 413b1–2.
26 Ibid. 414a31–2.

applicable to plants).[27] 'Living' is used more specifically for those entities that we would refer to as animals (cf. Gr. *zôon*).

Of the Neoplatonic commentaries on the *Isagoge*, that of Ammonius is the earliest and the briefest. In Ammonius's summary of the passage which contains the Tree of Porphyry, he explains the difference between ensouled and animal (i.e. living).

> For the animal is said to be ensouled and partaking of sensation (Gr. *aisthḗseōs metéchon*); ensouled is that which is reared, increases, and begets something similar to itself. Therefore plants, which partake of these faculties, are ensouled, but they are not animals.[28]

He then mentions creatures such as sponges, which seem to be in between plant and animal in that they have sensation, but are rooted like plants (i.e. they do not move). For Ammonius, what makes an animal different from something ensouled is sensation. This definition of 'animal' as that which has sensation and of 'ensouled' as what we would refer to as living (i.e. growth) goes back to Aristotle and employs a different notion of soul than that of Christian sources, which do not usually attribute a soul to animals.

The commentaries on the *Isagoge* attributed to Elias and David, two shadowy figures of the sixth century, rationalize the statement of Ammonius quoted above by suggesting three divisions beneath ensouled (instead of 'animal' and 'not animal'): plant, animal-plant (*zōóphuton*, i.e. the sponge), and animal. All three have souls, but the animal-plant has sensation, while the animal has both sensation and movement.[29] For Aristotle and the commentators on the *Isagoge*, sensation and movement are properties that distinguish the animal from the ensouled. That the *Cause* associates movement with the living (i.e. the animal) makes sense in this context and fits with the later commentary tradition. However, its attribution of sense to soul does not.

The *Cause*'s lack of harmony with the Neoplatonic material stems from a Christian notion of the soul. While Neoplatonists understood there to be different levels of the soul and even a lower and a higher soul, one associated with the nutritive, the other containing the higher functions like those of the mind (Gr. *noûs*), Christians tended to understand the soul as a unified

27 See the so-called *scala naturae*, the gradual movement from soulless entity to animal at *Hist. Animal.* 588b4–589a3.

28 Ammonius, *In Isagogen* 79.4–7.

29 Elias, *In Isagogen* 64.27–35; David, *In Isagogen* 148.18–34, ed. A. Busse (CAG 18.2, 1904).

and singular entity. Although it skews the Tree in the process, the author's attribution of sense to soul points to his concern to protect and maintain the Christian idea of the soul. A similar confusion in the Tree can be found in that of Paul the Persian, a figure from earlier in the sixth century, whose *Introduction to Logic* was composed in Middle Persian and translated into Syriac in the seventh century. Paul's text introduces logic by summarizing the *Isagoge* and the *Organon*. Paul presents his own version of the Tree of Porphyry in the same place that the Tree appears in the *Isagoge*, that is, in his discussion of the concept of species.

> There is one genus which is called substance and this is divided into corporeal and incorporeal. Incorporeal is divided into souls, angels, and demons. Corporeal is divided into the animate (lit. ensouled) and the inanimate, the inanimate is divided into heaven and earth and into stones, wood and all things such as this. Animate is divided into living animate and not animate but only (living), such as trees. Animate life is then divided into domesticated animals, wild animals, fish, creeping things, and the human being. The human being is divided into individual persons, each of whom are human beings who differ from one another among numerable persons.[30]

Paul has made several changes to Porphyry's schema. What is relevant to our discussion is that he seems to have two conceptions of the soul: one as the capacity for life, as in the Tree of Porphyry, but another which includes the higher functions, which animals and humans have, such as movement and sensation. Furthermore, he also places souls themselves, the entities which 'ensoul' corporeal beings, in a separate subgroup of incorporeals. It is interesting that Paul, or at least the translator of his text, is willing to distort the Tree even though it is in a section of his text, as in the *Isagoge*, aimed at introducing the reader to the notions of genus and species. Furthermore, 'rational' has been removed from the Tree. This may be because of the existence of a separate group of incorporeals, such as angels, which are also rational. Perhaps Paul does not want to make rational a species of body. In any case, the multiple meanings of 'soul' in this text reflect the tension between a Christian and a philosophical psychology.

The *Cause* attributes sensation to the soul apparently because it too maintains a Christian notion of the soul, understanding it to be a more complex entity with higher faculties than the simple philosophical notion of

30 Paul the Persian, *Introduction to Logic*, 6.25–7.6 (Syriac) / 7–8 (Latin version). On this 'Tree of Porphyry', see Javier Teixidor, *Aristote en Syriaque: Paul le Perse, logicien du VIe siècle* (Paris: CNRS, 2003), 82–83.

soul, which is often employed to describe the simple nutritive faculty of all 'living' beings. The division of rational into spiritual (or 'pneumatic') and psychic seems to be a Christian addition to the Tree deriving ultimately from 1 Cor 2:14–15.[31] This division shows up in the ascetic writings of the early Syriac monastic writer, John the Solitary, who attributes to human beings a corporeal, a psychic, and a pneumatic state.[32] His threefold system shows up in later Syriac texts as well.[33] Like the Tree found in Paul the Persian's *Introduction*, the Tree in the *Cause* seems to use 'soul' and its cognates in more than one way. Further divisions under 'rational' appear in the later Neoplatonic commentators as well. Ammonius states that the rational is a genus of the mortal and the mortal a genus of man.[34] The later Elias divides the rational up into God, angel, and man.[35]

Despite the clear dependence on Greek philosophical texts and ideas at the School of Nisibis as well as at other less well attested East-Syrian schools, it is important to emphasize that the East-Syrians were not engaged in philosophy per se. For example, Dimitri Gutas argues that philosophy died in Late Antiquity and only appeared again in the 'Abbasid period, as is exemplified in the work of al-Kindi.[36] His argument is based upon the premise

31 For 'psychic' see Gerhard Kittel, ed., *Theological Dictionary of the NT* (Grand Rapids, MI: Eerdmans, 1964–76), vol IX; for the importance of this division for so-called Gnostics, see Elaine Pagels, *The Gnostic Paul: Gnostic Exegesis of the Pauline Letters* (Philadelphia: Fortress Press, 1975), 59.

32 S. Dedering, ed., Johannes von Lykopolis, *Ein Dialog über die Seele und die Affekte des Menschen* (Arbeten utgivna med understöd av Vilhelm Ekmans Universitetsfond 43; Uppsala, 1936), 13.12

33 For example, Joseph Ḥazzāyā, *Lettre sur les trois étapes de la vie monastique*, ed. and trans. P. Harb and F. Graffin, PO 45:2 (1992).

34 Ammonius, *In Isagogen* 79.12–14.

35 Elias, *In Isagogen* 63.27; see also 65.22ff: 'Some also have a problem with how it is that the animal is divided into the rational and the irrational and the rational into the mortal and the immortal. For it is also possible to divide again the mortal into the rational and the irrational. Since then the thing which is divided tends to be more general than the things into which it is divided, both the rational will be more general than the mortal and the mortal more general than the rational, which is odd. To this we say that there is no subdivision of mortal and immortal but an epi-division or secondary division of the animal, so that we might say of the animal that there is rational and irrational, and again of the animal that there is mortal and immortal, as it is possible to be divided into other things … the rational is divided into God and man.' See also 66.2ff.

36 Dimitri Gutas, 'Geometry and the Rebirth of Philosophy in Arabic with al-Kindi', in *Words, Texts and Concepts Cruising the Mediterranean Sea: Studies on the Sources, Contents and Influences of Islamic Civilization and Arabic Philosophy and Science*, ed. R. Arnzen and J. Thielmann (Louvain: Peeters, 2004), 195–209.

that philosophy in its Western classical sense exists only within a circumscribed space of reason. Philosophy does not consist simply of philosophical arguments and ideas, but requires a certain foundation in reason. While one might argue that Gutas's position raises the bar too much for determining what counts as philosophy and avoids the internal perspective of the specific intellectual cultures under examination, his general point is accurate. The East-Syrian use of Aristotle and the Neoplatonic commentary tradition on his logical works should not be mistaken for philosophy. As the example of the Tree of Porphyry and its incorporation into the *Cause* demonstrate, the East-Syrian appropriation of philosophical terms and concepts consisted of a pragmatic selection of what would ultimately be useful only to issues of theological and devotional concern.

APPENDIX III
THE LITERARY DEPENDENCE OF THE *CAUSE OF THE FOUNDATION OF THE SCHOOLS* ON THE *ECCLESIASTICAL HISTORY*

The relationship between the *Cause* and the *Ecclesiastical History* is certainly puzzling.[1] Although the two texts were written within approximately twenty years of one another, within the same institution, and perhaps by the same author, nevertheless there are discrepancies in the information they provide. Ignoring the issue of authorship, the possible ways of explaining the texts' relationship are: 1) the *Cause* and the *Ecclesiastical History* come from the same milieu and thus, unsurprisingly, say similar things; 2) the *Cause* and the *Ecclesiastical History* share a similar source; or 3) the *Cause* depends on the *Ecclesiastical History*. Of these three options, the first seems to be the least likely because of specific parallels, however few, in phraseology between the two texts. The problem with the second position is that the *Ecclesiastical History* usually does little to disguise its dependence on its sources and it does not seem to be quoting from other texts in its 'Life of Narsai', the portion where it most often overlaps with the *Cause*.[2] Moreover, the 'Life of Narsai' has certain similarities to the 'Life of Abraham of Bēt Rabban',[3] which follows it, suggesting that the 'Life of Narsai' is not a wholly different source incorporated into the body of the *Ecclesiastical History*. However, at this point it is not possible to determine whether positions two or three are more likely: the texts are clearly related to one another, but it is not certain whether this is through dependence on a third text.

The *Cause* and the *Ecclesiastical History* overlap specifically in their treatment of the lives and careers of Narsai and Abraham of Bēt Rabban. Despite these overlaps the two works differ in their style of presentation. In fact, a look at their respective treatments of the life of Narsai may help to characterize the general tendencies of each text. The *Ecclesiastical History* presents Narsai as one in a long list of persecuted Christians who have

1 See comments at Baumstark, *Geschichte*, 136 n. 8.

2 Barhadbeshabba, *La second partie de l'histoire ecclésiastique*, Chapter 31, pp. 588–615.

3 Ibid., pp. 616-31.

confessed their faith in the face of adversity since the time of the conversion of Constantine. However, from the highly philosophical and even Evagrian language in the 'Life of Narsai', it seems that the text understands its hero as a kind of spiritual superman, whose natural philosophical aptitude, purity, and wisdom gave him a head start on the path of learning from a preternaturally young age. In contrast, the Narsai described in the *Cause* establishes the formal scholastic hierarchy of offices, founds the School of Nisibis, and serves as a key figure in the transmission of the School's learning, particularly the school tradition and the exegesis of Theodore of Mopsuestia. Despite these particulars he is presented in a more stereotyped form as one of a number of heads of the School, and he stands out primarily only because he is the first within an institutional succession.

Although the *Cause* and the *Ecclesiastical History* are different in genre and intent, when placed side by side a number of verbal similarities are apparent (I have included parallels below).[4] These two texts use similar language when they describe the head of the School of the Persians prior to Narsai.[5] However, the former attributes this position to Qyorā and the latter to Rabbula. The discrepancy between the names of the two heads is even more striking when we consider the possibility that both names may derive from the enemies of the adherents of traditional Antiochene theology, that is, the two Miaphysite bishops of Edessa: Cyrus (Syr. Qurā), who closed the School of the Persians in 489, and the notorious Rabbula (d. 435/6 CE). Despite these inconsistencies, the parallels in wording and content suggest that these two passages are clearly related to one another. It is worth noting that for the different school offices mentioned in this passage the *Cause* uses abstract terms (e.g., *maqryānutā* for the *Ecclesiastical History*'s *qeryānā*) appropriate to the increase in certain morphologies in Syriac through the sixth century, in part due to the influence of texts translated from Greek.[6]

The texts also overlap closely in their description of Narsai's ascent to the position of leader at the School of the Persians.[7] After this point the

4 Employing a synoptic comparison, Hermann argues that the *Cause* uses the *Ecclesiastical History*, however not 'slavishly' (Hermann, 'Die Schule von Nisibis vom 5. bis 7. Jahrhundert', 94).

5 *Cause* 382.3–7; Barhadbeshabba, *La second partie de l'histoire ecclésiastique*, 598.10–14.

6 Sebastian Brock has a number of articles on translation in antiquity, specifically Greek to Syriac, e.g., 'The Syriac Background to Ḥunayn's Translation Techniques', *Aram* 3 (1991): 139–62 (repr. in *From Ephrem to Romanos*, Chap. 14).

7 *Cause* 383.7–384.4; Barhadbeshabba, *La second partie de l'histoire ecclésiastique*, 598.14–599.12.

Ecclesiastical History provides an extended description of the events leading to Narsai's removal, or rather flight, from Edessa. This description includes unflattering information about Narsai, which the *Cause* would perhaps have left out even if its treatment were more extensive.[8] In contrast, the *Cause* interjects here an addition to the original narrative, an update of sorts about two other important figures of the day, Barṣaumā of Nisibis and Ma'nā of Rewardashir.[9]

The texts agree on specific details in their description of Narsai's exodus from Edessa and arrival at Nisibis.[10] However, in its description of events the *Cause* characterizes the affair as a communal matter. It uses the word 'assembly' (Syr. *knushyā*) for what was uprooted and brought from Edessa, the same term used throughout the *Cause*'s history of the various institutions of learning since creation. In contrast to the *Cause*'s depiction of the exodus as an institutional phenomenon, in the earlier *Ecclesiastical History* it is a personal affair. Despite this difference both texts recount the pronoucement Barṣaumā, the bishop of Nisibis, made to Narsai on his arrival in Nisibis.[11] The *Cause* states that Narsai led the School for forty-five years; the *Ecclesiastical History*, for forty years.

In both texts the prosperity of the School of Nisibis is described.[12] Then the career of the leader of the School subsequent to Narsai, Elisha bar Qozbāyē, is addressed.[13] According to the *Cause*, Elisha succeeded Narsai; however, the *Ecclesiastical History* suggests that Abraham of Bēt Rabban led the assembly briefly but was deposed and replaced by Elisha, only to lead the School again later. The texts have a number of verbal parallels in their description of Abraham.[14]

As stated above, there are two possible explanations for the numerous

8 For example, the fact that Narsai fled in secret, something for which the *Ecclesiastical History* seems to feel obliged to apologize (Barhadbeshabba, *La second partie de l'histoire ecclésiastique*, 604.5–7).

9 *Cause* 384.1–2.

10 *Cause* 384.3–10; Barhadbeshabba, *La second partie de l'histoire ecclésiastique*, 605.5–606.11.

11 *Cause* 384.10–386.3; Barhadbeshabba, *La second partie de l'histoire ecclésiastique*, 606.11–608.7. There are specific verbal overlaps in these two speeches.

12 *Cause* 386.4; Barhadbeshabba, *La second partie de l'histoire ecclésiastique*, 608.7–14.

13 *Cause* 387.4–387.7; Barhadbeshabba, *La second partie de l'histoire ecclésiastique*, 620.1–5.

14 *Cause* 387.8–388.2; Barhadbeshabba, *La second partie de l'histoire ecclésiastique*, 616.1–11; also *Cause* 389.1–11; Barhadbeshabba, *La second partie de l'histoire ecclésiastique*, 630.7. Note the long stretch between the two passages in the *Ecclesiastical History*, as opposed to their proximity in the *Cause*.

instances of overlap both in content and in language between the *Cause* and the *Ecclesiastical History*. First, the author of the *Cause*, whether he was also the author of the *Ecclesiastical History* decades before or not, wrote with the *Ecclesiastical History* open next to him. However, this does not account for the discrepancies between the two texts. The second explanation is that the two texts rely on the same source or sources. The library of the School of Nisibis perhaps had numerous documents chronicling the history of the School. The historical introductions to the statutes of the School may serve as an example of this.[15] This source in fact even mentions an archive at the School.[16] One could argue that the strong verbal overlaps between the *Cause* and the *Ecclesiastical History* were due to the paraphrasing of these different sources. This would also help to explain some of the more unexpected discrepancies between the two texts, such as the Qyorā/Rabbula problem and the differences regarding length of tenure of office. However, as stated above, one argument against this would be that the *Ecclesiastical History* in other places often quotes openly from sources, leaving the seams of these interpolations apparent.[17]

15 E.g., *Statutes of the School of Nisibis*, 51–72.

16 Ibid. 54, Syriac *bēt arkē* (= Gr. *tà archeîa*).

17 A full study needs to be done on the *Ecclesiastical History* and its sources. The only close study of this text remains Abramowski's *Untersuchungen zum Liber Heraclides des Nestorius*, which examines its central chapters for information on Nestorius.

SYNOPTIC COMPARISON OF THE *CAUSE OF THE FOUNDATION OF THE SCHOOLS* AND THE *ECCLESIASTICAL HISTORY*

Verbal similarities are underlined and significant differences are marked in boldface.

Qyorā/Rabbula

Cause 382.3–7

The head and exegete of that school (*eskolē*) was an enlightened (*saggi nuhrā*) man whose (lit. his) name was **Qyorā**, who was completely a person of God. To such an extent was this man swallowed up by love for the business (of the school), that he embraced the complete practice of interpretation (*mphashshqānutā*), of reading-instruction (*maqryānutā*), and of vocalization (*mhaggyānutā*), as well as church homily. Although he was fasting and abstinent, nevertheless he would strenuously complete all this labour.

Ecclesiastical History 598.10–14

There was an exegete then at that time in Edessa. They say about him that he was an enlightened (*saggi nuhrā*) man. His name was **Rabbula**. This man was adorned with all things, with truth learning and perfect virtue in manner of life. He bore all the work of the school, reading (*qeryānā*) as well as elementary instruction (*hegyānā*) and interpretation (*pushshāqā*). He also had confidence in speech.

Narsai

Cause 383.7–384.4

After that man, the exegete of the school, took his rest, then the whole brotherhood asked Mār Narsai to stand at the head of the assembly and to fill its needs, because among all of them there was no one there like him. When Mār Narsai refused, he said to them: 'I myself am not able to bear the whole labour the school, as our master did. For he was rich in two things: in bodily health and in spiritual grace with old age. But if you make (someone else) reader and elementary instructor (*maqryānā wa-mhaggyānā*), perhaps I will be able to interpret.' After they did everything that he asked, then that blessed man led the assembly for a period of twenty years, while daily leading the choir and giving interpretation.

Then Barṣaumā came to Nisibis and was chosen to be bishop. Ma'nā went to Persia and received there the yoke of priesthood.

When the business of the assembly was proceeding in order, then Satan troubled and mixed them up, as is his habit.

Ecclesiastical History 598.14–599.12

After this holy man fulfilled his course, according to the will of God, and rested from his labour, there was an inquiry concerning who would be suitable for the work of teaching after him. All of them equally shouted, 'Mār Narsai the presbyter is suitable, not only because of his old age, his success, his work, and the elegance of his speech, but also because of his perfect and divine manner of life and his condescension towards everyone. After they compelled him with many (entreaties), he received only the work of teaching and made for himself a aeader and an elementary instructor (*maqryānā wa-mhaggyānā*) so that it would be easier for him to work at (interpreting) the meaning of the divine scriptures. He led the assembly for the long period of twenty years, in all things beneficial, and in all that time, there was no Satan nor evil presence. But it is not our set purpose to describe all his glories, lest our speech burden the audience.

When Satan saw that his kingdom was already despoiled, his side brought low, and his force diminished, he then began to stir up trouble and fear by means of evil men. He found as the symposiarch for his error the local bishop whose name was **Cyrus**, a man heretical

Cause 384.4–10

When Mār Narsai migrated from there, he came to Nisibis and settled in the Monastery of the Persians. For his thought was to go down to Persia. Barṣaumā, after he heard this, sent his archdeacon and he ordered that he enter the city with great honour. After he entered and the two of them greeted one another and attended to one another for a few days, Barṣaumā entreated him, if he desired, to settle there and make an assembly of the school in that city, while he (Barṣaumā) would help him with all the necessities. As it was difficult in the eyes of Mār Narsai, then Barṣaumā said to him:

Ecclesiastical History 605.5–606.11

The holy one, after he arrived in Nisibis, did not enter the city. For he thought that he would perhaps be hindered from his intended goal, which was in truth what happened. But he went to the Monastery of the Persians, which lay to the east of the city. For his intention was to go down to the east, that is, to the interior of Persia, in order that he might provide instruction there and plant the seed of the learning of the fear of God even if (only) in a few who were there. When he was thinking to do this, three clergymen happened on the monastery and saw that the man was modest in his face and honourable and glorious in his radiant appearance, and they asked about him, who he was and what news he brought. Then after they learned the object of their question, they eagerly went in and informed Mār Barṣaumā about him. When he heard, he earnestly sent to him some men from the clergy, (saying) that if he ordered he could enter the city. After he was not persuaded to enter with them and gave as an excuse for this sometimes weariness, [606] at other times sickness, sometimes that he was a stranger, at other times that he was an unknown person, even sometimes that there was no need for him to enter, then the bishop again sent people, but this time his archdeacon[1] and ten of the clergy as an honour to him. When they went out and entreated him in many ways that he might see his friend, he thought that perhaps it might be a mark of shame and contempt for him to not enter. So he stood and entered with them.

After he entered the city, Mār Barṣaumā went out to meet him with much pomp and with comely honour he led him into the church. Then they conversed with one another for a little while. After he learned the cause of his migration from there, he requested that, if he desired, he should leave off his prior design and that which he intended to do far off would be accomplished there in proximity and by the interaction of the two of them planting the assembly of Mesopotamia, so as to offer a great benefit to both sides, to the Romans and the Persians at once. Then as if to someone who was resisting, the bishop said to that holy one:

Both texts then turn to Barṣaumā's speech to Narsai on his arrival in Nisibis.

Cause 384.10–386.3

'Do not think that your removal from Edessa and the scattering of the assembly were accidental, oh my brother, but rather that it was the providence of God. If it is (the case) that you should liken this to that which occurred in Jerusalem after the ascension of our Lord, you would not be mistaken. For also the band of Apostles was there and the gift of the spirit and the signs which were done and the different powers. Because they were not worthy, their *house was forsaken desolate*, according to the saviour's word. The Apostles then went *out to the ways* of the Gentiles *and to the narrow paths* of paganism, and *gathered everyone whom they found, good and evil.* They made students, baptized and taught, and in a short time the gospel of our Lord flew through all the world. It seems to me that the scattering of this (i.e. your) assembly is similar. If you listen to me and settle here, everywhere there will be a great benefit from you. For there is no city in the Persian realm which is able to receive you like this one. It is a great city, set in the borderlands, and from all regions they (i.e. people) are gathered unto it. When they hear that there is an assembly here, especially that you yourself are its leader, many will throng here, especially because now heresy has begun openly to gaze out from its surroundings in Mesopotamia. You will be as a shield to us and a strenuous labourer. Perhaps between you and me we will be able to expel evil from our midst. For it is said: *Two good men are*

Ecclesiastical History 606.11–608.7

'Do not think that this deed is human, master. For although they planned evil against you and completed their satanic plan, nevertheless that hidden providence, which sees everything, did not turn away from you. But it did what was expedient for the purpose of providence, just as in the time of Joseph and in the time [607] of the Apostles. Just as at one time the assembly migrated from Antioch to Daphne and from there to Edessa, so also now I think that it has migrated from Edessa to here because the ones who were reading were not worthy. For, behold, also the Apostles endeavoured much to plant the gospel in Judea. Because that rabid nation was not worthy of this lasting good, when they thought to harm them by expelling them from their midst, it rather turned out to be a benefit for the Apostles since they were not chastised along with them in Titus's punishment. But by this cause they went over to the gentiles. Then they *went out to the ways and the narrow paths.* They *compelled* the gentiles *to enter* the messianic banquet. Thus now also it seems to me that this has happened. Because the Romans were not worthy of receiving the truth nor of enjoying the shining rays of the light of true faith, and are going to earn punishment for their sins; on account of this they incited a war against you, that you yourself would be saved like Lot from punishment, while they will be destroyed like the harmful Sodomites. But you also, like the Apostles, busy yourself and plant here the word of *better than one, in that there is a better reward in their labour. If one becomes strong, two of them will stand against him.*'

Orthodoxy. For if you do this, the two sides will easily benefit, since it is close enough for your students to come here [608] to you. Furthermore, Persians frequent here because of the climate of the place, and because the place is bountiful in all kinds of products it is easy for the brothers to live and succeed in learning scripture, especially since I myself will be a helper to you in this business. For although it happens that brave fighters are vanquished and flee from their enemies, yet whenever they do not depart to far away but reside at the side of a nearby place, this is a sign of their victory and the health of their soul. In this way also if you reside here in the neighbourhood of Edessa, it will be a sign of your victory and a disgrace unto your enemies.'

The *Cause* states that Narsai led the School for forty-five years; the *Ecclesiastical History*, forty years. The prosperity of the School of Nisibis is then described:

Cause 386.4–11
After he (i.e. Barṣaumā) put his (i.e. Narsai's) mind to rest with (words) such as these, then he (i.e. Narsai) consented to do this. At once he commanded and did all the things that were necessary and useful for the school. In a short time they increased to such an extent – not only Persian and Syrian brothers who were near by, but also a majority of that assembly of Edessa came to it – so that as a result glory ascended to God. From this cause also assemblies increased in the Persian realm. Edessa grew dark and Nisibis grew light; the Roman realm was filled with error, and the Persian realm with knowledge of the fear of God. He led this assembly forty-five years. He also composed up to three hundred homilies, and more including his other writings.

Ecclesiastical History 608.7–14
After the holy one heard these words, his thought was inclined a little and he promised him that if it was possible he would do this. That Barṣaumā, as soon as he heard this, rejoiced greatly. Then he bought for the school a caravansary on the side of the church. Because there was a school there before, and an exegete from Kashkar whose name was Simeon, a great and excellent man, there was no hindrance in this matter, but the prior students busied themselves with learning. In a short time brothers began to gather from all regions because of this holy one.

Both texts then describe the careers of the subsequent leaders of the School.

Elisha bar Qozbāyā

Cause 387.4–7
Mār Elisha from the village of Qozb, a great man, trained in all the subjects of the ecclesiastical and profane books, received the work of interpretation. (It was) for seven years. He also composed many writings: a refutation of the charges of Magianism, a disputation against heretics, commentaries on all the books of the Old (Testament) according to the Syriac tongue.

Ecclesiastical History 620.1–5
After this blessed one died, the glorious one succeeded him and led this assembly for twenty years. Then the brothers as well as the citizens caused him trouble and made in his place as teacher Elisha of Bēt ʻArbāyē, from the village of Qozb, a great as well as learned man. He led the assembly for four years and he also composed many didactic and exegetical writings. He resolved the charges put forward by the Magi, that is, those who are against us.

According to the *Cause*, Elisha succeeded Narsai; however, the *Ecclesiastical History* suggests that Abraham led the assembly briefly but was deposed and replaced by Elisha only to lead the School again later.

Abraham of Bēt Rabban

Cause 387.8–388.2

After this blessed man was gathered unto his fathers in peace and in deep old age, then Mār Abraham received his labour – servant, kin and [74] cellmate (*bar qelāytā*) of Mār Narsai. This man, so they say, they would formerly call Narsai, and after his father brought him to this blessed man, he changed his name and called him Abraham.

Ecclesiastical History 616.1–11

For he was a kinsman of of Mār Narsai and of the same stock as well as from the same village (*bar qritēh*). The name of his father was Bar Sāhdē. After he reached fifteen years of age, he was moved by divine instigation to let go of and abandon all the desirable things of this world and to concern himself with spiritual labour. When he heard about Mār Narsai, where he was and what his work was, he asked his father that they (i.e. his family) might conduct him to him. Then after his father was persuaded and brought him to Nisibis and Mār Narsai was informed about him, that he was his kinsman, he asked what his name was. His father said, 'Narsai, like your own name'. Immediately he changed his name and called him Abraham and said, 'There should not be two Narsais in one cell'. [Abraham metaphor continued]

There is a long stretch in the *Ecclesiastical History* between the above passage and the following one.

BRIEF GLOSSARY OF SELECTED TERMS

Antiochene Theology A form of Christology (i.e. the theological understanding of the person(s) of Christ) associated with the city of Antioch which emphasized within the incarnation the persistence of the human nature of Christ as distinct from the divine. Its more famous and influential proponents are Diodore of Tarsus, Theodore of Mopsuestia, Nestorius, and Theodoret of Cyrrhus. The enemies of these Dyophysites condemned them as 'Nestorians'. It is often set against Alexandrian theology or Christology, which focuses more on the unity of the divine and the human in Christ (Miaphysitism).

Dyophysites Those who emphasized the dual nature of the incarnation. They have been unfairly called 'Nestorians', after Nestorius and his followers, who refused to employ the term 'Theotokos' for the Virgin Mary and rejected the views of Cyril of Alexandria.

East-Syrian This is a less offensive term than 'Nestorian' for the 'Church of the East', that is, the Dyophysite church in the Sasanian Empire, especially after it developed its own distinct ecclesiastical hierarchy in the fifth and sixth centuries.

Elementary instructor (*mhaggyānā*) This was the office of elementary instruction. It entailed the teaching of the alphabet and, as the name suggests, how to vocalize a text.

Exegete (*mphashshqānā*) There was only one holder of this office, which we could also render as 'the interpreter'. Apart from offering 'interpretation' (*pushshāqā*), he was also the nominal head of the School.

Instructor (*bādoqā*) It is not clear whether those with this title had a special place within the School. Etymologically the title suggests that this is someone who looked deeply into things, perhaps the meaning of scripture, but also possibly into the nature of things.

Miaphysites This is used instead of the more commonly recognized 'Monophysite'. To call certain Christians 'monophysite' is to suggest that they acknowledge only one nature in the incarnation, while 'miaphysite' places an emphasis on the incarnate word's unity of nature, which derives originally from two distinct natures.

Reader (*maqryānā*) This instructor offered more advanced lessons than the elementary instructor. As the name suggests, he would teach the students to read, perhaps by reading aloud first with the students repeating after him. He may have offered some interpretation of the text as well. It is not clear where the boundaries were between his position and the former elementary instructor and the latter exegete.

School (*eskolē*) This term, obviously deriving from the Greek *scholé* and cognate with our word 'school', was applied to a diversity of centres of learning, from informal gatherings at village churches to distinct instititutions such as the School of Nisibis.

Steward (*rabbaytā*) This title, meaning literally 'the chief or headman of the house', was given to the office of the one who was responsible for the mundane, day-to-day workings of the School, including economic matters.

Syriac The Aramaic dialect of Edessa, which became the dominant literary dialect among Christians in Mesopotamia and parts of Syria.

Teacher (*mallphānā*) This generic term seems to have also been applied to certain figures at the School, but it is not clear how it fits within the institutional organization.

Tradition (*mashlmānutā*; transmit: *ashlem*; *mashlem*) The School of Nisibis seems to have had an oral 'tradition' deriving from the School of the Persians in Edessa. 'Tradition' and the verb from which it derives ('transmit') are employed in the sources to describe the process of transmission of this exegetical tradition. The word *mashlmānutā* can also have a more concrete meaning, when it is used to refer to a collection of 'traditions'. In such cases it can mean 'commentary'.

West-Syrian This refers to Syriac Christian Miaphysites, although this term becomes problematic when used for the period before such identities had fully developed.

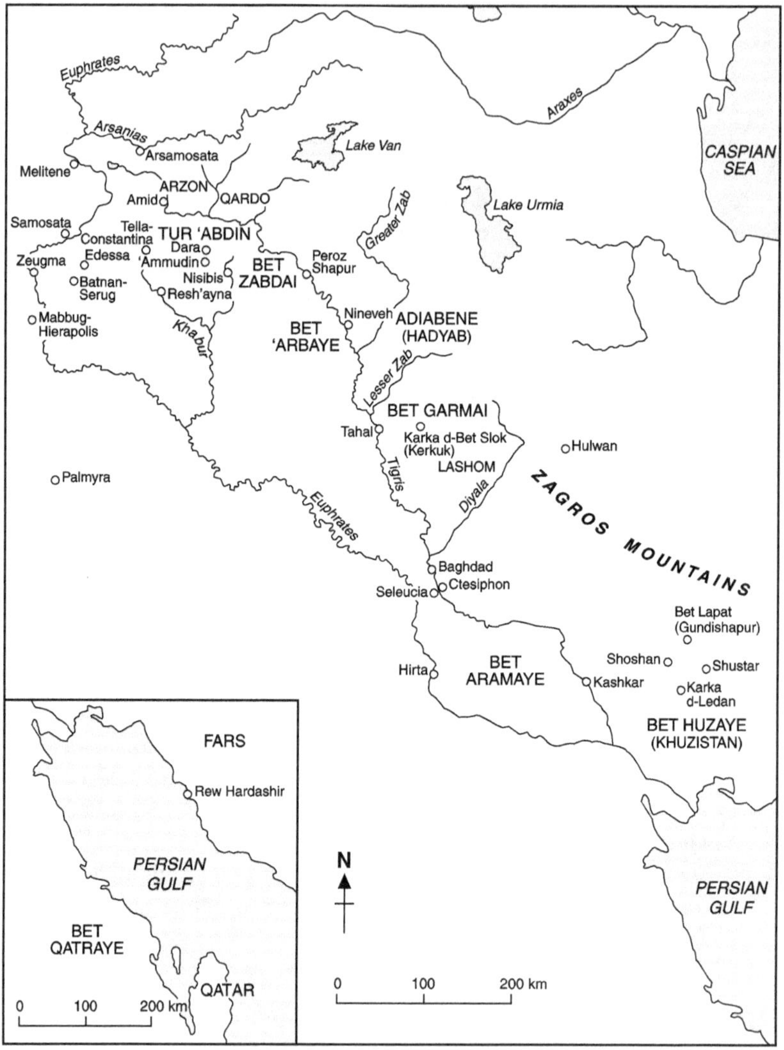

Map 1 Sasanian Mesopotamia and the north-western Roman frontier

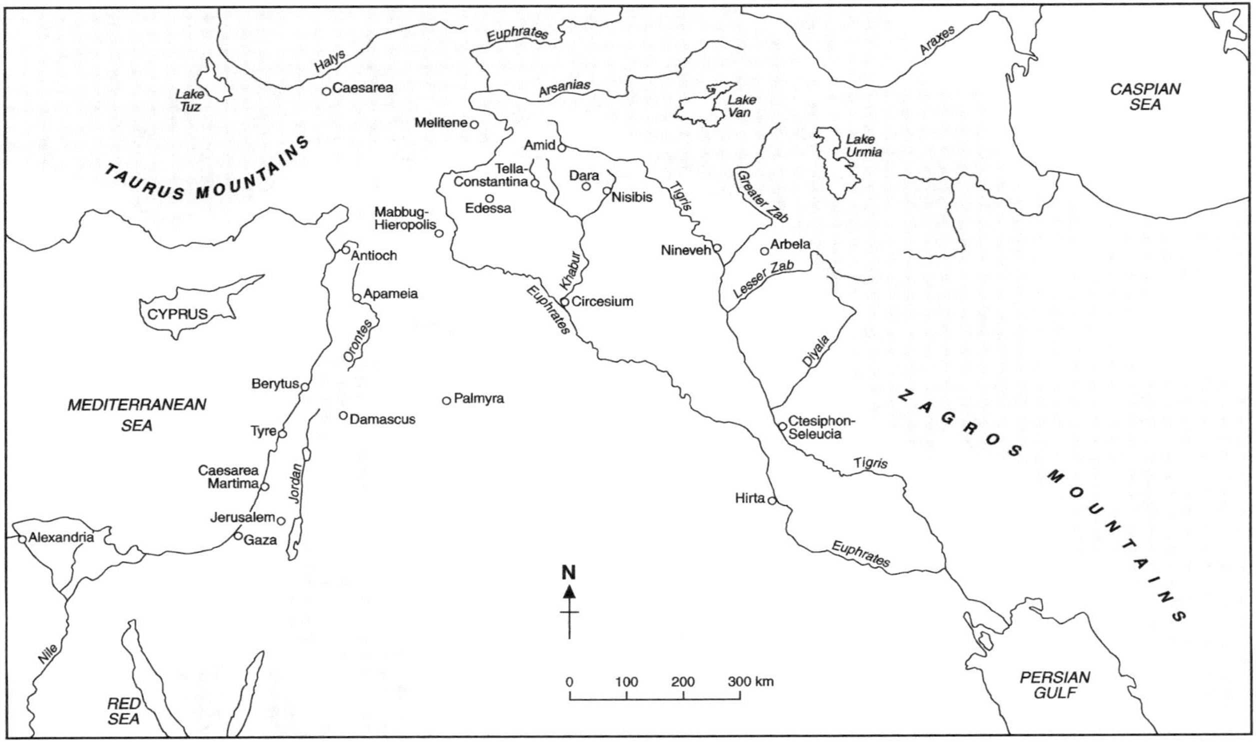

Map 2 The Late Antique Near East

BIBLIOGRAPHY

Primary Sources

'Abdisho', *Catalogue*. Ebediesu, *Enumeratio librorum omnium ecclesiasticorum*, in *Bibliotheca Orientalis* III.1.1–362.

Acta martyrum et sanctorum syriace, ed. P. Bedjan (7 volumes; Paris, 1890–1897; repr. Hildesheim: O. Harrassowitz, 1968).

Acts of the Council of Chalcedon, trans. Richard Price and Michael Gaddis (Translated Texts for Historians 45; Liverpool: Liverpool University Press, 2005).

Ammonius, *In Categorias*, ed. A. Busse (CAG 4.4, 1895).

—— *On Aristotle's* Categories, trans. S. M. Cohen and G. Matthews (Ithaca, NY: Cornell University Press, 1991).

—— *In De Interpretatione*, ed. A. Busse (CAG 4.5, 1897)

—— *On Aristotle's On Interpretation 1–8*, trans. D. Blank (Ithaca, NY: Cornell University Press, 1996).

—— *In Isagogen*, ed. A Busse (CAG 4.1, 1985).

Aphrahat, *Demonstrations. Aphraatis Sapientis Persiae Demonstrationes*, ed. J. Parisot, *Patrologia Syriaca* 1–2 (Paris, 1894, 1907).

Bābai the Great, *Commentary on the Kephalaia Gnostica*, in Wilhelm Frankenberg, ed., *Euagrius Ponticus* (Abhandlungen der königlichen Gesellschaft der Wissenschaften zu Göttingen, Philologisch-historische Klasse, New Series 13.2; Berlin: Weidmannsche Buchhandlung, 1912), 8–471.

Barhadbeshabba 'Arbaya, *La second partie de l'histoire ecclésiastique*, ed. F. Nau, PO 9:5 (1913).

Barhadbeshabba 'Arbaya, *La première partie de l'histoire*, ed. F. Nau, PO 23.2 (1932).

Bibliotheca Orientalis. J. S. Assemani, ed., *Bibliotheca Orientalis Clementino-Vaticana, in qua manuscriptos codices syriacos recensuit* I-III (Rome, 1719–28).

Cause. Addai Scher, ed., Mār Barḥadbeshabba 'Arabaya, *Cause de la fondation des écoles*, PO 4:4 (1908).

Cave of Treasures. S.-M. Ri, ed., *La Caverne des Trésors. Les deux recensions syriaques* (CSCO 486–87; Louvain: Peeters, 1987).
Chronicle of Arbela. P. Kawerau, ed. and trans., *Die Chronik von Arbela* (CSCO 467–68; Louvain, 1985).
Chronicle of Edessa. Chronicon Edessenum, ed. I. Guidi, *Chronica Minora I*. 1–13 (1–11) (CSCO 1–2; Louvain: Peeters, 1903).
The Chronicle of Joshua the Stylite, ed. William Wright (Cambridge: Cambridge University Press, 1882).
—— *The Chronicle of Pseudo-Joshua the Stylite*, ed. Frank R. Trombley and John W. Watt (Translated Texts for Historians 32; Liverpool: Liverpool University Press, 2000).
Chronicle of Siirt. Histoire Nestorienne (Chronique de Séert), ed. A. Scher, J. Périer, P. Dib and R. Griveau, PO 4:3; 5:2; 7:2; 13: 4 (1907–1919).
Cosmas Indicopleustes. *Christian Topography*. Cosmas Indicopleustes, *Topographie chrétienne*, ed. Wanda Wolska-Conus (SC 141, 159, 197; Paris, 1968–73).
Cyrus of Edessa, *Six Explanations of the Liturgical Feasts*, ed. and trans. W. F. Macomber (CSCO 355–56; Louvain, 1974).
Eusebius of Caesarea. *Ecclesiastical History. Eusebius Werke 2.1–3: Die Kirchengeschichte*, ed. E. Schwartz (Leipzig: Hinrichs, 1903–1909).
Eusebius of Caesarea, *Ecclesiastical History* (Syriac). W. Wright and N. McLean, eds., *The Ecclesiastical History of Eusebius in Syriac* (Cambridge: Cambridge University Press, 1898).
Elias, *In Isagogen* 64.27–35, ed. A. Busse (CAG 18.1, 1900).
Evagrius of Pontus, *Kephalaia Gnostica. Les six centuries des 'Kephalaia Gnostica' d'Évagre le Pontique*, ed. Antoine Guillaumont PO 28 (1958).
Furlani, Giuseppe, 'Due scoli filosofici attribuiti a Sergio di Teodosiopoli (Rêsh'aynâ)', *Aegyptus* Anno VII 10 (1926): 139–45.
Ḥenānā of Adiabene, *On Golden Friday*. In Scher, ed., *Traités*.
—— *On Rogations*. In Scher, ed., *Traités*.
Hoffmann, J. G. H., *De Hermeneuticis apud Syros Aristoteleis* (Leipzig, 1873).
Isaac of Nineveh, *Second Part*. Isaac of Nineveh (Isaac the Syrian), '*The Second Part*', *Chapters iv–xli*, ed. and trans. S. Brock (CSCO 554–55; Louvain, Peeters, 1995).
Ishai, *On the Martyrs*. In Scher, ed., *Traités*.
Isho' bar Nun, *Questions on the Pentateuch*. Ernest G. Clarke, ed., *The Selected Questions of Isho bar Nun on the Pentateuch* (Leiden: Brill, 1962).

Ishodad of Merv, *Commentary on Gospels*. Margaret Dunlop Gibson, ed., *The Commentaries of Isho'dad of Merv, Bishop of Hadatha of Assyria (c. 850 A.D.) on the New Testament* (3 volumes; Cambridge: Cambridge University Press, 1911).

Jacob of Sarug, *Against the Jews. Homélies contre Juifs*, ed. M. Albert, PO 38.1 (1976).

—— *Homilies. Homiliae selectae*, ed. P. Bedjan (Paris; Leipzig: O. Harrassowitz, 1905–1910).

—— Letters. *Iacobi Sarugensis Epistulae quotquot supersunt*, ed. G. Olinder (CSCO 110; Paris-Louvain, 1937).

John of Ephesus, *Lives of the Eastern Saints*, ed. E.W. Brooks, PO 17: 1–307; 18: 511–698; 19: 152–285 (1923–1926).

John Philoponus, *In Categorias*, ed. A. Busse (CAG 13.1, 1898).

—— *De Opificio Mundi*, ed. and trans. Clemens Scholten (Freiburg/New York: Herder, 1997).

—— *In de Anima*, ed. M. Hayduck (CAG 15, 1897).

Life of Abā. Paul Bedjan, ed., *Histoire de Mar-Jabalaha et trois autres Patriarches, d'un prêtre et deux laïques nestoriens* (Paris/Leipzig: O. Harrassowitz, 1895), 206–87.

Narsai, *Homiliae et Carmina. Narsai doctoris syri homiliae et carmina*, ed. Alphonse Mingana, I–II (Mosul: Typis Fratrum praedicatorum, 1905).

—— *Homilies on Creation*. Narsai, *Homélies sur la Création*, ed. and trans. Ph. Gignoux, PO 34:3, 4 (1968).

—— *Metrical Homilies*. F. G. McLeod, 'Narsai's Metrical Homilies on the Nativity, Epiphany, Passion, Resurrection and Ascension', PO 40:1 (1979).

Nestorian Christological Texts. Luise Abramowski and Alan E. Goodman, *A Nestorian Collection of Christological Texts, Cambridge University Library Ms. Oriental. 1319* (University of Cambridge Oriental Publications 18 [Syriac text] and 19 [Introduction, translation, indices]; Cambridge: Cambridge University Press, 1972).

Paul the Persian, *Introduction to Logic*. J. P. N. Land, ed., 'Pauli Persae Logica', *Anecdota Syriaca* (Leiden) 4 (1895): 1–32 (1–30).

Philoxenus, *Three Letters*. A. A. Vaschalde, ed., *Three Letters of Philoxenus* (Rome: R. Accademia dei Lincei, 1902).

Porphryry, *Isagoge*, ed. A. Busse (CAG 4.1, 1887).

—— *Isagoge* (Syriac). Sebastian Brock, 'The earliest Syriac translation of Porphyry's Eisagoge. I Edition', *Journal of the Iraqi Academy, Syriac Corporation* 12 (1988): 316–66.

Scher, ed., *Traités. Traités d Išaï le Docteur et de Ḥnana d'Adiabène sur les Martyrs, le Vendredi d'Or et les Rogations*, ed. A. Scher, PO 7 (1909): 5–91.

Simplicius, *In Categorias*, ed. C. Kalbfleisch (CAG 8, 1907)

Sinkewicz, Robert E., trans., *Evagrius of Pontus: The Greek Ascetic Corpus* (Oxford: Oxford University Press, 2003).

Statutes of the School of Nisibis, ed. and trans. A. Vööbus (Stockholm: Estonian Theological Society in Exile, 1961).

Synodicon Orientale ou recueil des Synodes Nestoriens publié, traduit et annoté, ed. and trans. J.-B. Chabot (Notices et extraits de la Bibliothèque Nationale, Tome 37; Paris: Imprimerie Nationale 1902).

—— O. Braun, trans., *Das Buch der Synhados oder Synodicon Orientale*. Stuttgart: J. Roth, 1900; repr. Amsterdam: Philo, 1975).

Syriac and Arabic Documents regarding Legislation relative to Syrian Asceticism, ed. A. Vööbus (Papers of the Estonian Theological Society in Exile 11; Stockholm: Estonian Theological Society in Exile, 1960).

Theodore of Mopsuestia, *Fragments*. E. Sachau, ed., *Theodori Mopsuesteni Fragmenta Syriaca* (Leipzig: G. Engelmann, 1869).

—— *Commentary on the Nicene Creed*. Alphonse Mingana, ed., *Commentary of Theodore of Mopsuestia on the Nicene Creed* (Woodbrooke Studies 5; Cambridge, 1932).

Thomas of Marga, *Book of Governors*: *The Historia Monastica of Thomas Bishop of Marga A. D. 840*, 2 volumes, ed. and trans. E. A. Wallis Budge (London: Kegan Paul, 1893; Piscataway, NJ: Gorgias Press, 2003).

Secondary Literature

Abramowski, Luise, 'Zu den Schriften des Michael Malpana/Badoqa', in *After Bardaisan: Studies on Continuity and Change in Syriac Christianity in Honour of Professor Han J. W. Drijvers*, ed. G. J. Reinink and A. C. Klugkist (OLA 89; Louvain: Peeters, 1999), 1–10.

—— *Untersuchungen zum Liber Heraclides des Nestorius* (CSCO 242; Secrétariat du CorpusSCO: Louvain, 1963).

Barsoum, Ignatius Aphram, *History of Syriac Literature and Sciences*, trans. Matti Moosa (Pueblo, CO: Passeggiata, 2000).

Becker, Adam H., *Fear of God and the Beginning of Wisdom: The School of Nisibis and the Development of Scholastic Culture in Late Antique Mesopotamia* (Philadelphia, 2006).

—— 'The Dynamic Reception of Theodore of Mopsuestia in the Sixth

Century: Greek, Syriac, and Latin', in *Greek Literature in Late Antiquity: Dynamism, Didacticism, Classicism*, ed. Scott Fitzgerald Johnson (Aldershot: Ashgate, 2006), 29–47.

Brock, Sebastian P., *From Ephrem to Romanos* (Aldershot: Ashgate, 1999).

—— 'Some Uses of the Term Theoria in the Writings of Isaac of Nineveh', *PdO* 20 (1995): 407–19

—— *The Luminous Eye: The Spiritual World Vision of St. Ephrem* (repr. Kalamazoo, MI: Cistercian, 1992).

—— *Studies in Syriac Christianity* (Aldershot/Brookfield, VT: Ashgate, 1992).

—— 'The earliest Syriac translation of Porphyry's Eisagoge. I Edition', *Journal of the Iraqi Academy, Syriac Corporation* 12 (1988): 316–66.

—— 'The Christology of the Church of the East in the Synods of the Fifth to Early Seventh Centuries: Preliminary Considerations and Materials', in *Aksum-Thyateira: a Festschrift for Archbishop Methodios*, ed. G. Dagras (London: Thyateira House, 1985; repr. in Brock, *Studies in Syriac Christianity*), 125–42.

—— 'Syriac Historical Writing: A Survey of the Main Sources', *Journal of the Iraqi Academy Syriac Corporation* 5 (Baghdad, 1979–80) (repr in Brock, *Studies in Syriac Christianity*, Chap. 1), 1–30

Brockelmann, Karl, *Lexicon Syriacum* (Hildesheim: Georg Olms, 1995).

Chabot, J.-B., 'L'école de Nisibe, son histoire, ses statuts', *JA*, series 9 vol. 8 (1896): 43–93

de Halleux, André, 'La dixième lettre de Philoxène aux monastères du Beit Gaugal', *LM* 96 (1983): 5–79.

—— *Philoxène de Mabbog. Sa vie, ses écrits, sa théologie* (Louvain: Imprimerie Orientaliste, 1963).

Doran, Robert, *Stewards of the Poor: The Man of God, Rabbula, and Hiba in Fifth-Century Edessa* (Kalamazoo, MI: Cistercian, 2006).

Dillemann, Louis, *Haute Mésopotamie Orientale et Pays Adjacents* (Paris: Librairie Orientaliste Paul Geuthner, 1962).

Drijvers, Hans J. W., 'The School of Edessa: Greek learning and local culture', in *Centres of Learning: Learning and Location in Pre-modern Europe and the Near East*, ed. Jan Willem Drijvers and Alasdair MacDonald, Brill's Studies in Intellectual History, vol. 61 (Leiden: Brill, 1995), 49–59.

Fiey, J.-M., *Communautés syriaques en Iran et Irak des origines à 1552* (London: Ashgate, 1979).

—— 'Médie Chrétienne', *PdO* 1 (1970): 357–84 (repr. in *Communautés syriaques*, Chap. 4).

—— 'Diocèses syriens orientaux du Golfe Persique', Mèmorial Mgr Gabriel Khouri-Sarkis (Louvain, 1969) (repr. in *Communautés syriaques*, Chap. 2)

Garsoïan, Nina, *L'Église Arménienne et le Grand Schisme d'Orient* (CSCO Subsidia 574; Louvain: Peeters, 1999)

Gero, Stephen, *Barṣauma of Nisibis and Persian Christianity in the Fifth Century* (CSCO 426; Louvain: Peeters, 1981).

Ginzburg, Louis, *Legends of the Jews* (7 volumes; Philadelphia, The Jewish Publications Society of America, 1909–38).

Glenthøj, Johannes Bartholdy, *Cain and Abel in Syriac and Greek Writers (4th–6th Centuries)* (Louvain: Peeters, 1997).

Grillmeier, Aloys and Theresia Hainthaler, *Jesus der Christus im Glaube der Kirche* 2/3 (Freiburg: Herder, 2004).

Harvey, Susan Ashbrook, *Asceticism and Society in Crisis: John of Ephesus and 'The Lives of the Eastern Saints'* (Berkeley: University of California Press, 1990).

Hermann, T., 'Die Schule von Nisibis vom 5. bis 7. Jahrhundert', *Zeitscrift für die neutestamentliche Wissenschaft* 25 (1926): 89–122.

Hoyland, Robert, *Seeing Islam As Others Saw It: A survey and evaluation of Christian, Jewish and Zoroastrian writings on early Islam* (Studies in Late Antiquity and Early Islam 13; Princeton: Darwin Press, 1997).

Hugonnard-Roche, Henri, *La logique d'Aristote du grec au syriaque. Études sur la transmission des textes de l'*Organon *et leur interprétation philosophique* (Paris: Vrin, 2004).

Kaufman, Stephen A., *The Akkadian Influence on Aramaic* (Chicago: University of Chicago Press, 1974).

Labourt, Jérôme, *Le Christianisme dans l'Empire Perse, sous la Dynastie Sassanide (224–632)* (Paris: V. Lecoffre, 1904).

Löw, Immanuel, *Aramäische Pflanzennamen* (Leipzig, 1881).

Macomber, William, 'The Manuscripts of the Metrical Homilies of Narsai', *OCP* 39 (1973): 275–306.

Mingana, Alphonse, *Réponse à M. l'abbé J.-B. Chabot, à propos de la chronique de Barhadbšabba* (Mosul, 1905).

Molenberg, Corrie. 'The Silence of the Sources: The Sixth Century and East-Syrian "Antiochene" Exegesis', in *The Sixth Century – End or Beginning?*, ed. Pauline Allen and Elizabeth M. Jeffreys (Byzantina Australiensia 10; Brisbane: Australian Association for Byzantine Studies, 1996), 145–62.

Ortiz de Urbina, Ignacio, *Patrologia Syriaca* (Rome: Pontificium Institutum Orientalium Studiorum, 1958).

Payne Smith, Jessie, ed., *A Compendious Syriac Dictionary, founded upon the Thesaurus Syriacus by R. Payne Smith* (Winona Lake, IN: Eisenbrauns, 1998).

Ramelli, Ilaria, 'Barhadbeshabba di Halwan, *Causa della fondazione delle scuole*: traduzione e note essenziali', *'Ilu. Revista de Ciencias de las Religiones* (Madrid, Universidad Complutense) 10 (2005): 127–70.

Reinink, Gerrit J., *Syriac Christianity under late Sassanian and Early Islamic Rule* (Aldershot: Ashgate, 2005).

—— '"Edessa Grew Dim and Nisibis Shone Forth": The School of Nisibis at the Transition of the Sixth-Seventh Century', in J. W. Drijvers and A. A. MacDonald, eds., *Centres of Learning: Learning and Location in Pre-modern Europe and the Near East* (Studies in Intellectual History 61; Leiden: Brill, 1995), 77–89 (repr. in Reinink, *Syriac Christianity under late Sassanian and Early Islamic Rule*, Chap. 1).

Rubenstein, Jeffrey, *The Culture of the Babylonian Talmud* (Baltimore, MD: Johns Hopkins University Press, 2003).

Samir, Samir Khalil, *Alphonse Mingana, 1878–1937, and his contribution to early Christian-Muslim studies* (Birmingham: Selly Oak Colleges, 1990).

Symposium Syriacum III 1980, ed. René Lavenant (OCA. 221; Rome, 1983),

Scher, Addai, 'Étude supplémentaire sur les écrivains syriens orientaux', *Revue de l'Orient Chrétien* 11 (1906): 1-33.

Shaw, Teresa M., *The Burden of the Flesh: Fasting and Sexuality in Early Christianity* (Minneapolis, MN: Fortress Press, 1998).

Tamcke, M., *Der Katholikos-Patriarch Sabrīšō I. (596-604) und das Mönchtum* (Europaische Hochschulschriften Reihe 23; Theologie, vol. 302; Frankfurt am Main, 1988).

Vööbus, A., *History of the School of Nisibis* (CSCO 266; Louvain, 1965).

Winter, Engelbert and Beate Dignas, *Rom und das Perserreich: Zwei Weltmächte zwischen Konfrontation und Koexistenz* (Berlin: Akademie, 2001).

Wright, William, *Catalogue of Syriac Manuscripts in the British Museum acquired since the year 1838* (London, 1870–72; repr. Piscataway, NJ: Gorgias Press, 2002).

—— *A Short History of Syriac Literature* (London: A. & C. Black, 1894; repr. Piscataway, NJ: Gorgias Press, 2001).

INDEX OF BIBLICAL REFERENCES

Genesis
1 117
1:1 103, 105
1:3 n187 117, n188 118
1:26 115
2:17 123
2–3 123
3:4–5 124
3:18–19 117
4:5 66
4:12 125
4:15 125
6:3 85
6:9 125
8:21–22 125
12:1 126
17:4 73
18:16–19:29 64
18:19 126
22:17 126
22:18 25
28:12 120
32:8 122

Exodus
20:19 126
31:18 n187 118
32:17–18 127
32:26 127
32:27–29 128
32:29 128
34:29–35 128

Leviticus
18:5 128

Numbers
35.13–14 62

Joshua
10:12 116

Judges
15:20 72
21:25 129

1 Samuel
19:8–17 62

2 Samuel
15:13–31 62

1 Kings
3:12 130
4:31 130, 147
4:33 130
4:34 130
5:4 58
18:43 131
19:1–18 53
19:3 131
21 61, 66

2 Kings
4:12 131
4:25 131
4:38 131
5:20 131
6:1–3 131
20:11 116

Ezra
7:6 142

Job
38:7 118

Psalms
1 123
1:2 49
1:3 76
17:27 69
18:16 69
19:10 53
19:11 53
27:12 81
33:5 95
37:28 81
45:2 142
82:6 115
89:3 95
89:8 96
103:20 114
111:10 52
119:23 59
119:64 95
119:97 50
119:103 53

Proverbs
1:7 132

4:10 130
14:15 49
25:3 131

Ecclesiastes
2:12 130
3:3 130
4:4 67
4:9 152
4:17 130
7:23 130
7:23–24 104
11:10 49
12:1 49
12:13–14 131

Sirach
16:3 60

Isaiah
26:20 62
38:8–9 116

Jeremiah
5:3 59, 136
7:28 59
10:12 96
36:19–26 62
48:13 136

Ezekiel
1:1–28 158
20:25 128

Daniel
1:10 53
2:21 96
7:10 121
9:21 114
11:34 96

Jonah
4:6–11 124

Micah
7:2 59, 136

Matthew
5:2–3 139
5:16 160
5:17 138, 139
6:11 157
6:23 108
10:28 54
10:32 60
11:8 77
11:11 137
11:13 137
11:27 103, 105
11:29 137
12:24 25
13:2–3 139
13:52 156
21:22 72
22:10 152
22:11 159
22:12–13 159
23:38 151
25:31 79
25:36 79
26:20–30 140
26:28 140
28:19–20 140

Mark
3:22 25
7:25 71
14:12–25 140
14:15 140
14:24 140
14:49 139
16:20 140

Luke
3:2 25
3:23 139
6:17 139
6:39 108
11:15 25
12:31 158
14:23 64, 151
15:8–10 108
16:16 137
22:7–23 140
22:12 140
22:20 140

John
1:4 108
1:29 137
1:51 114
3:30 137
8:44 125
10:33 25
11:48 139
12:19 139
12:35 109
12:43 143
16:12–13 140
17:6 105
18:1 140
18:13–14 25
18:23–24 25

Acts of the Apostles
141
4:6 25
8:9 26
9:15 96
11:26 141
15 141
17:27 114
18:11 141
19:7–8 141
19:9–10 142
28:31 141

Romans
1:19 105
1:21 133

1:22 132, 136
1:25 132
7:15 51
11:33 94, 96
12:19 60, 62
16:27 96

1 Corinthians
2:10 105
2:11 103
2:14–15 179
9:22 60
9:26 158
9:27 75

2 Corinthians
3:12 141
7:4 141
11:29 78, 82, 141

Galatians
1:10 60
2:1–14 141
2:10 26
3:6–9 25
6:2 60

Ephesians
1:21 121, 122
2:2 45, 116, 121
3:8 94
4:22–24 75, 160

Philippians
1:20 141
3:20 158

Colossians
1:16 121, 122
3:9–10 75, 160, 75, 160
4:5–6 159

1 Timothy
6:7 157

2 Timothy
4:8 72
4:16 82

Titus
2:7 55
2:7–8 59

Philemon
8 141

Hebrews
1:14 120

James
1:12 72

INDEX OF PROPER NAMES

Aaron 129
Abā 161, 162, 171
'Abdisho' bar Berikā of Nisibis 12, 16 40
Abel 88, 124–5
Abraham 25, 73, 85, 88, 126, 154–5
Abraham bar Qardāhē 164
Abraham of Bēt Rabban 7, 8, 11, 15, 43, 153–5, 163–4
  life of 18, 46, 47, 73–85, 181, 183, 191
  accused by enemy brothers 80–1
  asceticism 76–7
  death 85
  defence of the Doctors of the Church 82–4
  early life and training under Narsai 73–4, 75
  Jews attack 81–2
  on learning and the body 74–6
  work at the school 77–80
Abraham of Media 33, 35
Abraham of Nisibis 155
Abshalom 62
'Abshoṭā of Nineveh 32
Acacius of Bēt Ārāmāyē 32, n61 32, 35, 38
Achaea 141
Adam 88, 89, 125
Addai 34
Addai the Apostle 149–50
Aetius 42
Ahriman 136
Aksenāyā 34, 148
  see also Philoxenus
al-Kindi 179
Alexander of Alexandria 144, n432 144
Alexander of Constantinople 42
Alexandria 1, 6, 36, 42, 88, 134–5, 142–3, 144, 174
Amida n58 54, 70
Ammonius 177, 179
'Amr ibn Mattā 4
Anastasius, Emperor 23, 37, n116 37
Antioch 6, 24, 27, 29, 36, 64, 71, 141, 144, 145, 174, 188
Apollinaris of Laodicea 38, n120 38
Arabia 22, 141
'Arabistān 12
Aristotle 91, 92, n152 114, 132, 134, 172, 176–7, 180
Arius 38
Arius of Alexandria 42, 45, 144
Artemon 26, 27, 29, 38
Arzon 164
Asclepius 133
Ashoqar 135
Assemani, Joseph Simeon 17, 21
Athanasius of Alexandria 42, 145, n433 145
'Ayn Addad 70
'Ayn Dulbā 49
'Ayn Qennē 34

Bābai, Catholicos 22, 23, 39
Babel 134
Baghdad 14, 166, 167, 168
Bar Sāhdē 73, 191

Bardaiṣan 6
Barḥshabbā of Bēt 'Arbāyē 4, 11–16, 167, 168, 170
see also Cause of the Foundation of the Schools; *Ecclesiastical History* (subject index)
Barḥadbeshabbā of Hulwān 11–14, 15, 167
Barḥadbeshabbā of Qardu 34
Barsamyā, Bishop of Edessa 44
Barṣaumā, Bishop of Nisibis 2, 7, 32, 35, 38, 56, 63–5, 66–7, 99, 147, 149, 151–2, 164, 183, 186–7, 190
Bashtasp 135
Basil, Bishop of Caesarea 43, 145, n439 145
Baumstark, A. 15
Benjamin of Bēt Ārāmāyē 34
Berlin 163
Bēt Ārāmāyē 36, 39
Bēt 'Edrai 36
Bēt Garmai 34, 35
Bēt Kaphtarāyē 70
Bēt Lāpāt 35
Bēt Nuhādrā 36
Bithynia 42

Cain 66, n138 66, 88, 124–5
Caiphas 25, 26
Cassiodorus 3
Chabot, J. B. 169, 171
Cilicia 27, 28
Coakley, J. F. 170
Constantine, Emperor 27, 36, 37, 182
Constantinople 22, 29, 147, 148
Corinth 141
Ctesiphon 36
Cyril of Alexandria 43
Cyrus, Bishop of Edessa 2, 5, 34, 58, 61, 182, 186

Dadisho' of Bēt Qatrāyē 12
Damascus 141
Daniel 53, 54, 114, 121
Daphne 64, 188
David 49, 62, 69, 129, 136
David (6th-century author) 175, 177
De Halleux, A. 23
Democritus 134–5, n338 134–5
Dhu Nuwas 22
Diodore of Tarsus 6, 27–8, n28 27, 29, 38, 39, 43, 83, 93, 145–6

Ebion 26, 27, 29, 38
Edessa 2, 5–7, 9, 31, 34–5, 55–7, 59, 61, 64, 65, 72, 99, 149–50, 151, 163, 173–4, 182–3, 188–90
Egypt 62, 126, 134, 164
Elias (6th-century author) 175, 177, 179, n35 179
Elijah 53, 131
Elisha bar Qozbāyē 8, 153, 164, 183, 190–1
Elisha of Bēt 'Arbāyē 76, n24 76
Elisha the prophet 131
Emmanuel 54–5, n53 54
Ephesus 30, 36, 43, 141
Ephrem the Syrian 6, 144, 149–50
Epicurus 134–5, n338 134–5
Eudoxius the Arian 42
Eunomius the Arian 42
Eusebius of Caesarea 40–1
Eustathius, Bishop of Antioch 42, 144, n428 144, 145
Eutyches 29, n44 29, 38
Evagrius of Pontus 91–2, n194 118–19, 145, n441 145
Eve 67, 122, 124
Ezalyā of Kephar Māri 33

Fiey, J.-M. 15, 169
Flavian, Bishop of Antioch 43, 145
Frashoqar 135

Gabriel (Archangel) 114, 121

Gabriel (teacher) 56
George the Arian 42
Germanicia 29
Gero, Stephen 15–16
Gibeon 116
Greater Armenia 37
Gregory, Bishop of Neocaesarea 42
Gregory of Nisibis 40
Gurzan 37
Gutas, Dimitri 179–80

Hainthaler, T. 23
Hannan 25, 26
Haran 62, 126
Harris, Rendel 170
Ḥazqi'el 162
Helen (mother of Constantine) 44
Helen of Troy 44
Ḥenānā of Adiabene 4, 7, 8, 10, 13, 14–16, 86, 155–7, n521 155, 162, 169
Hermann, T. 15
Hezekiah 156
Horeb, desert of 128
Hormizd 39, 135–6
Hulwān 12

Ibas of Edessa 30–1, n50 30, 33, 34, 35, 38
Ibn at-Tayyib 4–5
Isaiah 116
Ishai 161, 162
Isho'dād of Merv 13–14
Isho'denaḥ of Basra 40
Isho'yahb of Arzon (Isho'yahb I) 8, 14, 155, 164
Israel 129
Italy 3

Jacob 62
Jacob Burd'ānā 21–2
Jacob of Nisibis 144, 163
Jacob of Sarug 69
Jeremiah 62, 136
Jerusalem 141, 151
Jesus 24, 37, 88, 90, 99, 158
'humanity' of 6, 25–6, 27, 28–31, 37–8, 45, 144
imitation of 91
life on earth 45
as the Master Teacher 136–41
see also Son (subject index)
Jezebel 66, n137 66
Job 118
John the Apostle 108
John the Baptist 88, 137
John bar 'Amrāyē 70
John of Bēt Garmai 32
John of Bēt Rabban 8, 153–5, 163–4
John of Bēt Sāri 35
John Chrysostom 145, n440 145
John, Bishop of Constantinople 43
John of Ephesus 21
John the Solitary 179
John of Tella 21–2
Jonah 74
Joseph 64, n119 64, 188
Joseph, Catholicos 161–2
Joshua bar Nun 88, 116, 127, 129
Jovian, Emperor 6
Judea 64
Julian the Apostate 6
Justin, Emperor 23
Justinian, Emperor 23, 83, n67 83, 84, n71 84

Karka d-Ledan 161
Kashkar 65, 161, 190
Kavad 70, n171 70
Kephar Māri, Bēt Zabdai 54–5, 67
Khusrau I Anushirvan 154, n509 154, 161–2
Khuzistān 33, 35
Kidron valley 140

Labourt, J. 170–1
Lēdān 35
Lot 64
Luke 141

M'altā 49, 73
Mamai 66–7
Ma'nā, Bishop of Rewardashir 32, 35, 149, 151, 183, 186
Mani 38
Mārā of Qardu 32
Marcion 29, n43 29, 38
Māri of Bēt Hardashir 31, n54 31
Māri of Tahāl 38–9
Mārī ibn Sulaymān 4–5
Mariam 129
Mark 140
Māron Elitā 31
Mārutā, Bishop 36–7
Mary the *Theotokos* 35, 39
Mary the Virgin 27, 29–30
Maximinus 43
Meletius, Bishop of Antioch 42
Memnon of Ephesus 43
Mesopotamia 1–3, 6, 11, 44, 63, 152, 173, 188
Michael 164
Michael (Archangel) 121
Mikā 32–3
Mingana, Alphonse 14, 15, 17, 165, 167, 168–71
Moses 62, 74, 88, 98, 126–9
Mount Sinai 126, 137

Najran 154
Narsai 2, n7 2–3, 5, 7–9, 11, 18, 43, 46–72, 93, 99, 147, 149–53, 163–5, 168–70, 181–2, 186–91
- arrival in Edessa 55–6
- arrival in Nisibis 62–3, 187
- death 72, n180 72
- early years 49–53
- failed attempts to convert 58–60
- heals boy harassed by a demon 71–2
- inspired to write by Jacob of Sarug 69
- leadership in time of persecution 53–4
- the Leprous One 33, n76 33, 35, 38
- persuaded to stay in Nisibis 63–5
- public accusation and flight 60–2
- residence at Kephar Māri 54–5
- Satan's assault on in Nisibis 66–8
- scholastic asceticism 68–9
- slandered 58–60, 71
- takes over the School 57–8
- training of Abraham of Bēt Rabban 73–4, 75
- trouble with Persian authorities 70–1

Nau, François 15, 40, 45, 167
Nero 142
Nestorius 29–30, n41 29, 35, 38, 43, 45, 58, 83–4, 147
Nicaea 36
Nisibis 2–3, 12, 56, 61–8, 72–3, 80, 149, 151, 162–4, 183, 187, 190
Noah 88, 125

Origen of Alexandria 92
Ortiz de Urbina, I. 15

Pāpā 33
Palestine 126
Paul, Bishop 84, n71 84, 162
Paul the Persian 174, 178, 179
Paul, St 51, 60, 62, 75, 82, 88, 96, 103, 105, 114, 120, 141–2, 156, 157, 158, 159
Paul of Samosata 27, 28, 29, 38, 39, 58
Paul (son of Qaqay) 33, 35
Peroz 35, 38, 70
Persia 23, 25, 31, 35, 63, 71, 73, 151, 152, 187
Persian Empire 5, 154–5, 188
Peter, St 88, 137, 142

Philo of Alexandria 92, 142–3, n420 143, 144
Philoxenus of Mabbug 21–2, 23, 93
Plato 132–4, n317 132, 173, 174
Porphyry of Tyre
  Isagoge 172–4, 177, 178
  Tree of 172–80
Proclus 43
Pusai (son of Qurti) 35
Pythagoras 135

Qaphar of Lādab 70
Qashwi 79
Qozb 76, 190
Qritā 34
Qyorā 149–50, 182, 184, 185

Rāmisho 161
Rabban Surin 163–4
Rabbula, Bishop of Edessa 57, n73 57, 148, n460 148, 182, 184, 185

Sabrisho‘, Catholicos 10
Salibā ibn Yuhannā 4–5
Samuel 129
Saul 62
Scher, Addai 14, 15, 17, 163, 165–9
Seleucia 36
Seleucia-Ctesiphon 22, 161
Sergius of Rēsh‘aynā 173
Severus of Antioch 21–2
Shoshan 161
Shushtar 35
Siirt 165, 166
Simeon bar Ṣabba‘ē 42
Simeon of Bēt Arsham 21–24
  anaphora 22
  ‘The Disputer’ 22
Simeon (exegete from Kashkar) 65, 190
Simon (Peter) 140
Simon Magus (the Sorcerer) 26, n13 26, 27, 28, 29, 38
Socrates 173, 174
Socrates Scholasticus 45
Solomon 88, 129–31, 147

Tfinkdji, J. 167
Thecla 147
Theodora 22
Theodore of Mopsuestia 6, 9, 13–14, 18, 28–9, 35, 38, 43, 58, n36 78, 83–4, 88, 90–3, n185 117, 145, 146–8, n444 146, 150, 156, 182
Theodoret of Cyrrhus 30–1, n48 30
Theodosius the Great 36
Theodosius the Younger 36
Theodoulos 147
Timothy 49
Titus 64, 188

Valens, Emperor 145
Valentinian 44
Valley of Aijalon 116
Vivarium 3
Vööbus, Arthur 4, 8, 15, 167, 168, 169
  History of the School of Nisibis 7
Vosté, J.-M. 166, 167

Walker, Joel 170
Wardashir 161

Yazdegird 37

Zabargan the *marzbān* 39
Zaroqar 135
Zeno, Emperor 2, 5, 34, n90 34, 36
Zoroaster 135–6
Zurwān 135–6, n346 135

SUBJECT INDEX

'Abbasid period 3, 179
Accident 172, 175, 176
action, perfection of 111–12
administrators 8
allegorical exegesis 6
Alqosh 155 167
Amida, church of 54
angels 87, 88, 107, 108, 114–16, 133
  diligent 88, 121–2
  lazy 88, 120–1
  orders of 121–2, n217 121
  as rational beings 178, 179
  schools of 86, 88, 118–22
animals 174, 176–8
  sacrifice 133, 136
animate 173–5, 178
anti-Miaphysite regimes 23
Antiochene theology 6, 24, 91, 182
  see also Dyophysite Christians; East-Syrians; Nestorianism
apophatic theology 92
Apostles 26, 36, 44, 60, 64–5, 77, 88, 141–2, 151–2, 157, 188
  see also disciples; specific Apostles
Arabic 3
Arabic sources 4–5
Arabs 10, 12
Arians 42, 45, 145
Aristotelian logic 2, 6, 8, 10, 91, 92, 172, 176–7, 178, 180
Aristotelian *Organon* 10, 92, 178
Armenian Council of Dvin (505/6) 23
asceticism 76–7, 179
astrology 134, n336 134
Athenian schools 1, 132–4

Babylonian Jewish academies (*yeshivot*) 3
Beelzebub 25
  see also Satan
being
  coming-into 74–5, 102, 106, n101 106
  essential 74
beings
  created 74–5, 95, 96–8, 106
  rational 95, 96, 107
bgadkephat letters 18
body 106–7, 173, 174, 175, 178
  ensouled 16–7, 173, 174, 175
  learning and 74–6
  weakness 97

canons of the School 4
Cappadocians 36
categories 176
Cause of the Foundation of the Schools (Barḥadbeshabbā) 4, 7, 8, 10, 11, 13–18, 24, 86–160
  Abraham 126
  Abraham of Bēt Rabban 153–5, 191
  Abraham of Nisibis 155
  angelic activity above 114–16
  Apostle Paul 141–2
  Arius of Alexandria 144
  Cain and Abel 124–5
  conclusion 159–60
  corporeal creation 112–14

Council of Nicaea 144
creation as reading lesson 117–20
diligent angels 121–2
distinction and learning 106–8
divine illumination 108–11
division of the sessions 157–8
Elisha bar Qozbāyē 153, 183, 190–1
exhortation 158–9
Fall 116–17
God's epistemological inaccessibility 103–6
God's grace towards the speaker and assembly 97–100
God's priority in existence 100–3, 107
Ḥenānā of Adiabene 155–7
human schools 122–57
influences on 91–3
Isho'yahb of Arzon 155
Jesus the Master Teacher 136–41
John of Bēt Rabban 153–5
Joshua 129
lazy angels cast from Heaven 120–1
literary dependence on the *Ecclesiastical History* 181–4
literary genre/mode 91
manuscript tradition of the 165–71
  A. 166, 167, 168
  Alqosh 155 167
  C. 166, 167
  M. 166, 167
  Ms 52 Notre-Dame des Sémences (Alqosh 65/Baghdad Chald. Mon. 181) 166, 167, 168–9
  Ms Ming. Syr. 547 168–9
  Ms Vat. Syr. 507 167–8
  Sharfeh Patr 80. 168
  Syriac Ms 394 Bibliothèque Nationale de France 167–8
  T. 166, 167
Mēmrā on the Holy Fathers 163–4
Moses 126–9
Narsai 150–2, 182–3, 186–9, 190–1
Noah 125
pagan schools 132–6
parts 89–91
Patrologia Orientalis edition 165–8
perfection of intelligence and action 111–12
Philo of Alexandria 142–3
Post-Apostolic Schools 142–3
Post-Nicene schools 144–5
preface 94–7
prophets 131
Qyorā 149–50, 182, 184, 185
School of Adam 122–4
School of Alexandria 142–3
School of Diodore of Tarsus 145–6
School in Edessa and removal to Persia 149, 151
Solomon 129–31
speech format 86–7
synoptic comparison with the *Ecclesiastical History* 185–91
Theodore of Mopsuestia 146–8
Tree of Porphyry 172–80
Chalcedonian orthodoxy 23
Chaldaeans 134, n336 134
  monasteries 166
Cherubs 121–2
Christian hagiography 45
Christianization 1, 3, 6
Christians
  in Antioch 141
  Dyophysite 24, n12 26
  from the East, immigration 6
  heterodox 10
  Nestorianization of Persian 21–39
  persecution 22
Chronicle of Arbela 169, 170
Chronicle of Siirt (*Nestorian History*) 5, 10, 13, 16, 165, 166
Church 44–5, 69
  Satan's opposition to 42, 44–5
Church of Antioch 6, 83

Church of the East 2–6, 9, 11, 13, 15–16, 24, 91
Church of Nisibis 83
cognitive faculties 109–11, n123 109, n124 109
corporeal creation 112–14
cosmology 134–5
Council of Ephesus 45
Council of Mār Gregory I 605 CE 13, 14, 16
Council of Nicaea 42, 144
created beings 74–5, 95, 96–8, 106
creation 87–8, 136
  angelic classroom of 88
  corporeal 112–14
  human authority over 114–16
  as reading lesson 117–20
cross 80–1
currency 79, n44 79
curriculum 8–10
Cyrilians 45

death sentences 60, n97 60
deceiver, the 116–17
decline of the school 10–11
demons 71–2
  of sleep n155 68
desire, fleshy 75
Difference 172
Diodorians 16
disciples 17, 44
  see also Apostles
divine light 87, 108–11
division of the sessions 157–8
doxographical literature 92
Dyophysite Christians 24, n12 26
  see also Antiochene theology; East-Syrians; Nestorianism

East-Syrian 'cause' literature 4, 10, 91
East-Syrian chronicles 12–13
East-Syrian schools 1–4, 8, 11, 86, 92, 179
East-Syrians 7, 9, 10, 22–4, 45–6, 91–2, 173, 175, 180
  see also Dyophysite Christians; Nestorianism; *see also* Antiochene theology
Ebionites n18 26
Ecclesiastical History (Barḥadbeshabbā of Bēt 'Arbāyē) 4, 7, 8, 11, 15–17, 40–85
  chapter one 44
  chapter summary 42–3
  chapter thirty one, Life of Narsai 46, 47–72, 181–3, 186–9, 190
  chapter thirty two, Life of Abraham of Bēt Rabban 46, 47, 73–85, 181, 183, 191
  chapter two 44–5
  heresy 42, 44–5, 58, 69
  influences 92
  literary dependence of the *Cause of the Foundation of the Schools* on 181–4
  preface 41
  sources 45–6
  synoptic comparison with the *Cause of the Foundation of the Schools* 185–91
Eden 88, 123–4
elementary instructors 8, 9
ensoulment 16–7, 106–8, 173, 174, 175, 176–8
Eucharistic communion 91
Eunomians 45
Eutychians 29
evil 58, 59, 69, 80, 95, 96, 112, 136, 142
  women as cause of 67, n142 67
  see also tree of knowledge of good and evil
exegesis 9–10
  allegorical 6
  biblical 2
  heterodox 10

exegetes 7–8, 9, 57, 90
existence 87, 100–3, 106, 107, 175–6

Fall 87, 116–17
falsehood 111
Father 37, 103, 137–8
  see also God
Flood mythology 125
foundation of the school 2
freewill 51, 91

Galatians 36
Gannat bussāmē (*Garden of Delights*) 13–14
Genus 172, 173, 176
God 25, 29, 30, 38, 42, 50, 179
  as cause of all things 107, 175
  and creation as reading lesson 117–20
  divine illumination of 108–11
  essence of 104, n83 104, 105, 106, 107, 108
  fear of 52–4, 59–60, 63, 73, 75–6, 94, 111, 131, 140, 152–3, 190
  goodness of 87, 94–5
  grace of 87, 89, 95, 97–100
  human capacity to know 87, 88, 103–6
  and the human schools 122–9
  and human traverse to heaven/ authority over creation 114–16
  Judgement of 131
  law of 49–50, n17 49, 88, 98, n44 98, 138, 139
  nature of 86, 87, 88, 89, 92, 103–6
  and the pagan schools 133, 135, 136
  Plato on 133
  power of 87, 94–6
  priority in existence 87, 100–3, 107
  as prototype of humanity 113, n143 113
  revelation 105
  and Solomon 130–1
  unknowability of 92
  wisdom of 87, 94–6, 109
  Word of 136
  wrath of 60, 62
  see also Father
gods 135–6
golden calf 127–8
good 112, 136
  see also tree of knowledge of good and evil
goodness 87, 94–5
grace 87, 89, 95, 97–100
Greek philosophy 3, 10, 88, 91–2, 172–7, 179–80

hagiography 45
heads of the school 9, 57, 90
  chronology 7–8
  see also specific heads
Heaven
  human traverse to 114–16
  kingdom of 137
  lazy angels cast from 120–1
heresy 7, 22, 144
  in the *Ecclesiastical History* 42, 44–5, 58, 69
  Macedonian 27–8, n29 27–8
  Simeon of Bēt Arsham on 23–4, 25, 27–30
heterodox theology 10
Himyarites 22
'History of the Holy Fathers Who were Persecuted because of the Truth, The' 12
History of the School of Nisibis (Vööbus) 7
Holy Spirit 27, n29 28, 36, 37, 44, n233 123, 141
homonyms n98 106
hospices 78–80
human nature, diversity of 95, n18 95
human schools 86, 88, 89–90, 122–57

icons 80
idolatry 80–1
  see also golden calf
ignorance 96, 110, 111, 112
immortality 107, 108
intelligence 111–13
  perfection of 111–12
interpretation 9
interpreters (*bādoqā*) 8, 40
Iraq War 166
Isagoge (Porphyry of Tyre) 172–4, 177, 178
Islam 3
Israelites 98, 126

Jacobites 21
Jacob's ladder 114
Jews 10, 22, 25–6, n10 25, n12 26, n14 26, 114, 139
  attack on Abraham of Bēt Rabban 81–2
  institutionalization of learning 3
Judgement, of God 131

kataphatic theology 92
Khuzistan Chronicle 12–13
Khuzites 23, 35–6, 70–1
knowledge n152 114
  contemplative 50, n24 50
  human of God 87, 88, 92, 103–6
  and the perfection of intelligence 111

Late Antiquity 1, 3, 172, 179
law, God's 49–50, n17 49, 88, 98, n44 98, 138, 139
learning
  and the body 74–6
  and Christianization 1, 3
  Greco-Roman institutions 1
  level of 8–9
'Letter' of Simeon of Bēt Arsham 16–17, 18, 21–39
  anathemas against dissenters 37–9
  apostasy of the Khuzites and the Persians 35–6
  date 23
  genealogy of Nestorianism 25–31
  on heresy 23–4, 25, 27–30
  Orthodox faith 36–7
  parts 23
  and the 'School of the Persians' 21, 23, 24, 31–5
Levites 127
literacy, basic 8, 9
liturgy 9
living beings 173–9
logic 2, 6, 8, 91, 92, n141 112, 172, 176–8, 180

Macedonian heresy 27–8, n29 27–8
Magi 53, 76, 190
Manichees 133, n332 133–4
Marcionites 29
mēmrē 69, 70, 163–4
Miaphysites 21–2, n12 26, 182
  see also anti-Miaphysite regimes
Middle Ages 1
mimesis n19 50
mind 87
  as captain and purification of the faculties 109–11
  rationality 87
Mingana Fragment 161–2, 169, 170–1
Monastery of the Persians, Nisibis 62–3, n115 63, 151, 186
Monastery of Rabban Mornizd 166
movement 176–7
Ms 52 Notre-Dame des Sémences (Alqosh 65/Baghdad Chald. Mon. 181) 166, 167, 168–9
Ms Ming. Syr. 547 168–9
Ms Vat. Syr. 507 167–8
Ms Vatican Syriac 135 17, 21, 23

natural philosophers 135
Neoplatonism 1, 10, 92, n141 112, 172–5, 177, 179–80
Nestorianism 6
  and the Christian community in Persia 21–39
  genealogy of 25–31
  see also Antiochene theology; *Chronicle of Siirt*; Dyophysite Christians; East-Syrians
New Testament 9, 28, 156
non-rational, the 174, 175, n17 175
Notre-Dame des Sémences monastery 166, 167

Old Testament 9, 28, 138, 156
order 100–1
origins of the School of Nisibis 5–7
  and the *Cause of the Foundation of the Schools* 89
  and the 'Letter' of Simeon of Bēt Arsham 23, 24
orthodoxy 65, 69, 78, 82, 189
  Chalcedonian 23
  Syrian 22

pagans 44, 53, 80
  schools 90, 132–6
Parable of the Lost Coin 108, n112108
Parthian Empire 24
Passover 141
patristic literature 91, 92–3
perception n152 114
Persians 58–9, 61, 63, 65, 70–1, 99, 187, 190
Pharisees 139
plague 154, n512 154
plants 176–7
Platonic spirituality 92
polyonyms n101 106
Post-Apostolic Schools 142–3
Post-Nicene schools 88
power, of God 87, 94–6
prayer 157
predicables 172
Property 172
Psalters 9, 53, n46 53, 80

rational beings 95, 96, 107
rational, the 173, 174, 175, 178–9, n35 179
rationality 108–9, 111–13, 116
readers (*maqryānā*) 8, 9
reading 9, 117–21, 122–4
  metaphors of 117–20, n194 118–19
revelation 105
rise/importance of the school 2–3, 5
Roman Empire 152, 155, 190
Romans 27, 34, 37, 58, 63–4, 71, 80, 82–3, 161, 187
Rome 26, 142

sacrifice, animal 133, 136
salvation 97, n34 97
Samaritans 26, n14 26
Sasanian Empire 1–3, 6, 10–11, 21, 24, 170, 173
Satan 42, 44–5, 53, 58, 89, 99, 121, 124–5, 142, 151, 162
  assault on Abraham of Bēt Rabban 80–2
  assault on Narsai in Nisibis 66–8, 70, 71
  see also Beelzebub
scholastic asceticism 68–9
School of Adam 122–4
School of Alexandria 142–3
School of Diodore of Tarsus 145–6
'School of the Persians', Edessa (School of Edessa) 2, n5 2, 5–7, 9
  and *Cause of the Foundation of the Schools* 88, 90, 182
  and the *Ecclesiastical History* 54, 56, 182
  and the 'Letter' of Simeon of Bēt

Arsham 21, 23, 24, 31–5
School of Seleucia 11, 171
school year 90
schoolmen 8
sensation 176–7, 178–9
Seraphs 121
Severans 45
Sharfeh Patr 80. 168
sleep 68, n155 68
sociability of study 8–9
Sodomites 64, 188
Son 37, 38, 103, 105
as created being 144
see also Jesus (names index)
soul 50–2, 75, 87, 108, 109, 110–11, 133, 176–9
appetitive/active/effectual portion n25 50, 109, n125 109–10, 110–11, n129 110, n132 110, n141 112
Christian understanding of the 177–9
first cause/origin 51, n27 51
intellectual/cognitive portion 50, n22 50, 110, n129 110, n141 112
passive 50, n23 50, n25 50, 52, n37 52, n39 52
as principle of movement 176
as principle of sensation 176, 178–9
Species 172, 173, 175, 178
speech 92, 107
spiritual 175–6, 179
spirituality, Platonic 92
staters 79, n44 79
stewards (*rabbaytā*) 8
substance 173, 174, 175–6, 178
suffering 97–8, n39 98
Synodicon Orientale 13
Syriac alphabet, transliteration 18–19
Syriac Ms 394 Bibliothèque Nationale de France 167–8
Syriac sources 5
Syrian Orthodox Church 22

teachers (*mallphānā*) 8
ten (number) 119, n196 119
ten commandments 127, 128
theology
Antiochene 6, 24, 91, 182
apophatic 92
heterodox 10
kataphatic 92
thought n152 114
Tigris 81
time n83 104
Torah 137
tree of knowledge of good and evil 123–4, n239 123
Tree of Porphyry 92, 172–80
Trinity 44
truth 111–12

'Umri 34

Vatican library 167–8

Watchers 121
weakness 95, 96, 97
West-Syrians 7, 21, 23, 46, 93, 173
wisdom
of God 87, 94–6, 109
of Solomon 129–31, 147
women, as cause of evil 67, n142 67
Word of God 136
wrath, of God 60, 62

youth 74

zervanism 135–6, n346 135, n347 136
zodiac 134
Zoroastrians 10, 88, 92, 135–6

www.ingramcontent.com/pod-product-compliance
Lightning Source LLC
Chambersburg PA
CBHW062222300426
44115CB00012BA/2179
* 9 7 8 1 8 4 6 3 1 1 6 1 1 *